Educational Resiliency
Student, Teacher, and School Perspectives

A volume in
Research in Educational Diversity and Excellence
Series Editors: Hersh C. Waxman and Yolanda N. Padrón

Educational Resiliency

Student, Teacher, and School Perspectives

Edited by

**Hersh C. Waxman,
Yolanda N. Padrón,
and Jon P. Gray**

**INFORMATION AGE
PUBLISHING**

80 Mason Street • Greenwich, Connecticut 06830 • www.infoagepub.com

Library of Congress Cataloging-in-Publication Data

Educational resiliency : student, teacher, and perspectives / edited by Hersh C. Waxman, Yolanda N. Padrâon, and Jon Gray.
  p. cm. – (Research in educational diversity and excellence)
Includes bibliographical references and index.
  ISBN 1-931576-08-4 (pbk.) – ISBN 1-931576-09-2 (hardcover)
  1. Children of minorities–Education–United States. 2. Children with social disabilities–Education–United States. 3. School improvement programs–United States. 4. Resilience (Personality trait) I. Waxman, Hersholt C. II. Padrâon, Yolanda N. III. Gray, Jon (Jon P.) IV. Series.
  LC3731.E43 2003
  371.93–dc22

                                                        2003021159

Copyright © 2004 Information Age Publishing Inc.

All rights reserved. No part of this publication may be reproduced, stored in a retrieval system, or transmitted, in any form or by any means, electronic, mechanical, photocopying, microfilming, recording or otherwise, without written permission from the publisher.

Printed in the United States of America

CONTENTS

part I
Issues and Reviews of Research

1. Introduction and Overview
   Hersh C. Waxman, Jon P. Gray, and Yolanda N. Padrón   3

2. Resilience: Emerging Social Constructions in Educational Policy, Research, and Practice
   Joel H. Brown   11

3. Promoting Educational Resilience for Students At-Risk of Failure
   Hersh C. Waxman, Jon P. Gray, and Yolanda N. Padrón   37

4. Resilience Research and Practice: National Resilience Resource Center Bridging the Gap
   Kathy M. Marshall   63

part II
Studies of Students' Resiliency

5. A Longitudinal Look at the Literacy Development of Children Prenatally Exposed to Crack/Cocaine
   Diane Barone   87

6. Achieving Success: An Agentic Model of Resiliency
   Ruth Silva and Judy Radigan   113

7. Mathematics Learning Environment Differences between Resilient, Average, and Nonresilient Elementary Students
Hui-Li Chang   *137*

8. The Student–Teacher Axis: Idiosyncratic Credit and Cutting the Slack
Sue McGinty   *157*

9. The Relations of Teacher Education Students' Resiliency, Work Motivation, and School-Level Resilience
Jon P. Gray   *175*

part III
Schools, Programs, and Communities That Enhance Resiliency

10. Presenting a Resilience Paradigm for Teachers
Sybil Wolin   *189*

11. Developing Resilient Learning Communities to Close the Achievement Gap
Robert Stephen Topf, Virginia Frazier-Maiwald, and Martin L. Krovetz   *205*

12. Resilient Communities: The Interplay between Community Development and Child Development Through Effective School Reform
Héctor H. Rivera   *227*

13. Promoting Resiliency in Youth, Educators, and Communities
Doris "Annie" Henry, Mike M. Milstein   *247*

14. Future Directions for Educational Resiliency Research
Hersh C. Waxman, Ann Brown, and Hui-Li Chang   *263*

Contributing Authors   *275*

part I

ISSUES AND REVIEWS OF RESEARCH

CHAPTER 1

INTRODUCTION AND OVERVIEW

Hersh C. Waxman
University of Houston

Jon P. Gray
Lamar University

Yolanda N. Padrón
University of Houston

Research on resilience has been widely conducted in the areas of developmental psychopathology, psychology, sociology, and anthropology during the past few decades. In education, conceptual and empirical work on resilience has recently gained similar recognition as a framework from which we can attempt to understand why some students become successful in school, while similar students from the same socially and economically disadvantaged backgrounds and communities have not been successful (Waxman, Gray, & Padrón, 2002).

Some average-ability students do well in inner-city schools despite coming from at-risk environments, and it is important to know why these resilient students succeed while other students (i.e., nonresilient students) from equally stressful environments do not. This approach focuses on the predictors of academic success rather than on academic failure. The resiliency perspective also may help us design more effective educational interventions because it enables us to specifically identify those "alterable" factors that distinguish resilient and nonresilient students. In addition, resilience has gained recognition as an important intervention framework in promoting skills and characteristics associated with student success in school.

Thus, the construct of "educational resilience" is not viewed as a fixed attribute of some students, but rather as alterable processes or mechanisms that can be developed and fostered. In other words, this approach does not focus on attributes such as ability, because ability has not been found to be characteristic of resilient students (Benard, 1997; Gordon & Song, 1994; Masten, Best, & Garmezy, 1990). On the other hand, there have been several alterable processes or characteristics that have been found to be associated with resiliency in children. Benard (1997), for example, found that there were four attributes or personal characteristics that resilient children typically display: social competence, problem-solving skills, autonomy, and a sense of purpose. McMillan and Reed (1994) also described four other factors that appear to be related to resiliency: (1) personal attributes such as motivation, aspirations, and goals; (2) positive use of time (e.g., on-task behavior, homework completion, participation in extracurricular experiences); (3) family life (e.g., family support and expectations); and (4) school and classroom learning environment (i.e., facilities, exposure to technology, leadership, and overall climate).

For several reasons, there has been a shift in resiliency research toward education. While there is still an important research emphasis placed on resiliency and psychopathology, the educational community has adopted resilience as a "strength-based" or "solution-based" approach. Educational researchers and practitioners alike have explored and investigated resilience to seek answers and to improve educational and social outcomes for children and youth. The demographic shift in our schools, the political climate, and the learning environment associated with student success create a scenario in which educational resilience offers far-reaching implications.

Resiliency research is not only aligned with the objectives of the No Child Left Behind Act (NCLB), it provides the means for the essential achievement of that legislation—effectively addressing the specific problems and local conditions of the culturally and linguistically diverse minority students that are in danger of being left behind. This legislation has enabled educators to focus on what can be done to reduce the achievement gaps between white and minority students and high- and low-income students. By focusing on students' strengths, educational resilience provides an important foundation for promoting excellence for *all* students. The educational community and the school itself are at the forefront of providing all students with positive school and classroom learning environments. More than any institution except the family, schools can provide the supportive environmental conditions that foster resiliency in today's youth and tomorrow's adults (Henderson & Milstein, 1996).

OVERVIEW OF BOOK

This book is the first volume in the series *Research in Educational Diversity and Excellence*. The mission of this series is to bring issues of diversity and educational risk to the forefront of national attention in order to assist the nation's diverse students at risk of educational failure to achieve academic excellence. This series focuses on critical issues in the education of linguistic and cultural minority students and those placed at risk by factors of race, poverty, and geographic location.

The purpose of the present book is to summarize and discuss recent perspectives, research, and practices related to educational resilience. There are three distinct parts of the book. The first part, "Conceptual Issues and Reviews of Research," focuses on issues related to defining resiliency as well as reviewing classical and recent studies in the area of educational resiliency. Part II, "Studies of Students' Resiliency," focuses on recent resiliency findings including methodological issues and implications of individual and school-level resilience. The final part, "Schools, Programs, and Communities that Enhance Resiliency," concentrates primarily on interventions and instructional programs that foster resiliency in youth and the schools they attend.

PART I: CONCEPTUAL ISSUES AND REVIEWS OF RESEARCH

This part consists of three chapters that highlight critical conceptual issues in the field as well as review relevant research. In Chapter 1, "Resilience: Emerging Social Constructions in Educational Policy, Research, and Practice," Joel Brown examines resilience from a sociopolitical and psychosocial perspective. His discussion examines resilience, its current social construction, and current implications for policy and program development. Specifically, two forms of resilience research are identified, the "specifist" and "generalist" approaches.

In "Promoting Educational Resilience for Students At Risk of Failure," Waxman, Gray, and Padrón provide an alternative approach to the study of risk. The authors discuss issues related to defining resiliency, review several classical and recent resilience studies, and examine the factors related to student success. The authors also focus on the implications of resilience research for educational practice.

Part I concludes with a chapter by Kathy Marshall, "Resilience Research and Practice: National Resilience Resource Center Bridging the Gap," that examines the transition from classical resilience research to the practical approach used in educational settings today. Marshall also offers promising supportive information for practitioners to foster resilience in our nation's schools.

PART II: STUDIES OF STUDENTS' RESILIENCY

This part consists of five chapters that focus on research on students' resiliency. These studies vary in their focus and methods, but share a common perspective that examines factors that promote students' resiliency. In Chapter 4, "A Longitudinal Look at the Literacy Development of Children Prenatally Exposed to Crack/Cocaine," Diane Barone contends that resilience is an important contributor to the literacy development of high-risk students. She explains that resiliency and family stability are present in high-risk students that have the ability to read and write.

In Chapter 5, "From Risk to Success: An Agentic Model of Resiliency," Ruth Silva and Judy Radigan explore the social realities of a group of students who were deemed "at risk." The authors utilize a conceptual model based on Giddens's (1994) notion of foundational agency to explain their proposed agentic model of resiliency.

In "Mathematics Learning Environment Differences between Resilient, Average, and Nonresilient Elementary Students," Hui-Li Chang examines differences between resilient and nonresilient elementary students' perceptions of their learning environment. Additionally, she reports key factors that resilient students identify as important in overcoming adversities and helping them on the pathway of success.

Sue McGinty studied young resilient women at a Midwest high school in "The Student–Teacher Axis: Idiosyncratic Credit and Cutting the Slack." She reveals that resilient students and teachers work together to make the educational system successful.

In the final chapter in Part II, "Relations of Teacher Education Students' Resiliency, Work Motivation, and School-Level Resilience," Jon Gray explores the resilience concept in teacher education students and university teacher education programs. His focus is to empirically link positive individual characteristics like resiliency and work motivation to the campus-level learning environment. Also, the implications of the association between these factors are discussed in terms of practicality for both schools and students.

PART III: SCHOOLS, PROGRAMS, AND COMMUNITIES THAT ENHANCE RESILIENCY

In the concluding part of the book, there are four chapters that focus on schools, teachers, programs, and communities that enhance resiliency. Sybil Wolin, in "Presenting a Resilience Paradigm to Teachers," advocates a new resilience paradigm that offers a more optimistic approach than the risk paradigm. Specifically, she focuses on four obstacles that teachers encounter when shifting to the resilience paradigm. More importantly, she offers solutions to these obstacles based on her many years of experience and service to teachers and school districts.

In "Developing Resilient Learning Communities to Close the Achievement Gap," Robert Topf, Virginia Frazier-Maiwald, and Martin Krovetz advocate resilience as an integrated approach to foster success. The authors offer supportive information from a school district in San Jose, California. Resilience is discussed from the viewpoints of students, teachers, family members, and school leaders.

In "Resilient Communities: The Inner-Play between Community Development through Effective School Reform," Hector Rivera examines the social component of resilient communities. He shares his experiences with the Zuni Pueblo community in New Mexico and explores the concept of resilience in promoting school reform for Native Americans.

In "Promoting Resiliency in Youth, Educators, and Communities," Annie Henry and Mike Milstein describe the six resiliency factors that emphasize the importance of resiliency in schools today. The authors present an updated resiliency model, applications of their work, and provide insights for strategies that promote resiliency.

In the concluding chapter, Hersh Waxman, Ann Brown, and Hui-Li Chang discuss future directions for resiliency research. They discuss needed research in the field as well as new areas that present opportunities for further research.

SUMMARY

The purpose of this book is to make available information for improving our understanding of some new directions for research on educational resiliency. The book describes some of the conceptual and research-based approaches that successfully work in improving the resiliency of students and teachers. This book also illustrates several ways we promote educational resiliency to improve teaching and student learning. We maintain that conceptual and empirical work on resiliency can be a critical component for improving the role of teachers and administrators, policymakers, parents, and other educators. Although recognition of the uniqueness of each school and classroom situation will always need to be considered, the accumulation of research evidence over time and across studies provides consistent findings that enhance our understandings of improving student learning. In other words, more conceptual work and research on resiliency may allow us to change and improve the education of teachers and consequently improve the education of students.

There are, of course, many unanswered questions about promoting resiliency over the long term. We hoped to be able to provide a synthesis both of what we think we know and what we need to know. We were probably less successful in developing this synthesis, not because of the quality of the chapters, but because of the lack of information that can be brought to bear. As we will point out in the Conclusion, there is much work to be done. We hope that these chapters will encourage others to join us in the continuing search to answer some of the interesting questions related to promoting resiliency in schools.

We want to thank the U.S. Department of Education, Office of Educational Research and Improvement, which provided support for our resiliency research through a grant to the National Center for Research on Education, Diversity, and Excellence (CREDE). During the past 8 years, we have conducted research with approximately 2,000 elementary and secondary school students from about 50 classrooms in several schools identified as having large proportions of English language learners (i.e., > 80%) as well as having students from high-poverty families (~ 90% received free or reduced-cost lunches). Our CREDE research has included descriptive, correlational, and experimental studies, using both qualitative and quantitative research methods (Padrón, Waxman, Brown, & Powers, 2000). This research has helped us formulate many of the ideas, perspectives, and findings that we describe in this book.

I (Hersh Waxman) also would like to thank the late Margaret Wang, former Director of the Temple University Center for Research in Human Development and Education, National Research on Education in the Inner Cities, and Mid-Atlantic Laboratory for Student Success. It was the work of Margaret and her colleagues (Wang & Gordon, 1994; Wang, Haertel, & Walberg, 1998) that shaped the direction of research on educational resilience and contributed greatly to the knowledge base in the field. Margaret's many contributions, including a passion for her work and her commitment to educating *all* students, have made an immeasurable difference in the lives of children, teachers, administrators, and policymakers.

We also would like to thank all the authors who gave generously of their time to the chapters in this volume. We chose many individuals who were prominent in the area of resiliency and who had already written some of the most critically acclaimed books in the field (e.g., Barone,1999; Brown,

D'Emidio-Caston, & Benard, 2000; Henderson & Milstein, 1996; Krovetz, 1999; McGinty, 1999; Milstein & Henry, 2000; Wolin & Wolin, 1993). We gained knowledge from reading their current thoughts about resiliency as well as a renewal of energy and enthusiasm about the potential benefits of continuing to promote resiliency in schools. We also gained a sense of direction about what questions need to be answered next, and we hope that others who read these chapters will share these outcomes.

ACKNOWLEDGMENT

This research was supported in part by a U.S. Department of Education, Office of Educational Research and Improvement grant from the National Center for Research on Education, Diversity, and Excellence. The opinions expressed in this chapter do not necessarily reflect the position, policy, or endorsement of the granting agency.

REFERENCES

Barone, D. (1999). *Resilient children: Stories of poverty, drug exposure, and literacy development.* Newark, DE: International Reading Association and National Reading Conference.

Benard, B. (1997). *Turning it around for all youth: From risk to resilience* (ERIC/CUE Digest No. 126). New York: ERIC Clearinghouse on Urban Education.

Brown, J. H., D'Emidio-Caston, & Benard, B. (2000). *Resilience education.* Thousand Oaks, CA: Corwin.

Gordon, E. W., & Song, L. D. (1994). Variations in the experience of resilience. In M. C. Wang & E. W. Gordon (Eds.), *Educational resilience in inner-city America: Challenges and prospects* (pp. 27–43). Mahwah, NJ: Erlbaum.

Henderson, N., & Milstein, M. M. (1996). *Resiliency in schools: Making it happen for students and educators.* Thousand Oaks, CA: Corwin.

Krovetz, M. L. (1999). *Fostering resiliency: Expecting all students to use their minds and hearts well.* Thousand Oaks, CA: Corwin.

Masten, A. S., Best, K. M., & Garmezy, N. (1990). Resilience and development: Contributions from the study of children who overcome adversity. *Development and Psychopathology, 2,* 425–444.

McGinty, S. (1999). *Resilience, gender and success at school.* New York: Peter Lang.

McMillan, J. H., & Reed, D. F. (1994). At-risk students and resiliency: Factors contributing to academic success. *The Clearing House, 67,* 137–140.

Milstein, M. M., & Henry, P. A. (2000). *Spreading resiliency: Making it happen for schools and communities.* Thousand Oaks, CA: Corwin.

Padrón, Y. N., Waxman, H. C., Brown, A. P., & Powers, R. A. (2000). *Improving classroom instruction and student learning for resilient and non-resilient English language learners* (Research Brief No. 7). Santa Cruz, CA: Center for Research on Educational Diversity and Excellence.

Wang, M. C., & Gordon E. W. (Eds.). (1994). *Educational resilience in inner-city America: Challenges and prospects* (pp. 45–72). Hillsdale, NJ: Erlbaum.

Wang, M. C., Haertel, G. D., & Walberg, H. J. (1998). *Building educational resiliency.* Bloomington, IN: Phi Delta Kappa Educational Foundation.

Waxman, H. C., Gray, J., & Padrón, Y. N. (2002). Resiliency among students at risk of failure. In S. Stringfield & D. Land (Eds.), *Educating at risk students* (pp. 29–48). Chicago: National Society for the Study of Education.

Wolin, S. J., & Wolin, S. (1993). *The resilient self.* New York: Villard.

CHAPTER 2

RESILIENCE

Emerging Social Constructions in Educational Policy, Research, and Practice

Joel H. Brown
The University Of Oklahoma and
Center for Educational Research and Development (CERD)

Forty-five years of wisdom tells us that resilience makes a difference in the quality of life, particularly with young people. Other than in the home, schools and classrooms provide the richest opportunities to connect with them. In these settings, facilitation of resilience may make *the* difference between participation or alienation, mobilization or stagnation, and life success or failure. By almost invisibly transitioning from risk to resilience, education is inching toward change (Brown, 2001a, 2001b). This chapter explores the policies, programs, and youth impact surrounding the educational transition from risk to resilience.

Following a description of the evidence to be presented in this chapter, the evolution of risk is chronicled. Resilience and its emerging conceptualization(s), practices, and youth outcomes are then developed into two conceptually distinct categories, one called the "Specifist" approach and another called the "Generalist" approach. When appropriate, examples are provided. At this chapter's conclusion, findings and implications are discussed. Throughout the chapter, the following main points will be made:

- The effect of a school-based risk focus on young people results in youth labeling, cognitive dissonance, and likely reduced adult credibility.
- The important distinction(s) between risk and a "Generalist" orientation toward resilience are; (a) a deficit versus strengths-based view of young people and; (b) a problem remediation versus capacity building focus in practice.
- Despite being a distinct perspective, the development and application of resilience is evolving in a pattern similar to the application of risk.
- A general process-oriented, nondidactic approach to facilitating resilience offers an essential dimension of school reform. This is achieved by professional and explicit facilitation of individual and societal connectedness in a mutually rewarding and pro-youth climate.

EVIDENCE AND LIMITATIONS

For this chapter, hundreds of policy, program, and research documents were examined. Some evidence represents landmark research or documents. Other evidence represents important but rarely considered information. Overall, the information considered for this chapter is limited by the following sociopolitical or psychosocial dimensions of risk and resilience: (a) relationship(s) to youth development or education or; (b) policy, practice, or youth impact evidence. Evidence is considered valid only after contradictory information, spurious relations, and rival explanations are considered and subsequently ruled out (Kirk & Miller, 1986; Sanders, 1994). Unless otherwise stated, exemplars presented throughout the chapter represent the conclusions drawn from an examination of this evidence. For more comprehensive reviews of the risk and resilience literature, please see Brown (2001a, 2001b), Brown and Horowitz (1993), and Brown, D'Emidio-Caston, and Benard (2000).

RISK

For well over 20 years, risk has come to represent a primary, if not *the* primary, social construction or perception of young people in education and related environments (Berger & Luckmann, 1967). In its ideal state, those adhering to this orientation suggest that if leaders (en masse) or practitioners (in individual cases), can identify risky environments or young people possessing risk factors, they can then be assisted to reduce their risk and prevent life failure (Hawkins, Catalano, & Miller, 1992; Hawkins, Lishner, Jensen, & Catalano, 1987). This is identified as a "Specifist" approach.

The impact of risk, however, involves more than this ideal. What came to be called a "risk orientation," coined in 1995 (Brown & D'Emidio-Caston, 1995), was found to include a constellation of less-than-ideal dimensions. Researchers such as Baizerman and Compton (1992), Blue-Swadener and Lubeck (1995), Brown (2001a, 2001b), Brown and Horowitz (1993), Fine (1993), Placier (1993), and Richardson (1990) connected the risk research with politics and policies, and the lives of young people. Through their research, terms such as "at-risk youth" and "high-risk youth" came to be powerful indicators of this general perception of youth experiencing, or believed to be heading, for life challenges.

For two reasons, then, the following examination of risk as a stepparent of resilience is instructive. First, it situates risk in a historical context. Second, an examination of risk illustrates the main pattern of development that resilience follows.

"A Nation At Risk": Codifying A Deficit Youth View?

In April 1983, the National Commission on Excellence in Education issued a landmark report titled "A Nation At Risk: The Imperative for Educational Reform." Assertions like the following drew attention to the challenges facing America and its educational system:

> If an unfriendly foreign power had attempted to impose on America the mediocre educational performance that exists today, we might well have viewed it as an act of war. We have even squandered the gains in student achievement made in the wake of the Sputnik challenge. Moreover, we have dismantled essential support systems which helped make those gains possible. We have, in effect, been committing an act of unthinking, unilateral educational disarmament.

Since the launch of *Sputnik* Soviet satellites in 1957, when American Education responded by engaging in a rapid succession of major science and math initiatives, few reports drew as much attention as this one. Filled with Cold War language, the authors identified American youth as primed for failure. No less than 10 "risk" factors placing American children in danger for future failure were noted. For example, it was described that the "average achievement of high school students on most standardized tests is now lower than 26 years ago when Sputnik was launched" (National Commission on Excellence in Education, 1993). In addition to noting specifics on what could be done to improve education by continually associating the risks young people face with the Cold War, the report may have popularized and codified the term "at risk" when referring to young people.

The Paradox of Risk: The Search for Risk Factors Evolves Into a General Youth Deficit Perspective

The two and one-half decades following the publication of "A Nation at Risk" caused and coincided with a large undertaking having a paradoxical effect; the scientific search for specific risk factors identifying "at-risk" youth, evolving into a general perception of young people as being "at risk" for some type of failure.

In the years since the "Nation at Risk" report, the social science community produced voluminous evidence correlating risk factors with negative youth outcomes. Factors such as rebellious youth attitudes or unclear familial expectations were two of many associated with negative life outcomes such as school failure or drug use (Hawkins et al., 1987). Additional research suggested that the more risk factors young people possessed, the more likely they were to experience a host of negative outcomes (Newcomb & Bentler, 1988).

When considering this evidence, it is important to consider that the risk factor research is largely associative. For example, where a correlation between a risk factor such as "youth rebelliousness" and an outcome such as drug experimentation is found, it does not mean that a student's rebelliousness *causes* drug use. In reality, this could be the case, that youth rebelliousness causes drug experimentation. Or it could be that drug experimentation causes youth rebelliousness. Finally, it could be that some other factor or factors, such as youthful curiosity, actually causes drug experimentation. In fact, under correlation research, one, another, many, none or unknown factors could be responsible for these outcomes. Because much if not most risk factor research is based on correlations, there is serious cause for pause, reflection, and consideration of whether there ever existed a sound basis for its widespread implementation in schools and/or programs (Bruvold, 1990; Manski, Pepper, & Petrie, 2001).

Despite this questionable evidence, as risk researchers consulted with policymakers, policies supporting identification and assistance of "at-risk" and "high-risk" youth were developed and implemented across the country. Funding streams, such as the Title IV, Safe and Drug Free Schools and Communities Act facilitated implementation of programs like this: "OSAP [Office of Substance Abuse Prevention] intends to fund applications that target youths with multiple risk factors, and propose comprehensive, multilevel prevention/intervention strategies that address clearly specified risk factors" (OSAP, 1989, p. 4). At the state level, in order to receive federal support, states asked many of their school districts to identify the numbers and types of "at-risk" youth in their schools. The following example comes from California:

Extensive research on risk factors offers a clear direction for prevention programs.... In planning prevention programs, begin by reviewing the following list of risk factors and protective factors. Determine which risk factors are most significant in your school community. Then inventory the resources that might be available to you in reducing these risk factors and increasing protective factors. With this information you can formulate objectives and activities that are designed to deal with the most important problems facing your students. (California State Department of Education, 1992, p. viii)

While noting protective factors as "available resources," this state policy language went on to list the following 36 "risk factors" associated with youth failure, which are reproduced in Figure 2.1.

Family risk factors:	lack of clear expectations for behavior; lack of monitoring; inconsistent or excessively severe discipline; lack of caring; parental drug, alcohol, and tobacco use; positive parental attitudes toward use; low expectation for children's success; family history of alcoholism.
School risk factors:	lack of clear policy regarding drugs, alcohol, and tobacco; availability of drugs, alcohol, and tobacco; school transitions; academic failure; lack of student involvement; little commitment to school.
Community risk factors:	economic and social deprivation; low neighborhood attachment and community disorganization; community norms and laws favorable to drug, alcohol, and tobacco use; availability of drugs, alcohol, and tobacco.
Individual/peer risk factors:	early antisocial behavior; alienation and rebelliousness; antisocial behavior in late childhood and early adolescence; favorable attitudes toward drugs, alcohol, and tobacco use; greater influence by and reliance on peers rather than parents; friends who use drugs, alcohol, and tobacco, or sanction use; early first use.
High risk factors:	(for the purposes of these guidelines, the federal definition of high risk will be used) any student who is at high risk of becoming or who has become a drug abuser or an alcohol abuser and is a child who has one or more of the following characteristics: is identified as a child of a substance abuser; is a victim of physical, sexual, or psychological abuse; has dropped out of school; has become pregnant; is economically disadvantaged; has committed a violent or delinquent act; has experienced mental health problems; has attempted suicide; has experienced long-term physical pain due to injury; has experienced chronic failure in school; has been placed on probation, formal or informal, or has served time in a juvenile detention facility.

Figure 2.1. Thirty-six risk factors associated with youth failure (California State Department of Education, 1992, pp. viii–ix).

These federal and state policy examples signify a compelling commitment to the risk factor approach. To procure funding, school districts needed to "determine which risk factors are [were] most significant" in their communities." The more youth that could be identified in each risk category, the higher the likelihood that districts could procure badly needed discretionary funding. Indeed, billions have been spent on these kinds of risk-based programs (U.S. General Accounting Office [GAO], 1996).

The large number of risk factors related to youth failure translated into a "risk orientation" or a deficit perception of young people. A school leader typified such a perception: "We are addressing the risk factors that show up, with the idea that it's real hard for me to point out which of our kids are not at risk" (Brown & D'Emdio-Caston, 1995, p. 13).

Under this funding approach, a transfer of the model from risk based policies into problem remediation programs occurred. Wide ranging programs such as "Just Say No" drug prevention and its variant offshoots were implemented across the country. This includes implementation of highly touted yet ineffective programs such as Drug Abuse Resistance Education (DARE) and Life Skills Training (Brown, 2001a, 2001b; Clayton, Catarello, & Johnstone, 1996; Ennett, Tobler, Ringwalt, & Flewelling, 1994; GAO, 1997; Gorman, 1998; Lynham et. al., 1999; Rosenbaum & Hansen, 1998). The problem remediation practices found in such programs are characterized by strategies to reduce risk through fear arousal, rewards, or coercion. Except under the most stringent conditions of monitoring, each of these "social influence" strategies attempting to mold or modify behavior have repeatedly found to be ineffective in the long term (Brown, D'Emidio-Caston, & Pollard, 1997; Raven, 1965).

If one steps back to examine the research, policies, and programs of risk, they give the illusion of incorporating a wide variety of perspectives and services. Yet, there is one primary social construction shared as part of a "Specifist" risk orientation: an operating assumption defined by a disease view of young people. Under this deficit approach, it is presumed that some aspect of youthful functioning is abnormal, thus the focus is on preventing youth failure. As this deficit perception of young people was translated from research to policy, problem remediation programs such as DARE usually followed.

Zero Tolerance

Perhaps the ultimate problem remediation practice is a zero tolerance policy. Such policies mandate "predetermined consequences or punishments for specific offenses" (Heaviside, Rowand, Williams, & Farris, 1998). These policies can be traced to the late 1980s, and the first Bush presidency:

School-based prevention programs should be reinforced by tough, but fair policies on use, possession, and distribution of drugs.... We cannot teach them that drugs are wrong and harmful if we fail to follow up our teaching with real consequences for those who use them.... Policies like these have been criticized for adding to the dropout problem. But experience shows that firm policies fairly enforced actually reduce the numbers of students who must be expelled for drug violations; most students choose to alter their behavior rather than risk expulsion. (The White House, 1989, pp. 50–51)

Under such policies, young people were to be removed from school for offenses such as any drug use or any violence. The U.S. General Accounting Office (1997) found that such policies have been implemented in more than 90% of American schools. Little evidence regarding zero tolerance is available. However, in 1998, the only year for which national data is currently available, 3.2 million, disproportionately minority young people, were removed from school under such policies (United States Department of Education [DOE] Office of Civil Rights, 2000).

Despite its widespread implementation, only a few of the researchers noted above connected these research, policy, and practice constructions of risk. Perhaps even fewer considered the impact of risk-oriented programs on young people, particularly from their own perspective(s).

Youth Impact of the Specifist Risk Approach

During the 1990s, our research team conducted one of the largest and most comprehensive evaluations of risk-based programs to date. It included in-depth examination of more than 75 school districts and 120 schools. Nearly 400 program school leaders and 250 young people in 40 focus groups were interviewed in-depth. This research also includes surveys of over 5,000 randomly selected youth. The contribution to the existing knowledge base was threefold: First, to examine risk as it was practiced. Second, to shift the research methods from primarily youth survey research containing correlations to predictive statistics, combined with a deep understanding of the risk-related educational culture through ethnographic research. Third, the perceptions of those developing and delivering programs were compared with the young people receiving the programs. Based on this change in the ways in which risk-based research was conducted, a heretofore undocumented magnitude and scope of the impact of risk oriented programs was discovered.

Results showed that a risk orientation had a negative youth impact. Beginning in fifth grade and by 12th grade, nearly all interviewees were aware that they or their peers were labeled as being at risk. They also experienced substantial cognitive dissonance as a result of risk-based programs (Brown et al., 1997). Cognitive dissonance was found in young people experiencing the conflict of seeing potentially troubled peers being removed from school rather than helped by people in their school (Brown & D'Emidio-Caston, 1995). Dissonance was also found in the conflicts young people experienced between the prevention information received in school as compared with their life experiences outside of school. These forms of dissonance were resolved by coming to believe that adults did not care about them, likely resulting in a decrease in adult credibility (Brown, 2001a; D'Emidio-Caston & Brown, 1998). As one young person noted, "If they suspect you of smoking or having drugs on you or whatever, if they see a kid like that in their school then, instead of suspending them and getting them out of school, why don't they help them?" (Brown & D'Emidio-Caston, 1995, p. 21). Young people concluded, "I don't think the schools are for like helping it's just for getting the bad kids out" (Brown & D'Emidio-Caston, 1995, p. 21). The cognitive dissonance experienced by young people in such risk-based programs is referred to as "disintegrative sharing" (Brown, 2001b). Across risk-oriented programs, the dissonance occurred precisely at the time youth/adult connections become of paramount importance, the transition from elementary to middle school (Eccles, 1991).

The concerns about the youth impact of risk-based programs were most serious in "Life Skills Training" programs (Botvin, Baker, Dusenbury, Botvin, & Diaz, 1995). Here, the dissonance occurs when programmers give the appearance of helping young people develop life and decision-making skills, when, in reality, young people learn that there is only one right choice to make—to abstain from risk-taking behaviors (Brown, 2001a). The dissonance from Life Skills Training was likely such serious impact that previously unreported results revealed a pattern of increased drug use among those receiving 50% or less of the program (Brown, 2001b).

The quantitative evidence supported the logically coherent statements made by young people. Among numerous findings, results showed that traditional factors such as gender, course grades, school attendance, and drug use did not explain the negative impact that risk-based prevention had on young people. Instead, the negative findings were best explained by the methods of social influence students described as experiencing in risk-based programs, that is, fear arousal, coercion, or rewards.

These findings were of such significant concern that a recent National Academy of Science report specifically discussed and supported them (Manski et al., p. 218). It followed such a discussion with the following conclusion about these types of prevention programs:

> Research is needed on a wider array of programs.... Until the results of such research are available, policy makers have only a weak information base on which to base policy decisions and are likely to continue to fund and operate ineffective prevention programs and programs of unknown effectiveness. (Manski et al., 2001, pp. 234–235)

Summary and Conclusions about the Specifist Risk Orientation

The development and application of the Specifist approach to risk in schools serves as an example in the relationship between research, policy, practice, and youth impact. Under what Thomas Kuhn in the "Structures of Scientific Revolutions" (1962) might have referred to as "normal" practices of science, ignoring contradictory evidence of its ineffectiveness, while nearly 25 years of mostly correlation risk research has produced apparently new evidence, such as additional risk factors correlated with some form of youth failure (Brown, 2001b). The publication volume of risk research may have been confused with research soundness. With the advice and consent of risk experts, the evidence was translated into premature policies and practices. So many factors were produced that its compelled implementation resulted in a general, yet narrow perception of young people—a deficit view of them producing ineffective programs, such as DARE or Life Skills Training, where every young person is "at risk." This Specifist perspective is so prevalent that it is referred to as the "risk orientation," a way of viewing young people. Risk orientation remains a dominant context in education, responsible for the significant amount of dissonance young people experience in schools.

RESILIENCE

When carefully considered, one body of evidence mitigates the utility, if not the validity of risk orientation. It is resilience. Resilience offers a more than 40-year pro-youth development perspective with a long-term scientific track record. Following a brief introduction, two different social constructions of resilience are developed. Its emerging application(s) are subsequently explored.

The Emergence of Resilience: Medicine and Developmental Psychopathology

Early findings supporting resilience emerged from medical and developmental psychopathology. For example, Hinkle (1974) followed people who had coronary disease. Over a 20-year period, he found that a few individuals who had experienced major life difficulties similar to others exhibited different illness patterns. It appeared that human processes of invulnerability were at work:

> The healthiest members of our samples often showed little psychological reaction to events and situations which caused profound reaction in other members of the group...the frustration of apparent important desires, or the failure to obtain apparently important goals produced no profound or long lasting reaction. (p. 40)

Since that time, other researchers located similar findings in psychosocial environments (Anthony 1970, 1974a, 1974b, 1984; Anthony & Cohler, 1987; Bleuer, 1978). In the transition from medicine to psychosocial research, a key conceptual distinction was also emerging. Those taking the psychosocial perspective shifted from examining invulnerability to risk, to examining strengths. As Anthony and Cohler (1987) noted, "Here, in this book, our major concern is with the elements of strength" (p. xi).

This early work evolved in two directions. In one direction, the Specifist perspective of resilience, researchers and practitioners have and continue to identify specific youth and conditions under which resilience occurs. This perspective is part of a traditional view of resilience: strength in the context of risk.

In the second approach to resilience, the Generalist perspective, participants articulate a general strengths perspective and wholistic view of the individual over one's life cycle, largely independent of a risk orientation. Each perspective is explored.

Resilience: The Specifist Perspective

Currently, resilience appears to be developing primarily in a Specifist manner. Its application in education bears an uncanny resemblance to the pattern of development of the risk orientation in schools. The policy example from California, described earlier and reproduced here, provides initial support for this assertion:

> Extensive research on risk factors offers a clear direction for prevention programs.... In planning prevention programs, begin by reviewing the following list of risk factors and protective factors. (California Department of Education, 1992, p. viii)

In this policy example, resilience is situated alongside "Extensive research on risk factors..." From the policy perspective, it is found that resilience is nearly always socially constructed as connected with risk. The research perspective is highly similar to the policy perspective—many participants also situate resilience with risk. According to Kuhn, a dimension of "normal science" is taking a next "logical" research step when considering previous research.[1] In the case of risk, those conducting such work might view risk on a linear continuum. On one end, risk is found. Perhaps in the middle of this continuum is an examination of vulnerability, and then, at the other end of the continuum, resilience is found. This construction has been developed by researchers calling for an extension of "normal" scientific practices into resilience:

> There is, however, a need for still greater specificity in defining the construct, since adjustment levels often vary considerably even within the broad domain of manifest competence. The current evidence indicates, then, that notions of "overall" resilience are of questionable utility...it would be more useful if discussions were presented in specific domains of successful coping. (Luthar, 1993 p. 442)

The kinds of "discussions" specifying "domains of successful coping" called for above are found at arguably the leading resilience organization in the United States, the Search Institute. The Institute developed an inventory of "30 original developmental assets," which was later expanded to 40. (Please see Figure 2.2.)

These 30 assets bear more than a passing resemblance to other initiatives, particularly the 36 risk factors described by the California State Department of Education. Many assets appear to represent the opposite of risk factors. This perspective does not reflect the longitudinal evidence

Support:	Family support, Parents as social resources, Parent communication, Other adult resources, Other adult communication, Parent involvement in schooling, Positive school climate
Boundaries:	Parental standards, Parental discipline, Parental monitoring, Time at home, Positive peer influence
Structured Time Use:	Involved in music, Involved in extracurricular activities, Involved in community organizations, Involved in church or synagogue
Educational Commitment:	Achievement motivation, Educational aspiration, School performance, Homework
Positive Values:	Values helping people, Is concerned about world hunger, Cares about people's feelings, Values sexual restraint
Social Competencies:	Assertiveness skills, Decision-making skills, Friendship-making skills, Planning skills, Self-esteem, Positive view of the future

Figure 2.2. Thirty original developmental assets (Benson, 1997, p. 252).

identifying resilience as a distinct social construction that is indicated by protective factors (Brown, 2001a; Brown & Horowitz, 1993).

On their website, the Search Institute goes on to suggest that most children do not experience a sufficient number of these assets in order to thrive:

> ...while the assets are powerful shapers of young people's lives and choices, too few young people experience enough of these assets. The average young person surveyed experiences only 18 of the 40 assets. Overall, 62 percent of young people surveyed experience fewer than 20 of the assets. In short, most young people in the United States do not have in their lives many of the basic building blocks of healthy development. (Search Institute, Developmental Assets: An Overview, n.d.)

Based on the inventory it developed, through sales of assessment packets, information services, training, and curriculum to interested parties, the Institute's work helps define who is resilient. It does so largely by correlating specific assets with, for example, demographic characteristics of young people. In form, research methods, and content, the Search Institute's work on resilience bears a resemblance to work patterns conducted with risk.

Overall, it is too early to tell how this construction of resilience will ultimately be implemented or what its long-term practice effects will be. However, judging by its evolution alongside the development of risk, resilience is primarily developing on a Specifist trajectory.

Resilience: A Generalist Perspective

In addition to the Specifist approach to resilience, another track is emerging. Many of those working on this track recognize that resilience, although borne of risk and vulnerability, is distinct from a risk orientation. Here, resilience evolves into a strengths-based approach to a global view of the whole child, not at a given point in time per se, but long term, as it evolves over one's life. This evolutionary shift and youth orientation is referred to as a "Generalist" resilience perspective. As Moriarty (1987) noted:

> Resilience as I have conceived of it, in terms of recovery over a shorter or long time, involves global aspects of the whole child—growth and growth drive.... Resilience, like competence and adaptation as outcomes of coping, is an evaluative concept, not a unitary trait. The resilient child is oriented toward the future, is living ahead, with hope. (p.101)

On the policy level, no explicit and large-scale Generalist examples supporting the above resilience perspective in practice could be located.

The Generalist perspective of resilience does, however, find substantial research support. For example, in longitudinal work, scientists such as Werner, Rutter, and Garmezy located the importance of resilience as a global construction over a life cycle. They found that approximately 60–70% of youth experiencing the challenging life conditions mature into adults who not only survive, but thrive (Garmezy, 1983, 1985, 1987, 1991; Rutter, 1979, 1981, 1985, 1987; Werner, 1986, 1987, 1989, 1990, 1993; Werner & Smith, 1977, 1982, 2001). Bonnie Benard (Brown et al., 2001), a leader in this field, notes three essential dimensions or protective factors comprising resilience: caring, connected relationships with an adult; opportunities for participation and contribution; and high self expectations.

When considering the longitudinal findings noted above, the importance of connectedness as the lynchpin for thriving is hard to overstate. For example, in longitudinal research, Resnick and colleagues (1997) found that "parent-family and perceived school connectedness were [was] protective against every health risk behavior measure except pregnancy" (p. 823). The protective factor of "connectedness" or bonds between infants, children, adolescents, and adults, any adults, is an essential component of what allows people to cope and to grow into successful people.

Not only is the evidence supporting resilience longitudinal, its Generalist construction crosses multiple lines of inquiry. This is described in our most recent book *Resilience Education*:

> It is important to take a moment to note the convergence of parallel lines of research. Long before resilience researchers were focused on the lifetime development of the whole child, progressive educators and developmental psychologists took this focus. Early childhood educators are familiar with the philosophical tradition that centers on the development of the whole child (Dewey, 1897, 1899, 1902; Montessori, 1912; Piaget, 1973; Steiner,1988; Kohlberg & Meyer, 1972, Bredekamp, 1986). Piaget's studies of how children develop their understanding of mathematics, time, moral judgment, etc. and Kohlberg's contributions to our understanding of moral development are often cited by educators who hold a wholistic, developmental approach to teaching and learning. This historical tradition in education and developmental psychology converges with resilience research to support a wholistic view of youth in the context of lifelong development. (Brown et al., 2000, pp. 12–13)

Across these disciplines, the evidence provides for a general transactional model of human development (Brofenbrenner, 1979). Under this model the process or the nature of the interaction between youth and adults in the context of the larger society itself is a significant part of what facilitates thriving development. Resilience is linked with a global view of the whole child, not just what they think, but essentially important, how they feel and relate to the world. These "feeling" dimensions of human perception and interaction have now been shown to be but a physiologically indispensable part of learning and resilient development (Brown, 1996, 2001a; Cline, Nechochea, & Brown, 1999).

Conceptually, the bottom line of the Generalist approach to resilience is that individual and social connectedness fosters resilience in most young people. In practice, those using a Generalist approach develop a nondidactic interactive process orientation. Connectedness serves as the means to locate strengths and interests to build on. Resilience, as this process orientation, is thoroughly and specifically described in *Resilience Education* (Brown et al., 2000).

The research on this Generalist track of resilience has been around for quite a while, yet its explicit development and application to education is in its infancy. Nevertheless, there is significant and relatively well-founded evidence suggesting the educational promise of resilience under the Generalist construct. An example of findings is summarized in a recent article:

> For example, the Child Development Program (CDP) studies have shown a number of significant outcomes with young people with whole-school interventions (e.g., educators, administrators, counselors, and community) initiated in elementary school that are highly significant by middle school. They include positive effects on their school-related attitudes and motives (e.g., liking for school, achievement motivation), social attitudes, skills, and values (e.g., concern for others, conflict resolution skills, commitment to democratic values), and involvement in problem behaviors (e.g., reduced drug use and violence related behaviors) (Battistich, Schaps, Watson, Solomon, & Lewis, 2000; Kendzior & Dasho, 1996; Solomon, Battistich, Watson, Schaps, & Lewis, in press; Watson, 1996; Watson, Battistich, & Solomon, 1997). These studies are showing that when compared with control groups, early evidence of the application of resilience to education reveals higher test scores, higher grades in core academic subjects, more involvement in positive youth school and community activities, and less misconduct at school than comparison students. (Brown, 2001a, p. 50)

When considering the Generalist resilience construct in education, there is promising but insufficient evidence regarding its impact. Clearer linkages between youth–adult connectedness and their relationship(s) and long-term positive outcomes must first be explored.

Calling for "clearer linkages" *does not* only mean working with resilience as it is often currently constructed under the Specifist approach. Let me specify what it might also mean in this case:

1. Absent the deficit and problem remediation constructs traditionally associated with such services, a pro-youth development orientation

toward young people's development may enhance the resilience of the majority of young people.
2. Employing predictive research methods examining relationship(s) between connectedness, the three core protective factors, and outcomes over at least a 3-year period.
3. Appropriately matching methods with research construction(s), for example, as opposed to linking resilience factors with a decrease in negative outcomes, linking resilience factors with competency-based outcomes such as skills development or demonstration(s).

DISCUSSION

Summary

Table 2.1 summarizes the dimensions of risk and resilience and their respective evolutionary patterns of development.

In review, the development and application of risk offers important insights into development of resilience. "Normal" research patterns associate, but do not clearly or consistently predict, youth failure. The large number of scientifically associated risk factors contributed to an overall policy and practice perception of risk. Nevertheless, in conjunction with policymakers, researchers helped make politically viable an assumption of deviance found in the risk factor model. First located in major policy statements, then transferred from the federal government to states and schools, the assumption of youth abnormality itself has had distressing consequences on young people's lives. Rather than assisting programmers in selecting youth for assistance, the increase in the number of risk factors allowed administrators and practitioners to generalize by labeling many or most young people as being at-risk for some kind of failure.

By fifth grade this risk orientation can be seen as a significant contributor to young people's cognitive dissonance about school and society, resolved by an apparent reduction in adult credibility. This dissonance begins to occur precisely at the time young people are in greatest need of youth adult connectedness—during the transition from elementary to middle school.

Most early applications of resilience in education follow a similar track to the development of risk. The policy language of resilience is often surrounded by risk. There have been significant calls for evidence supporting the specific dimensions and conditions defining resilient youth. As of this writing, the primary evidence supporting such specific applications of resilience is correlation, not consistently predictive of life success.

Table 2.1. Dimensions of Risk and Resilience

Dimensions	Research orientation and evidence	Policy orientation	Youth view, associated practices, and example program	Youth impact
Risk Specifist	Orientation: Identification of risk factors and youth possessing them 1. Evidence: Correlation(s) between risk factors and youth failure 2. No methodologically sound and consistently predictable relationship between risk factor identification and problem remediation	Theoretical identification and service of "at-risk" and "high-risk" youth Status: Large-scale implementation	Youth view. Deficit: "At risk" for life failure Practices: 1. Problem remediation: Didactic problem prevention orientation supported by zero tolerance policies 2. Decontextualized from social welfare Example: DARE	1. Labeling 2. Cognitive dissonance by fifth grade 3. Likely reduced adult credibility 4. Societal detachment
Resilience Specifist	Orientation: Identification of assets and youth possessing them 3. Evidence: Correlation(s) between assets and youth demographic characteristics 4. No methodologically sound and consistently predictable relationship between asset identification and capacity development	Theoretical identification and service of resilient youth. Associated with risk Status: Large-scale implementation	Youth view: Insufficient number of youth possess sufficient assets; consequently, at risk for life challenges Practices: 1. Problem remediation: Didactic problem prevention orientation related to assets development 2. May or may not be explicitly connected with social welfare Example: Search Institute Original Assets Development Program(s)	Inconclusive

Table 2.1. Dimensions of Risk and Resilience (Cont.)

Dimensions	Research orientation and evidence	Policy orientation	Youth view, associated practices, and example program	Youth impact
Resilience Generalist	Orientation: Extent to which protective factors predict development	Youth development and strengths based	Youth view: Resilience as a global trait over life span	Early longitudinal results:
	5. Evidence: Longitudinal, causation oriented	Status: Small-scale implementation or not implemented	Practices: Strengths based with process orientation	1. More positive school attitudes
	6. Promising but insufficient evidence of resilient school climate predicting positive youth outcomes		1. Development of affective and cognitive dimensions of connectedness(es) in the service of learning and development	2. Higher liking for school, achievement motivation, social attitudes, skills, and values, higher level of concern for others
			2. Recognizes mutuality between program deliverer and recipient	3. Improved conflict resolution skills
			3. Development and process explicitly connected with social welfare	4. Higher commitment to democratic values
			Example: Resilience education	5. Reduced involvement in problem behaviors, higher test scores
				6. Higher grades in core academic subjects
				7. More involvement in positive youth school and community activities
				8. Reduced misconduct

The Lessons of History in Process: Risking for Resilience

If the history of risk teaches us anything about resilience, it should at least alert us to its potential for misuse or negative politicization. Years ago, Garmezy (1987) alerted us as to this possibility:

> The concept of protective factors is potentially a political weapon. Resilient children and the countless numbers of successful adults who demonstrate their escape from poverty and disadvantage, can be used by political advocates of an ideological viewpoint that holds resiliency of some to be proof of its possession by all; that anyone can emulate such achievements if they only try harder.... The very fact of individual variations in competence suggests the need for greater assistance to some while lesser assistance may be directed to others. A wise society and a compassionate government see this position not as inconsistency, but rather as an exercise of mature, non-ideological judgment and equity.... Government, by providing protective factors, enables some who would otherwise be lost to a fruitful life to move above the threshold of competence needed to survive in an increasingly complex, technological, society. (p. 171)

Garmezy situates resilience in a larger context—as a Generalist construct linked with "equity," and thus the larger society. A connection between individual and larger society forms an essential distinction between the Generalist and Specifist approach to resilience. Rather than arguing for a view of resilience situated in determining who is resilient and who is not, Garmezy states the importance of establishing a "nonideological" and equitable resilience climate tied to the social welfare.

The Value of a Generalist Approach to Resilience: Reciprocity, Personal Responsibility, and System Development

Why is this link between individual and society in a general climate of resilience so important? Making such linkages contributes to the recognition of reciprocity and personal responsibility. Education is inextricably linked with social welfare. The moral or character dimension of education orients young people to recognize the "mutually supportive obligations of people to each other..." (Wickenden, 1965 p. 12). The risk orientation and the nascent Specifist construct of resilience detach young people from a mutually obligatory orientation by doing things to them rather than with them. Specifically, this often means what Boulding (1967) called a "unilateral transfer" of resources from provider to recipient, from school to young person, with little or no meaningful reciprocal responsibility. Under a risk orientation and arguably the emerging Specifist form of resilience, there are responsibilities that the young person has such as staying in school, proscribed labor such as erasing graffiti, or not violating other rules, and so on. Despite this, many of these obligations are punitively oriented, not seen as meaningful through young peoples' eyes. In terms of social influence, these methods of fear arousal, limited reward, or coercion have not resulted in personal development—change that becomes part of an individual or that does not have to be monitored in order to occur (Brown & Raven, 1994). Such a unilateral resource transfer without recognition of mutuality and meaningful opportunities for contribution will not transform those youth facing life's most serious challenges, let alone other young people, into societal participants. This is because many perceive no investment in a positive outcome. Those undergoing such challenges themselves do not see the potential rewards of a mutual and socially participatory life within school or societal membership. Those witnessing peers undergoing such challenges, often without assistance, come to believe that they live in an uncaring society, where the emphasis turns into self-reward. Situated on society's periphery, many young people feel no need to take responsibility for identifying their capacities in order to reciprocate. In summary, for these reasons, the evidence clearly suggests that connectedness is what fosters resilience.

As reciprocity and responsibility are important for children, there is a flip side. These elements are also essential for those working with young people, for example, educators, leaders, or any participants in learning environments. Reciprocity is part of the dynamic that maintains a healthy educational dynamic or social system. While discussing the importance of strategic reflection during resilience building, this is noted:

> Gaining the insight that comes from reflection on these issues helps us immensely with resilience education. It keeps the educator from burning out because s/he makes explicit a lifelong commitment to professional development for their own and their student's benefit. The educator comes to understand how s/he is growing. (Brown et al., 2000, p. 69)

With its focus on developing a general climate of resilience and explicitly developing human connections between social context, individual, and group, the Generalist perspective of resilience has a high potential for this kind of mutuality. As such, the Generalist perspective of resilience holds particular promise for meeting individual as well as societal needs.

CONCLUSIONS: RESPONDING TO RESILIENCES' FUTURE CHALLENGES IN EDUCATION

In sum, the Generalist approach to resilience is distinct from its Specifist counterpart. First, it is absent the deficit social construction and problem remediation practice focus found in the Specifist approach. Second, the Generalist approach is oriented toward youth development, not dependent on identifying who is at risk, each person's level of risk and ultimately, exiling those most in need of support. Finally, with its explicit process orientation focused on facilitating connectedness between youth and adult as well as society, where the specifist approach falls short, a Generalist approach to resilience in education offers the potential to contribute to a personally and mutually rewarding, evolving, and evolved social system.

There are numerous challenges to extensive development of resilience as is conceived of here. Two challenges are discussed. First, the ideal applied to the Generalist resilience program may not look like traditional curriculum or programs. Resilience is infused throughout the educational culture. Rather than a prescribed program typically found under specifist approaches, resilience education is a learning and development orientation made explicit by those working with young people so that they can then use this approach to develop their own path to personal responsibility, awareness and thus, resilience. While some may criticize resilience as being ambiguous, it is important to understand that an emphasis on context or a resilient climate *alone* has provided positive longitudinal evidence of positive long-term outcomes. Imagine what could be achieved when combining a resilient climate with a specific, yet nondidactic resilience education process orientation?

A second challenging aspect of implementing resilience in an educational environment is current school reform trends. While conceptually distinct from today's educational standards, accountability, and associated practices, the resilience-building process asks each individual to consider context and social welfare in an ongoing way. A resilience orientation then, supports an appropriate reform process for all involved.

Resilience education as part of a Generalist resilience approach represents more than just another program shift. It is a reasoned, scientifically supported conceptual and pro-youth development perspective, along with the specific, yet nondidactic means to implement it. As the esteemed Bonnie Benard has written numerous times (1994a, 1994b, 1987) when discussing resilience:

> I'd like to share with you an approach that has demonstrated effectiveness at facilitating the development within youths or adults of the belief that they are innately resilient—that they have the capacity to develop caring relation-

ships, to solve their own problems, to feel good about who they are, and to be optimistic about their future. (1994a, p. 1)

Without the research support evident in today's Generalist perspective of resilience, this conceptual shift was approached in the mid-1970s, but due to a minority yet vocal parents movement, never thoroughly implemented or evaluated (G. Brown, 1972/1990, 1975; J. Brown, 2001a). With an eye on these larger development patterns that can alleviate the errors made in the application(s) of risk, the accumulating resilience evidence suggests that the knowledge, process, and opportunity is available to create a pro-youth development educational system.

NOTE

1. For a comprehensive Kuhnian examination of development in risk and resilience, please see Brown, 2001b.

REFERENCES

Anthony, E.J. (1970). The impact of mental and physical illness on family life. *American Journal of Psychiatry*, 127, 138–146.

Anthony, E. J. (1974a). A risk-vulnerability intervention model. In E. J. Anthony & C. Koupernik (Eds.), *The child in his family: Children at psychiatric risk* (International Yearbook, Vol. 3). New York: Wiley.

Anthony E.J. (1974b). The syndrome of the psychologically invulnerable child. In E.J. Anthony & C. Koupernik (Eds.), *The child in his family: Children at psychiatric risk* (International Yearbook, Vol. 3). New York: Wiley.

Anthony, E. J. (1984). The St. Louis Risk Research Project. In N. F. Watt, E. J. Anthony, L. C. Wynne, & J. Roth (Eds.), *Children at risk for schizophrenia: A longitudinal perspective*. Cambridge, UK: Cambridge University Press.

Anthony, E. J., & Cohler, B. J. (Eds.). (1987). *The invulnerable child*. New York: Guilford Press.

Baizerman, M., & Compton, D. (1992). From respondent and informant to consultant and participant: The evolution of a state agency policy evaluation. In A. M. Madison (Ed.), *Minority issues in program evaluation* (New Directions in Program Evaluation, Vol. 53, pp. 5–16). San Francisco: Jossey-Bass.

Battistich, V., & Hom, A. (1997). The relationships between students sense of their school as a community and their involvement in problem behaviors, *American Journal of Public Health*, 87, 1997–2001.

Battistich, V., Schaps, E., Solomon, D., & Watson, M. (1991). The role of the school in prosocial development. In H. E. Fitzgerald, B. M. Lester, & M. W. Yogman (Eds.), *Theory and research in behavioral pediatrics* (Vol. 5). New York: Plenum Press.

Battistich, V., Schaps, E., Watson, M., Solomon, D., & Lewis, C. (2000). Effects of the Child Development Project on students drug use and other problem behaviors. *Journal of Primary Prevention, 21,* 75–99.

Benard, B. (1987). Protective factor research: What we can learn from resilient children. *Western Center for Prevention.* Portland, OR: Western Center for Prevention.

Benard, B. (1994b). *Fostering resiliency in urban schools.* San Francisco: Far West Laboratories.

Benard, B. (1994a, December). The health realization approach to resiliency. *Western Center News, 8*(1), 1–4.

Benson, P. (1998). *All kids are our kids.* San Francisco: Jossey-Bass.

Berger, P.L., & Luckmann, (1967). *The social construction of reality.* Garden City, NY: Anchor Books.

Bleuer, M. (1978). *The schizophrenic disorders.* New Haven, CT: Yale University Press.

Blue-Swadener, B., & Lubeck, S. (1995). *Children and families "at promise": Deconstructing the discourse of risk.* New York: State University of New York Press.

Botvin, G. J., Baker, E., Dusenbury, L., Botvin, E. M., & Diaz, T. (1995) Long-term follow-up results of a randomized drug abuse prevention trial in a white middle-class population. *Journal of the American Medical Association, 273,* 1106–1112.

Boulding, K. (1967). The boundaries of social policy. *Social Work, 12*(1), 7–21.

Bredekamp, S. (1986). *Developmentally appropriate practice in early childhood programs serving children from birth to age 8.* Washington, DC: NAEYC.

Brofenbrenner, U. (1979). *The ecology of human development.* Cambridge, MA: Harvard University Press.

Brown, G. I. (1972/1990). *Human teaching for human learning: An introduction to confluent education.* Highland, NY: The Gestalt Journal.

Brown, G. I. (Ed.) (1975). *The live classroom: Innovation through confluent education and Gestalt.* New York: The Viking Press.

Brown, J.H. (Ed.). (1996). *Advances in confluent education: Integrating consciousness for human change* (Vol. 1). Greenwich, CT: JAI Press.

Brown, J. H. (2001a). Systemic reform concerning resilience in education. *Association for Educational Communications and Technology, 45*(4), 47–54.

Brown, J. H. (2001b). Youth, drugs and resilience education. *Journal of Drug Education, 31*(1), 83–122.

Brown J. H., & D'Emidio-Caston, M. (1995). On becoming at-risk through drug education: How symbolic policies and their practices affect students. *Evaluation Review, 19*(4), 451–492.

Brown, J. H., D'Emidio-Caston, M., & Benard, B. (2000). *Resilience education.* Thousand Oaks, CA: Corwin.

Brown, J. H., D'Emidio-Caston, M., & Pollard, J. (1997). Students and substances: Social power in drug education. *Educational Evaluation and Policy Analysis, 19*(1), 65–82.

Brown, J.H., & Horowitz, J.E. (1993). Deviants and deviance: Why adolescent substance use prevention programs do not work. *Evaluation Review, 17*(5), 529–555.

California State Department of Education. (1992). *Healthy kids, healthy California: Drug, alcohol, tobacco, education (date) district application for funding*. Sacramento: California State Department of Education.

Clayton, R. R., Catarello, A. M., & Johnstone, B. M. (1996). The effectiveness of drug abuse resistance education (Project D.A.R.E.): 5-year follow up results. *Journal of Preventive Medicine, 25*(3), 1–12.

Cline, Z., Necochea, J., & Brown, J.H. (Eds.) (1999). *Advances in Confluent Education, Vol 2: Multicultural dynamics of educational change*. Greenwich, CT: JAI Press.

D'Emidio-Caston, M., & Brown, J.H. (1998). The other side of the story: Student narratives on the California Drug, Alcohol, Tobacco Education program. *Evaluation Review, 22*(1), 95–117.

Dewey, J. (1897). My pedagogic creed. *School Journal, 54*(3), 77–80.

Dewey, J. (1899). *The school and society*. Chicago: University of Chicago Press.

Dewey, J. (1902). *The child and the curriculum*. Chicago: University of Chicago Press.

Eccles, J. S., Midgley, C., Wigfield, A., Miller-Buchanan, C., Reuman, D., Flanagan, C., & MacIver, D. (1993). Development during adolescence: The impact of stage-environment fit on young adolescents' experiences in schools and families. *American Psychologist, 48*(2), 90–101.

Fine, M. (1993). Making controversy: Who's "at risk?" In R. Wollons (Ed.), *Children at risk in America* (pp. 91–110). New York: State University of New York Press.

Garmezy, N. (1983). Stressors of childhood. In N. Garmezy, & M. Rutter (Eds.), *Stress, coping and development in children* (pp. 43–84). New York: McGraw-Hill.

Garmezy, N. (1985). Stress resistant children: The search for protective factors. In *Recent research in developmental psychopathology (Journal of Child Psychology and Psychiatry*, Book Supp, Vol. 4). Oxford: Pergamon.

Garmezy, N. (1987). Stress, competence, and development: Continuities in the study of schizophrenic adults, children vulnerable to psychopathology, and the search for stress-resistant children. *American Journal of Orthopsychiatry, 52*(2), 159–175.

Garmezy, N. (1991). Resilience and vulnerability to adverse developmental outcomes associated with poverty. *American Behavioral Scientist, 34*, 416–430.

Gorman, D. M. (1998). The irrelevance of evidence in the development of school-based drug prevention policy, 1986–1996. *Evaluation Review, 22*(1), 118–146.

Hawkins, J. D., Catalano, R. F., & Miller, J. Y. (1992). Risk and protective factors for alcohol and other drug problems in adolescence and early adulthood: Implications for substance abuse prevention. *Psychological Bulletin, 112*, 63–105.

Hawkins, J. D., Lishner, D. M., Jenson, J. M., & Catalano, R. F. (1987). Delinquents and drugs: What the evidence suggests about prevention and treatment programming. In B. S. Brown & A. R. Mills (Eds.), *Youth at high risk for substance abuse* (pp. 81–131) (DHHS Publication No. ADM 87-1537). Washington, DC: US Government Printing Office.

Heaviside, S., Rowand, C., Williams, C., & Farris E., (1998, March). *Violence and discipline problems in U.S. public schools: 1996–97* [Online]. Washington, DC: National Center for Educational Statistics, U.S. Department of Education. Retrieved July 15, 1999 from: http://nces.ed.gov/pubs98/violence/

Hinkle, L. E. (1974). The effect of exposure to culture change, social change, and changes in interpersonal relationships on health. In B. S. Dohrenwend & B. P. Dohrenwend (Eds.), *Stressful life events*. New York: Wiley.

Kendzior, S., & Dasho, S. (1996, April). *A model for deep, long-term change in teachers' beliefs and practices*. Paper presented at the annual meeting of the American Educational Research Association, San Francisco.

Kohlberg, R., & Meyer, R. (1972). Development as the aim of education. *Harvard Educational Review, 42*, 449–496.

Kirk, J., & Miller, M. (1986). *Reliability and validity in qualitative research*. Newbury Park, CA: Sage.

Kuhn, T. (1962). *The structure of scientific revolutions*. Chicago: University of Chicago Press.

Luthar, S. S. (1993). Annotation: Methodological and conceptual issues in research on childhood resilience. *Journal of Child Psychology and Psychiatry, 34*, 441–443

Manski, C. F., Pepper, J. V., & Petrie, C. V. (Eds.). (2001). *Informing America's policy on illegal drugs: What we don't know keeps hurting us*. Washington, DC: National Academy Press.

Montessori, M. (1912). *The Montessori method*. New York: Frederick Stokes.

Moriarty, A. E. (1987). Further reflections on resilience. In E. J. Anthony & B. J. Cohler (Eds.), *The invulnerable child*. New York: Guilford Press.

National Commission on Education. (1983). *A nation at risk: The imperative for educational reform* [Online]. Washington, DC: U.S. Department of Education.

Newcomb, M., & Bentler, P. (1988). *Consequences of adolescent drug use: Impact on the lives of young adults*. Newbury Park, CA: Sage.

Office of Substance Abuse Prevention (OSAP). (1989). *Request for proposals for high-risk youth grants*. Washington, DC: Author.

Piaget, J. (1973). *To understand is to invent*. New York: Grossman.

Placier, M. L. (1993). The semantics of state policy making: The case of "at-risk." *Educational Evaluation and Policy Analysis, 15*, 380–395.

Raven, B. H. (1965). Social influence and power. In I. D. Steiner & M. Fishbein (Eds.), *Current studies in social psychology* (pp. 371–382). New York: Holt, Rinehart & Winston.

Resnick, M. D., Bearman, P. S., Blum, R. W., Bauman, K. E., Harris, K. M., & Jones, et al., (1997). Protecting adolescents from harm: Findings from the national longitudinal study on adolescent health. *Journal of the American Medical Association, 278*, 823–832.

Richardson, V. (1990). At-risk programs: Evaluation and critical inquiry. *New Directions for Program Evaluation, 45*, 61–75.

Rosenbaum, D. P. & Hanson, G. S. (1998). Assessing the effects of school-based drug education: A six-year multi-level analysis of project D.A.R.E. *Journal of Research in Crime and Delinquency, 35*(4), 381–412.

Rutter, M. (1979). Protective factors in children's responses to stress and disadvantage. In M.W. Ken & J.E. Rolf (Eds.), *Primary prevention of psychopathology, Vol. 3: Social competence in children*. Hanover, NH: University Press of New England.

Rutter, M. (1981). Stress, coping and development: some issues and some questions. *Journal of Child Psychology and Psychiatry, 22*, 323–356.

Rutter, M. (1985). Resilience in the face of adversity: Protective factors and resistance to psychiatric disorder. *British Journal of Psychiatry, 147,* 598–611.
Rutter, M. (1987). Psychosocial resilience and protective mechanisms. *American Journal of Orthopsychiatry, 57,* 316–331.
Sanders, J. R. (1994). *The program evaluation standards.* Newbury Park, CA: Sage.
Search Institute, developmental assets: An overview [Online]. (n.d.). Retrieved March 15, 2002, from: http://www.search-institute.org/assets
Solomon, D., Battistich, V., Watson, M., Schaps, E., & Lewis, C. (in press). A six-district study of educational change: Direct and mediated effects of the Child Development Project. *Social Psychology of Education.*
Steiner, R. (1988). *The child's changing consciousness and Waldorf education.* London: Steiner Press.
United States Department of Education, Office of Civil Rights. (2000). *1998 Elementary and secondary school civil rights compliance report.* Washington, DC: Author.
United States General Accounting Office. (1996, October,). *Drug and alcohol abuse: Billions spent annually for treatment and prevention activities* (No. GAO/HEHS-97-12). Washington, DC: Author.
United States General Accounting Office. (1997, June). *Substance abuse and violence prevention: Multiple youth programs raise questions of efficiency and effectiveness.* Statement of Carlotta C. Joyner, director education and employment issues, health, education, and human services division (No. GAO-T-HEHS-97-166). Washington, DC: Author.
Watson, M. (1996, April). *Giving content to restructuring: A social, ethical and intellectual agenda for elementary education.* Paper presented at the meeting of the American Educational Research Association, San Francisco.
Watson, M., Battistich, V., & Solomon, D. (1997). Enhancing students' social and ethical development in schools: An intervention program and its effects. *International Journal of Educational Research, 27,* 571–586.
Werner, E. E. (1986). Resilient offspring of alcoholics: A longitudinal study from birth to age 18. *Journal of Studies on Alcohol, 47*(1), 34–40.
Werner, E. E. (1987). Vulnerability and resiliency in children at risk for delinquency: A longitudinal study from birth to young adulthood: In J. D. Burchard & S. N. Burchard (Eds.), *Handbook of early intervention: theory, practice and analysis.* Cambridge, UK: Cambridge University Press.
Werner, E. E. (1989). High risk children in young adulthood: A longitudinal study from birth to 32 years. *American Journal of Orthopsychiatry, 59*(1), 72–81.
Werner, E. E. (1990). Protective factors and individual resilience. In S. Mesiels & J. Shonkoff (Eds.), *Handbook of early childhood intervention.* New York: Cambridge University Press.
Werner, E. E. (1993). Risk, resilience and recovery: Perspectives from the Kauai longitudinal study. *Development and Psychopathology, 5,* 503–515.
Werner, E. E., & Smith, R. S. (1977). *Kauai's children come of age.* Honolulu: University of Hawaii Press.
Werner, E . E., & Smith, R. S. (1982). *Vulnerable but invinceable: A Longitudinal study of resilient children and youth.* New York: McGraw-Hill.
Werner, E. E., & Smith, R. S. (2001). *Journeys from childhood to midlife: Risk, resilience, and recovery.* New York: Cornell University Press.

Werner, E. E., Bierman, J., & French, F. (1971). *The children of Kauai.* Honolulu: University of Hawaii Press.

White House, The. (1989). *National drug control strategy.* Washington, DC: Office of National Drug Control Policy.

Wickenden, E. (1965). *Social welfare in a changing world.* Washington, DC: U.S. Government Printing Office.

CHAPTER 3

PROMOTING EDUCATIONAL RESILIENCE FOR STUDENTS AT-RISK OF FAILURE

Hersh C. Waxman
University of Houston

Jon P. Gray
Lamar University

Yolanda N. Padrón
University of Houston

One of most formidable challenges facing public education is improving the education of the growing numbers of students at risk of academic failure (Pianta & Walsh, 1996; Waxman, Padrón, & Arnold, 1991). Students at risk of failure often face deleterious conditions caused by poverty, health, and other social problems that have made it difficult for them to improve their educational status. Consequently, one of our most pressing national educational priorities is closing the achievement gap and improving the academic performance for those students who are not successful in school. One area of research that has important implications for the educational improvement of students at risk of academic failure is that of examining "resilient" students, or students who succeed in school despite the presence of adverse conditions.

It is possible for students to be exposed to inappropriate educational experiences through their families, schools, or communities (Pallas, Natriello, & McDill, 1989). While educators cannot control community demographics and family conditions, they can change educational policy and practices to specifically address the educational needs of students at risk of academic failure (Comer, 1987). Policymakers, administrators, teachers, and parents need to know why some students are resilient and do well in school, while others from identical socioeconomic backgrounds, similar home environments, similar ability, and even from the same schools and classrooms do not do well academically. Examining these factors will allow us to investigate the circumstances that place these students at risk, as well as those processes or factors that foster success. One of the major advantages of the approach of studying educational success or resilience is that it shifts the focus of educational research and policy from school failure and predictors of school failure to school success and the predictors of academic success.

The purpose of this chapter is to explain how a perspective on educational resiliency might lead to educational improvements for students at risk of academic failure. This framework may help educators design more effective educational interventions that specifically take into account those "alterable" factors that promote students' resiliency. First, we discuss issues related to the definition of resiliency. Next, we review several classic resilience studies that helped develop the field. Then we examine several recent studies in the area of educational resiliency, specifically those that focus on differences between resilient and nonresilient students' characteristics, family background, and perceptions of the classroom and school environment. The final sections of the chapter focus on implications for educational practice and research.

ISSUES IN DEFINING RESILIENCY

Although most definitions of resiliency are similar, some delineation among definitions should be considered. Synonymous terms have been used interchangeably in describing resilient students and individuals. "Hardiness," "invulnerable," and "invincible," for example, are all terms that have been used to describe resilient characteristics (Wolin & Wolin, 1993). The common thread associated with the use of these terms is the focus on positive qualities or outcomes rather than focusing on negative concerns. The difference between the definitions of resilience is often rooted in the specific approach or context in which resilience is being studied. "High-risk" groups, for example, are typically defined by the factors that categorize the groups' label (e.g., poverty, family background, or abuse), while definitions that focus on the broader educational community are often based on the positive experiences that may be associated with individual adaptation (e.g., significant relationships, school perceptions, and school involvement). It is important to consider these different approaches when studying the resiliency construct. Furthermore, it also is important to recognize the specific context in which resilience is being examined before generalizing the resilience concept to larger educational resilience domains. All of these approaches are vital to the understanding of resilience. The resiliency concept needs to be more completely understood contextually before we can draw practical implications regarding building resiliency in our schools (Liddle, 1994).

Wolin and Wolin (1993) explained that the term "resilient" was adopted in lieu of earlier terms used to describe the phenomenon (such as invulnerable, invincible, and hardy) because "resilient" recognizes the pain, struggle, and suffering involved in the process of becoming resilient. The term "resiliency" generally refers to those factors and processes that limit negative behaviors associated with stress and result in adaptive outcomes even in the presence of adversity. Garmezy and Masten (1991), for example, defined resilience as "a process of, or capacity for, or the outcome of successful adaptation despite challenging and threatening circumstances" (p. 459).

One of the most widely used definitions of educational resilience is "the heightened likelihood of success in school and other life accomplishments despite environmental adversities brought about by early traits, conditions, and experiences" (Wang, Haertel, & Walberg, 1994, p. 46). While success is an educational variable that researchers often investigate and measure (e.g., cognitive, affective, and behavioral outcomes), "adverse conditions" is a phenomenon that educators often don't operationally define and study. Attending an at-risk school environment, for example, could be considered an adverse condition (Waxman, 1992), but there are other risk factors (e.g., poverty, drug abuse, sexual activity, coming from a single-parent home, having a sibling who has dropped out of school, or being home alone after school 3 or more hours a day) that may be equally as important to measure. This issue raises questions such as Should a successful student who has only one or two of these risk factors be considered a resilient student? Clearly, an educationally resilient student who has one or two risk factors is very different than a student who is extremely vulnerable to multiple high-risk behaviors (e.g., substance abuse, attempted suicide). Thus, the number of at-risk factors and the magnitude of risk factors are two important issues that should be addressed. Similarly, issues could be addressed regarding the measurement of resiliency. Should scoring in the top quartile on standardized test scores, scoring in the 95th percentile on standardized tests for a 3-year period, receiving a National Merit Scholarship, or graduating with honors from a prestigious school be weighted similarly or differently in a determination of resilience?

A similar issue regarding the measurement of resiliency applies to different identification procedures for distinguishing resilient from nonresilient students. Many resiliency studies have used students' academic achievement (e.g., grades and standardized achievement tests) as criteria for identifying resilient students. This approach has often been criticized, however, because of the potential limitations of measuring academic achievement (e.g., validity or reliability concerns). Furthermore, these studies often merely identify resilient students based on one achievement test, which may not be the best sample of students' overall academic achievement. Other resiliency studies have used teacher nomination as the criteria for determining resilient students. Not surprisingly, the dramatic differences found in most of these studies between resilient and nonresilient students may be consistent with teachers' expectations and attitudes toward the students. Thus, the use of teacher nomination to identify resilient students could be considered a limitation of the current research in the field because there is the danger that having teachers identify or classify students as nonresilient could impact their treatment of students and ultimately impact students' success (Storer, Cychosz, & Licklider, 1995). On the other hand, the teacher nomination approach may be one of the most valid identification procedures because teachers' decisions are typically based on a variety of indicators that are exhibited throughout the school year.

Whatever definition or criteria is used to describe educationally resilient students, we need to ensure that the term not be used to label or stigmatize students. This could easily occur if educators started to emphasize interventions specifically for nonresilient students, making the term "nonresilient" another negative label for these students. We also need to be aware that these labels often mask the diversity of those students who are being defined (Wehlage, Rutter, Smith, Lesko, & Fernandez, 1989). For example, there may be a wide range of characteristics among students who are categorized as either resilient or nonresilient. This diversity within categories or groups suggests that instructional- and school-based programs may impact students differently. Thus, one type of program that promotes resilience for some students may not be effective for others. The next sections describe some of the classic resilience studies, followed by current research in educational resiliency.

CLASSIC RESILIENCY STUDIES

The concept of resilience has been used to describe three major categories of phenomena in the psychological literature (Masten, Best, & Garmezy,

1990). The first category includes studies of individual differences in recovery from trauma. The second category is categorized by people from high-risk groups who have a better than expected outcome. The third major category of the resilience literature refers to a positive adaptation despite stressful experiences. The following studies have been identified as the pioneering work in identifying the resilience concept and contain aspects of all three categories of the resilience phenomena.

Rutter (1979) conducted an epidemiological study that reflects the first category of the resilience phenomena. He studied children whose parents were diagnosed as mentally ill on the Isle of Wight and in inner-city London. He followed 125 of these children over a 10-year period. Through an intensive interview process, he found that the offspring of mentally ill patients escaped relatively unharmed. They did not become mentally ill themselves or exhibit maladaptive behavior. Rutter started to question why so many children did not show signs of their adverse environmental conditions. He found that both individual differences and the child's school environment were important protective factors. Rutter suggested that genetic factors play a significant role in determining individual differences in personality characteristics and intelligence. He also found that the school environment contains important protective factors such as fostering a sense of achievement in children, enhancing personal growth, and increasing social contacts.

Werner and Smith (1977) conducted an important study that reflects the second category of the resilience phenomena. The focus of this longitudinal study was of a high-risk group of children born in 1955 in Kauai. One-third of this cohort ($n = 201$) was designated as high risk because they were born into poverty and lived in a family environment troubled by a number of factors such as biological and prenatal stress, family instability and discord, parental psychopathology, or other poor childrearing conditions. One third of these high-risk children ($n = 72$) grew up as competent, confident, and caring adults. Several differences were found when these children were contrasted with the at-risk children who did develop serious problems. These results were separated into three types of protective attributes that supported resilience: (a) dispositional attributes of the individual, (b) affectional ties with the family, and (c) external support systems in the environment. In early childhood, resilient children at high risk experienced fewer illnesses and were perceived as active, affectionate, and socially responsive by their parents. Resilient children displayed additional skills such as self-help skills, sensorimotor acquisition, and language development. In early adolescence, resilient children displayed adequate problem-solving skills, communication skills, and perceptual motor development. In their late teens, resilient individuals possessed high internal locus of control, an achievement-oriented attitude, and positive self-esteem. In adulthood, resilient individuals were able to relate to numerous sources of support within their environment (Werner & Smith, 1977).

In a follow-up study, Werner and Smith (1992) provide evidence that the resiliency process may be different for men and women. When their sample was 31 and 32 years of age, scholastic competence at age 10 was more strongly associated with successful transition into adult responsibilities for men than for women. Factors such as high self-esteem, efficacy, and sense of personal control at age 18, however, were more predictive of successful adult adaptation among the women rather than the men. Differences were also found with regard to loss of caregivers and the development of mental health problems. Within the first 10 years of life the men were more vulnerable to separation from the loss of caregivers, but in the second decade the adolescent women were found to be more vulnerable to chronic family discord and disturbed interpersonal relationships than men. They also found that women with mental health problems had more positive changes in life when compared to men.

The Project Competence study (Garmezy, Masten, & Tellegen, 1984) illustrates the third category of the resilience phenomena. Garmezy and his colleagues began Project Competence in order to better understand how resiliency impacted children when they experienced stressful life situations. The focus of the project was the effects of life "stressors" on competency levels experienced by elementary school students. For more than 10 years, approximately 200 children and their families were taken from a sample of 612 third- to sixth-grade students and participated in this study. Teacher ratings, peer assessments, and school record data assessed competence. Stress exposure was measured by a life event questionnaire. The researchers also intensively interviewed parents for 6 hours about the social structure of their family and their perspective about their child. In an exploratory multiple regression correlation analysis on the 200 participants that were identified as suffering from multiple stressful life conditions, they found that disadvantaged children with lower IQs and socioeconomic status (SES) and less positive family qualities were generally less competent and more likely to be disruptive. Garmezy and his colleagues, however, found that some of the disadvantaged children were competent and did not display behavioral problems. Because of this finding, they began to question why some children did not succumb to the adversity they faced and develop negative adaptations.

The results from these classic resiliency studies provide compelling evidence that many factors may help students at risk of failure become resilient in the face of adversity. These results also provide evidence that resilient individuals interpret stressful life experiences and trauma differently. The major theme that connects all of the previously mentioned results is the emphasis on both individual characteristics and environmental factors that may contribute to resilience. Evidence was also provided that the resiliency process may differ for men and women.

CURRENT EDUCATIONAL RESILIENCY RESEARCH

While it has been argued that the skills, opportunities, and relationships that promote resiliency can be provided in schools (Storer et al., 1995), only a few studies have examined resiliency in schools. Most of the research in this area has focused on comparing resilient and nonresilient students on important family and individual background characteristics, and key classroom processes that have been proposed to foster resiliency. Some of these researchers have found that there are dramatic differences between resilient and nonresilient students on a variety of background characteristics, personal attributes (e.g., motivation and future aspirations), and classroom processes (e.g., perceived learning environment and observed classroom behavior). This section highlights some of the recent educational resiliency research.

In a study designed to understand successful high school students, Reyes and Jason (1993) examined factors that distinguished the success and failure of Latino students from an inner-city high school. Based on their ninth-grade attendance rate and academic achievement, they identified 24 10th-grade students as being at high risk for dropping out of school, while 24 others were deemed to be at low risk of dropping out of school. They individually interviewed each participant on a number of topics covering four main areas: family background, family support, overall school satisfaction, and gang pressures. They found that there were no differences between the two groups as far as socioeconomic status, parent–student involvement, or parental supervision. Low-risk students, however, reported significantly more satisfaction with their school than high-risk students. On the other hand, high-risk students were more likely to respond that they had been invited to join a gang or brought a weapon to school.

In another study that used academic grades as criteria for resiliency, Gonzalez and Padilla (1997) examined factors that contributed to the academic resilience and achievement of 133 resilient and 81 nonresilient Mexican American high school students. From a population of over 2,000 Mexican American students from three high schools in California, they identified "resilient students" as students who reported that their grades so far in high school were "mostly A's." They identified "nonresilient students" as students who reported that their grades so far in high school were "mostly D's" or "mostly below D's." They found that resilient students had significantly higher perceptions of family/peer support, teacher feedback, positive ties to school, value placed on school, peer belonging, and familism than nonresilient students did. They also found that students' sense of belonging in school was the only significant predictor of academic resilience.

Alva (1991) used the term "academic invulnerability" to describe students who "sustain high levels of achievement motivation and performance, despite the presence of stressful events and conditions that place them at risk of doing poorly in school and ultimately dropping out of school" (p. 19). In her study that examined the characteristics of a cohort of 10th-grade Mexican American students, she found that resilient or invulnerable students (i.e., students who maintained a high grade point average in the 10th grade and were from a low socioeconomic background) reported higher levels of educational support from their teachers and friends and were more likely to "(a) feel encouraged and prepared to attend college, (b) enjoy coming to school and being involved in high school activities, (c) experience fewer conflicts and difficulties in their intergroup relations with other students, and (d) experience fewer family conflicts and difficulties" (p. 31).

The Center for Research on the Education of Students Placed At Risk (CRESPAR) has been involved in several studies focusing on educational resiliency. In a special issue on resilient students in *Education and Urban Society*, Lee, Winfield, and Wilson (1991) used 1983–84 reading assessment scores from the National Assessment of Educational Progress (NAEP) data to compare 661 high-achieving, eighth-grade, African American students to 1,894 low-achieving, eighth-grade, African American students. High-achieving students were those who scored above the overall population mean on reading performance, while low-achieving students were those who scored below the population mean. In terms of family or background characteristics, they found that high-achieving students were from a higher social class, younger, and had a higher proportion of working mothers than low-achieving students. In terms of school differences, they found that high-achieving students also were more likely to attend schools that were of higher socioeconomic status, were Catholic, had more curriculum exposure, higher student commitment, and a lower proportion of students in remedial reading than schools attended by low-achieving students. In terms of student academic behaviors, high-achieving African American students reported reading more pages per week, doing more homework, and having higher grades than low-achieving students did.

Nettles, Mucherach, and Jones (2000) reviewed several more recent CRESPAR studies that focused on the influence of social resources, such as parent, teacher, and school support, on students' resilience. They found that access to social resources such as caring parents, participation in extracurricular activities, and supportive teachers have positive benefits for students' academic achievement. In their own research with 75 fourth- and fifth-grade students, they found that students' perceived exposure to violence had a significant negative impact on their mathematics and reading achievement, while teacher support had a positive impact on mathematics achievement. Students' perceptions of stressful life events, however, did not have a significant effect on achievement.

In a series of studies conducted by the U.S. Department of Education National Research Centers; Center for Education in the Inner Cities (CEIC); and Center for Research on Education, Diversity, and Excellence (CREDE), Waxman, Padrón, and their colleagues examined differences between resilient and nonresilient elementary and middle school students from several urban school districts serving culturally and linguistically diverse students from low socioeconomic circumstances. In an initial study, Waxman and Huang (1996) compared the motivation and classroom learning environment of 75 resilient versus 75 nonresilient sixth-, seventh-, and eighth-grade students from an inner-city middle school located in a major urban city in the south central region of the United States. Educationally resilient students were defined as students who for a 2-year period scored at or above the 90th percentile on the standardized achievement test scores in mathematics. Nonresilient students were defined as students who scored at the 10th percentile or lower on the standardized achievement test scores for a 2-year period. Resilient students were found to have significantly higher perceptions of involvement, task orientation, rule clarity, satisfaction, pacing, and feedback than nonresilient students do. Resilient students also reported significantly higher social self-concept, achievement motivation, and academic self-concept than nonresilient students. On the other hand, there were no significant differences between the two groups on variables such as parent involvement, homework, and teacher support. One explanation why there were no differences found on the teacher support variable was that both resilient and nonresilient students had low perceptions of their teachers' support and there also was a great deal of variability of responses within the groups. On the other hand, one explanation for not finding significant differences between resilient and nonresilient students on their perceptions of parent involvement was that both groups' responses were very high and there was little variability within the groups.

Waxman, Huang, and Padrón (1997) compared the motivation and learning environment of resilient and nonresilient Latino middle school students from a multiethnic, metropolitan city located in the south central region of the United States. From the entire population of Latino students in the district, a stratified sample of 60 resilient and 60 nonresilient Latino students were randomly selected to be included in the study. Students identified as "gifted or talented" or "special education" were excluded from the population in order to avoid potential effects related to ability differences.

Students were classified as "resilient" if they: (a) scored on or above the 75th percentile on the district-administered, standardized Four-Step Problem Solving Test over a 20-year period and (b) reported receiving "A's" or "B's" in mathematics over a 2-year period. Students were classified as "nonresilient" if they: (a) scored on or below the 25th percentile on the Four-Step Problem Solving Test for a 2-year period, (b) reported receiving "C's," "D's," or "F's" for mathematics this year, and (c) "B's," "C's," "D's," or "F's" in mathematics the previous year. A stratified sampling technique was used in order to obtain an equal number of students by sex and grade within each student group (i.e., resilient or nonresilient).

The results indicated that there were no significant differences between the two groups on whether they spoke a non-English language before they started school. About 76% of the resilient students indicated that they spoke a language other than English before they started school, while about 67% of the nonresilient students responded that they also spoke a language other than English before starting school. There were, however, statistically significant differences between the two groups on the extent to which students were held back a grade in school. About 53% of the nonresilient students indicated that they were held back a grade in school as compared to only 13% of resilient students.

There were significant differences between the two student groups on their academic aspirations. Resilient students were significantly more likely to indicate that they were sure that they would graduate from high school and they were significantly more likely to respond that they would graduate college and attend graduate schools. About 78% of the resilient students indicated that they would graduate from high school as compared to only 43% of the nonresilient students. Similarly, over 90% of the resilient students indicated that they would graduate college or attend graduate school, as compared to only about 46% of the nonresilient students.

There were statistically significant differences between the two groups on two of the time allocation items. Resilient students reported that they spent significantly more time doing mathematics homework each week than nonresilient students did. Resilient students also indicated that they spent more time on additional reading than nonresilient students did. There were no significant differences between the two groups on the amount of time they spent watching television on weekends or during the weekdays, and on the amount of time spent listening to CDs, tapes, or the radio. There also were significant differences between the two groups on attendance records. Resilient students were less likely to report cutting or missing classes and being late for school than nonresilient students were.

The multivariate analysis and univariate post hoc tests revealed that resilient students had significantly higher perceptions of Involvement, Satisfaction, Academic Self-Concept, and Achievement Motivation than nonresilient students. The discriminant function analysis revealed that the variables of Academic Aspirations, Involvement, Academic Self-Concept, Expectations for High School Graduation, Not Being Held Back in School, and Satisfaction were related most highly to the overall discriminant function.

In another study, Waxman, Huang, and Wang (1997) focused on resilient and nonresilient students from four elementary schools from a large urban school district located in a major metropolitan city in the south-central region of the United States. Two fourth- and two fifth-grade classrooms were randomly selected from each of these four inner-city schools. Near the middle of the school year, teachers were asked to identify their population of students at risk (e.g., students from families of low socioeconomic status, living with a single parent, relative, or guardian). From this pool of at-risk students, teachers were told to select up to three "resilient" students (i.e., high achieving on both standardized achievement tests and daily schoolwork, very motivated, and excellent attendance) and three "nonresilient" students (i.e., low achieving on both standardized achievement tests and daily schoolwork, not motivated, and poor attendance) in their class. Each of these resilient and nonresilient students: (a) completed learning environment and motivation surveys, and (b) was observed using a shadowing observation technique. The shadowing observations consisted of narrative descriptions of (a) the physical environment of the classroom, (b) teachers' instructional approaches, behaviors, and attitudes toward students, and (c) students' observed attitudes, actions, mannerisms, and interactions. The shadowing observations were recorded on laptop computers that were programmed to provide observers with specific time prompts that told them exactly when they were to record the information (i.e., narrative comments) about each student. A sample of "average" students from each classroom also was included in the study.

Overall, resilient students perceived their classrooms much more favorably than nonresilient students did. Resilient students had higher academic self-concept and student aspirations than nonresilient students did. They also perceived their teachers as having higher expectations for them and providing them with more feedback and appropriate pacing than nonresilient students. Furthermore, resilient students reported that they were more involved and satisfied in their classrooms than nonresilient students were. They also perceived more task orientation and order and organization than nonresilient students did. For the most part, average students' perceptions were generally similar to resilient students.

There were several prevalent themes and issues that emerged from the shadowing and case study data. First, several important factors distinguished resilient from nonresilient students. Resilient students appeared to be persistent, attentive, demonstrated leadership skills, worked well with other students, frequently volunteered answers, and were often engaged in their schoolwork. Resilient students were generally more enthusiastic, energetic, and better behaved than nonresilient students. Resilient students received more teacher attention and praise than nonresilient students did. On the other hand, nonresilient students often appeared to be shy or timid, frequently tired, not attentive to the teacher, or bored. They were not as engaged in the activities of the class as resilient students and appeared to get started on their work more slowly. Furthermore, many nonresilient students appeared anxious, restless, easily distracted, and sometimes resistant to doing their work. A few of the nonresilient students were disruptive in the classroom, either disturbing other classmates by talking to them or making a loud enough commotion at their desks that the teacher needed to reprimand them. It should be mentioned, however, that there was much more variation (i.e., less homogeneity) among the behaviors of nonresilient students than resilient students.

While the primary focus of the shadowing data was to focus on resilient and nonresilient students, the instructional contexts that were prevalent in these classrooms also were observed. The findings revealed that the overall instruction in these inner-city elementary schools was whole-class instruction with students working in teacher-assigned activities, generally in a passive manner (i.e., watching or listening). There was very little small group work observed in any of the classrooms, and when it did occur, it would typically be one student working with another student. Teachers were observed keeping students on task most of the time, focusing on the task, communicating the task's procedures, and checking students' work. They also spent more time explaining than questioning, cueing, or prompting students. Teachers were not frequently observed encouraging extended student responses or encouraging students to help themselves or help each other. Generally, there was little engagement in the classroom and the intellectual level of the curriculum was low level, with very few authentic activities occurring. Very little of the content was related to students' interests or the world outside school. The predominant culture of classrooms observed was related to "getting work done," rather than an emphasis on authentic learning situations.

Another important finding from this study was that in the few classrooms where a great deal of student–teacher interactions occurred, it was much more difficult to ascertain differences between resilient and nonresilient students. The direct instructional approach that predominated in both reading and mathematics classrooms appeared to be much more suited to resilient students, who were motivated, attentive, volunteered answers, and received more teacher attention and praise than nonresilient students, who appeared bored, reluctant to answer questions, and at times reluctant to work during the direct instructional approach. Overall, the qualitative findings indicated that resilient students were much more successful in classrooms employing direct instruction than nonresilient students were. Although there were great observable differences in the academic behaviors of these two groups of students, no remediation, adaptive, or enrichment activities were observed in any classrooms. For the most part, teachers did not treat individual students differently; they focused on the whole class and directed instructional activities toward everyone at the same time.

Padrón, Waxman, and Huang (1999) compared the classroom instruction and learning environment of about 250 resilient, average, and nonresilient students in fourth- and fifth-grade classrooms from three elementary schools located in a major metropolitan area in the south-central region of the United States. Students in the three schools were predominately Hispanic (>75%) and most of them (>90%) received free or reduced-cost lunches. Near the middle of the school year, teachers were asked to identify their population of students at risk (e.g., students from families of low socioeconomic status, living with a single parent, relative, or guardian). Students identified as "gifted or talented" or "special education" were excluded from the population in order to avoid potential effects related to ability differences. From this pool of at-risk students, teachers were then told to select up to three "resilient" (i.e., high achieving on both standardized achievement tests and daily schoolwork, very motivated, and excellent attendance) and three "nonresilient" students (i.e., low achieving on both standardized achievement tests and daily schoolwork, not motivated, and poor attendance) in their class. Near the end of the school year, all the fourth- and fifth-grade students completed the My Class learning environment survey and trained observers also systematically observed the resilient and nonresilient students identified by teachers during regular reading and/or language classes.

They found that resilient fourth- and fifth-grade students perceived a more positive instructional learning environment and were more satisfied with their reading and language arts classrooms than nonresilient students. In addition, nonresilient students indicated that they had more difficulty with their classwork than both average students and resilient students. The observational results revealed that resilient students spent significantly more time interacting with teachers for instructional purposes, whereas nonresilient students spent more time interacting with other students for social or personal purposes. Resilient students were also observed watching or listening significantly more often than nonresilient students, whereas nonresilient students were observed more often not attending to task. The percentage of time that resilient students were on task was much higher than that of nonresilient students. Resilient students were also less often distracted or disruptive than nonresilient students.

Read (1999) interviewed several fourth- and fifth-grade teachers about the concept of resilient and nonresilient students. Teachers reported that they had no difficulty identifying resilient and nonresilient students in their classrooms. Several teachers shared specific examples of why certain students in their class were clearly resilient or nonresilient. The teachers also indicated that the resilience framework was a useful approach that helped them understand why certain students might be successful or unsuccessful in school. In addition, the study revealed several distinct patterns of behaviors that teachers thought distinguished resilient from nonresilient students. Most teachers, for example, indicated that lack of parental involvement, low student motivation, and low self-esteem were the major factors contributing to lack of success in nonresilient students, and the teachers similarly reported that the same factors (parental involvement, student motivation, self-esteem) contributed to the success of resilient students. The teachers, however, did not mention any school, program, or classroom factor (e.g., teaching practices) that contributed to the academic success or failure of nonresilient students. In addition, teachers reported that many instructional strategies were effective for resilient students. They could, however, mention only a few instructional strategies that they thought were effective for nonresilient students.

The previously described studies illustrate the growing body of research that has tried to address the issue of why some students succeed in school, while others are not successful. Most of the research, however, has been descriptive, causal-comparative, or correlational. There have been few experimental studies in this area. One exception is a recent project in the Center for Research on Education, Diversity, and Excellence (CREDE), where Padrón, Waxman, Powers, and Brown (2002) developed, implemented, and tested a teacher development program designed to improve the resiliency of low achieving English language learners (ELLs). The Pedagogy for Improving Resiliency Program (PIRP) was implemented in six fourth- and fifth-grade classrooms in an urban elementary school serving predominantly Hispanic ELLs from low socioeconomic backgrounds. The year-long PIRP consisted of training that incorporated several components designed to help classroom teachers improve their instruction and the learning of resilient and nonresilient ELLs.

The findings from the study revealed that the treatment teachers' classroom instruction exceeded that of the comparison teachers on some important aspects (e.g., explanations, encouragement of extended student responses, encouragement of student success, focus on the task's learning processes). Students in the treatment classes reported a more positive classroom learning environment than students in the comparison classes (e.g., higher cohesion, satisfaction, and teacher support as well as less friction), and had significantly higher reading achievement gains than students in the comparison classrooms. The only discouraging aspects of the The Pedagogy for Improving Resiliency Program related to issues that impacted teachers' implementation of the PIRP program, such as the district's emphasis on high-stakes testing.

Another quasi-experimental study by McClendon, Nettles, and Wigfield (2000) examined the effects of Promoting Achievement in School through Sport (PASS), an elective, year long course in high school, implemented with 900 students from 16 high schools in the West and Midwest. PASS classrooms feature protective or resiliency characteristics such as caring and support, high expectations, and encouragement of student engagement and involvement. The curriculum is self-paced, mastery based, and project oriented. Students in PASS were found to have significantly higher grades than the comparison group at the end of the school year. Classroom observations revealed that PASS had more indicators of authentic instruction (i.e., instructional practices that connect students to meaningful, real-life experiences) than non-PASS classrooms.

IMPLICATIONS FOR EDUCATIONAL PRACTICE AND RESEARCH

Most of the current research on educational resiliency has focused predominantly on minority students from low-income families. The findings have typically revealed that there are several classroom processes (e.g., learning environment and classroom instruction) and motivational aspects that significantly differ between resilient and nonresilient students. Despite coming from the same school environment and having similar home backgrounds and demographic characteristics, some students do exceptionally well in school, whereas others do very poorly. The results from these studies generally indicate that resilient students perceive a more positive instructional and classroom learning environment and are more satisfied with their classrooms. In addition, nonresilient students often indicate that they have more difficulty in their classwork than both average and resilient students do. The magnitude of these differences is both statistically and educationally significant. These findings provide a great challenge for classroom teachers who need to provide optimal learning environments for all of their students.

Implications for Practice

Theoretical and conceptual work in the area of resiliency has hypothesized that some of the processes and mechanisms could be developed and altered to facilitate students' resilient behaviors. Rutter (1987), for example, identified four processes that could be developed in order to facilitate resiliency: reducing risk impacts and changing students' exposure to risks, reducing the negative chain reactions that often follow exposure to risks, improving students' self-efficacy or self-esteem, and opening up or creating new opportunities for students. Masten (1994) similarly described four strategies for fostering resiliency, including reducing vulnerability and risk, reducing stressors, increasing available resources, and mobilizing protective processes. Finally, Swanson and Spencer (1991) also provided some specific suggestions for enhancing most of these resiliency processes. They maintained that to reduce the risk impact, educators should increase access to academically challenging programs for disadvantaged students; forge alliances between schools, churches, organizations, and businesses; and increase funding for early childhood programs. To reduce negative chain reactions, Swanson and Spencer argued that teacher training, teacher recruitment, and teacher retention need to be addressed and altered, and parent involvement in schools also needs to be increased. To improve students' self-efficacy, they argued that schools should recognize and demand academic performance and also redesign classrooms into heterogeneous ability groups rather than tracking students by ability level. Finally, in order to open up opportunities, they maintained that there should be increased funding for compensatory education, student financial aid, pilot programs, and updated technological equipment. They also called for integrating resources from schools, businesses, and communities to help students make a smooth transition from school to the work environment.

There are several positive action strategies that classroom teachers can use to foster resiliency in students. Bruce (1995), for example, cited several specific strategies that teachers could use to foster resiliency, such as providing social skills training and teaching students self-monitoring, self-evaluation, and self-reinforcing strategies. Furthermore, school districts like the Minneapolis Public Schools have developed policies for promoting resiliency and have trained most of their teachers in resilience strategies. They focus on five resilience strategies that schools and teachers are urged to implement: (1) offer opportunities to develop attachment relationships, (2) increase students' sense of mastery in their lives, (3) build social competencies as well as academic skills, (4) reduce the stressors children don't need to face, and (5) generate school and community resources to support the needs of children (North Central Regional Educational Laboratory, 1994). More proactive approaches like these are needed to foster resiliency in students and reduce the current educational gaps between resilient and nonresilient students.

Teacher support and expectations of students

Schools build resiliency in students through creating an environment of caring and personal relationships. The foundation of this relationship begins with educators who have a resiliency-building attitude (Henderson & Milstein, 1996). Teachers who model the resilient behaviors they desire from their students are often called "turnaround teachers" (Benard, 1997). Turnaround teachers provide and model three protective factors that buffer risk and enable positive development by meeting youth's basic needs for safety, love and belonging, respect, power, and accomplishment and learning (Benard, 1991). The three factors are: (1) caring relationships, (2) positive and high expectations, and (3) opportunities to participate and contribute.

Teachers can convey loving support to students by listening to students and validating their feelings, and by demonstrating kindness, compassion, and respect (Higgins, 1994; Meier, 1995). Benard (1997) explained that turnaround teachers refrain from judging, do not take students' behavior personally, and understand that students are doing the best they can. Turnaround teachers can also have an impact on overwhelmed families. Teachers can proactively seek referrals to social service agencies, offer assistance through provision of supplies, and seek out family members' concerns regarding basic needs.

Teachers' high expectations can structure and guide behavior, and they can challenge students beyond what they believe they can do (Delpit, 1996). Turnaround teachers focus on the strengths of all students, as well as assist youth that have been labeled by schools or oppressed by their families and/or communities. They especially empower overwhelmed youth to use their personal power to transform from victim to survivor. Turnaround teachers help students not to internalize the adversity in their lives, to see adversity as impermanent, and to see setbacks not as pervasive but as surmountable or temporary (Seligman, 1995). Furthermore, Seligman (1995) contends that turnaround teachers are student-centered, using students' strengths, interests, goals, and dreams as the beginning point for learning, thereby tapping students' intrinsic motivation for learning.

Resiliency is fostered when teachers provide meaningful opportunities for students to contribute their skills and energies (Henderson & Milstein, 1996). Turnaround teachers provide opportunities to participate and contribute by allowing students to express their opinions, make choices, problem-solve, work with and help others, and encourage students to "give back" to their community. They treat students as responsible individuals, allowing them to participate in all aspects of the school's functioning (Kohn, 1993). A key finding from the resilience research is that successful development and transformative power exists not necessarily in programmatic approaches but rather in the deeper level of relationships, beliefs, expectations, and willingness to share power. Schools need to develop caring relationships not only between educators and students but also between students, between educators, and between educators and parents (Benard, 1997).

Promoting school resilience

School environment is another critical component that can either promote the development of protective factors associated with individual resilience or create instead an organizational atmosphere or climate that can lead to teacher alienation, burnout, and dissatisfaction. In other words, the school environment can contribute to both risk and protective mechanisms. The role of schools, however, has received relatively little consideration in the study of the resilience process (Maughan, 1988). School resilience is defined as teachers' involvement in their jobs; peer cohesion, or how friendly and supportive teachers are to each other; and supervisor support, or the extent to which the administration is supportive of teachers and encourages teachers to be supportive of each other. In other words, schools build resiliency through creating an environment of caring personal relationships (Henderson & Milstein, 1996). Krovetz (1999) similarly argues that in order to build resilient schools, teachers must create time to develop professional relationships with other school members.

Administrators can create a school environment that supports teachers' resilience as well. Administrators can facilitate this nurturing environment in various ways. They can demonstrate positive beliefs, set expectations and trust teachers, and provide on-going opportunities for teachers to reflect, dialogue, and make decisions together (McLaughlin & Talbert, 1993). Promoting teacher and school resilience will facilitate the development of students' resiliency. Resilient students are the outcome or product of a resilient school climate. All stakeholders can facilitate resiliency in students by modeling the desired behavior or outcome themselves. They can promote caring relationships among colleagues, demonstrate positive beliefs, provide ongoing opportunities to reflect, and make decisions together (McLaughlin & Talbert, 1993).

Professional development of teachers

Another approach that has been found to be very effective for promoting resiliency is using feedback from classroom observation and learning environment measures to help teachers understand their current instructional strengths and weaknesses (Fraser, 1991; Stallings & Mohlman, 1988; Waxman, 1995; Waxman, Huang, & Padrón, 1995). One of the most influential components of the Pedagogy to Improve Resiliency Program, for example, was the provision of feedback profiles to the teachers that described differences between resilient and nonresilient students' perceptions of their learning environment and observed behaviors in the classroom (Padrón et al., 2002). These profiles contained the teachers' individual data from their classroom and a summary of the aggregated data across the elementary school. The class means for each of the indicators on both of the observation and survey instruments were presented for both resilient and nonresilient students, along with the overall school mean value. This allowed each teacher to compare their class means to the school's average. Feedback from these profiles was used to stimulate dialogue and discussion about instructional strengths and weaknesses in the school. The profiles also helped initiate discussion about specific instructional areas that needed to be improved in the school.

The feedback profiles provided some guidelines for practice; they were not attempts to tell teachers what to do. These profiles provided teachers with concepts and criteria that they could use to reflect about their own teaching (Nuthall & Alton-Lee, 1990). We did not view the feedback session as one where we would apply our research findings to specific rules or guidelines for teachers to follow. Rather, the observational and survey feedback was used as guides for teachers, to give them and their colleagues the opportunity to reflect on their practices on their own and decide what action to take. Quality teacher professional development is one of the keys to successful school reform and improving the education of at-risk students, and feedback from classroom observation and survey data can be a catalyst for this process.

Changing classroom instruction

Unfortunately, there are many children who live in socially and economically disadvantaged environments that would typically induce despair for most individuals. Some of these children at risk, however, have learned how to selectively ignore their external conditions and "redirect their attention to an inner life that is real only to themselves" (Csikszentmihalyi, 1997). Csikszentmihalyi (1997) referred to such children as "autotelics," arguing that they concentrate more, enjoy themselves more, have higher self-esteem, and see what they do as related to future goals. This autotelic personality is similar to the concept of resiliency and, according to Csikszentmihalyi, the key component for encouraging the development of such a personality is the ability to concentrate and control attention.

As previously described, prior research comparing resilient and nonresilient students has found that nonresilient students are engaged in their schoolwork significantly less than resilient students. The implications of these findings suggest that we need to help nonresilient students become more engaged and control their attention better. Two components that help individuals' control attention are (a) learning to manage or focus one's goals, and (b) providing immediate feedback on activities. Csikszentmihalyi (1997) refers to optimal experiences or "flow" as lessons or instructional activities that allow students to overcome challenging material by providing them with appropriate skills, relevant feedback, and clear goals. According to this perspective, classroom activities would ideally focus on flow experiences where students would be involved in challenging lessons that would help them develop new skills, as well as learn to control attention.

Classroom instruction for students at risk of academic failure, however, is typically the direct instructional model, where teachers teach to the whole class at the same time and control all of the classroom discussion and decision making (Waxman, Padrón, & Arnold, 2001). This teacher-directed instructional model emphasizes lecture, drill and practice, remediation, and student seatwork that consists mainly of worksheets (Stephen, Varble, & Taitt, 1993). Haberman (1991) argued that this overreliance on direct instruction in schools serving minority students constitutes a "pedagogy of poverty" (p. 290). He maintained that this teacher-directed instructional style leads to student complacency, passive resentment, and teacher burnout. Furthermore, he criticized this orientation because teachers are generally held accountable for "making" students learn, while students usually assume a passive role with low engagement in tasks or activities that are generally not authentic. In other words, classroom instruction that focuses on providing meaningful, flow-like experience for at-risk students is lacking.

Improving classroom instruction for nonresilient students centers on employing explicit teaching practices that have been found to be effective for students at risk of failure. Waxman and colleagues (2001), for example, described five explicit practices that have been shown to improve the education of at-risk students: (1) cognitively-guided instruction, (2) culturally responsive teaching, (3) technology-enriched instruction, (4) cooperative learning, and (5) instructional conversation. These research-based, instructional practices all stress a student-centered model of classroom instruction that emphasizes more active student learning, with teachers acting as facilitators of learning. Furthermore, these teaching practices may create "flow-type" instructional activities that are needed by many students at risk of failure.

Implications for Research

In the past decade, there have been many causal-comparative studies that have identified differences between resilient and nonresilient students. These studies have employed both primary and secondary quantitative data analyses, as well as extensive qualitative, ethnographic field methods.

There only have been a few naturalistic, longitudinal studies conducted that have examined the success of high-risk children (Pianta, Steinberg, & Rollins, 1995). Similarly, there have only been a small number of experimental studies that have investigated the impact of resiliency treatments on teacher and student outcomes.

Mixed methods approaches are needed to examine educational resiliency. Teacher self-report data, along with teacher, administrator, and student interview data, could all be used to help supplement the survey data and systematic classroom observation data that are generally used in resiliency research. Such data could help us understand, from different perspectives, the complexity of issues surrounding the educational improvement of students at risk of failure. More ethnographic studies also are needed in order to help us uncover "grounded theoretical" explanations of factors that impact resilient and nonresilient students.

Future studies should investigate other indicators of resiliency to see what processes can promote protective mechanisms in the classroom learning context (Nelson-LeGall & Jones, 1991), for example, argued that classroom help-seeking behavior is a strategy that allows learners to cope with academic difficulties; this becomes a protective mechanism in the classroom learning context. Clark (1991) similarly suggested that social identity and support networks are resilient behaviors that need to be fostered and developed by at-risk students, while Barbarin (1993) maintained that we need to focus on the coping processes students use to mediate risk factors. These variables and others, such as peer-group support, problem-solving skills, and students' cognitive learning strategies, need to be explored in future studies. Further studies should specifically examine how aspects of the classroom learning environment and instructional learning environment can be changed so that they can serve as a protective mechanism for at-risk students. Future research needs to include experimental studies that explicitly test interventions that promote resiliency for at-risk students. In addition, more affective or motivational training programs need to be developed and implemented in order to test their effects on students' cognitive and affective outcomes. These and similar issues should be examined so that we can continue to understand why some students at risk of academic failure are resilient and how we can help nonresilient students become more successful and resilient.

SUMMARY

While student success and failure is dependent upon a number of influential determinants, it is apparent that instructional practices and the classroom learning environment are contributing factors (Travis, 1995;

Waxman, 1992; Waxman & Huang, 1997). The findings from many of the research studies discussed in this report are discouraging in that they paint a bleak picture of nonresilient students who are not doing well in school. Many of the nonresilient students in these studies appear to have already "given up" on school and many indicated that they didn't plan to finish high school. Furthermore, given that teachers in several studies felt that they could easily distinguish the resilient from the nonresilient students in their classrooms, it is troubling that few remediation or corrective activities were employed to aid the nonresilient students. Although teachers were aware that nonresilient students were not doing well in their classrooms, there was no concerted effort to help them or address their specific learning needs.

It has been argued that resilient individuals seek environments that are supportive and conducive to growth (Masten, 1994). Students in disadvantaged school environments, however, often cannot choose which schools or classes they attend. Educators need to be aware of the concerns and problems facing these students and how schools contribute to these problems. In conclusion, it is apparent that some of the risks associated with students' failure in school are due to the particular school the student attends. This is an unacceptable situation and the solution to these problems will require collaboration among teachers, administrators, university faculty, parents, and the government (Futrell, 1988). In addition to this call to action, it will require a change in attitude that will make us aware of the severity of the problems facing students at risk *and* seriously committed to reversing the cycle of educational failure.

ACKNOWLEDGMENT

This research was supported in part by a U. S. Department of Education, Office of Educational Research and Improvement grant from the National Center for Research on Education, Diversity, and Excellence. The opinions expressed in this chapter do not necessarily reflect the position, policy, or endorsement of the granting agency.

REFERENCES

Alva, S. A. (1991). Academic invulnerability among Mexican-American students: The importance of protective resources and appraisals. *Hispanic Journal of Behavioral Sciences, 13*, 18–34.

Barbarin, O. A. (1993). Coping and resilience: Exploring the inner lives of African American children. *Journal of Black Psychology, 19*, 478–492.

Benard, B. (1991). *Fostering resiliency in kids: Protective factors in the family, school, and community.* Portland, OR: Western Regional Center for Drug Free Schools and Communities.

Benard, B. (1997). *Turning it around for all youth: From risk to resilience* (ERIC/CUE Digest No.126). New York: ERIC Clearinghouse on Urban Education.

Bruce, M. A. (1995). Fostering resiliency in students: Positive action strategies for classroom teachers. *The Teacher Educator, 31*(2), 178–188.

Clark, M. L. (1991). Social identity, peer relations, and academic competence of African American adolescents. *Education and Urban Society, 24*, 41–52.

Comer, J. P. (1987). New Haven's school community connection. *Educational Leadership, 44*(6), 13–16.

Csikszentmihalyi, M. (1997). *Finding flow: The psychology of engagement with everyday life.* New York: HarperCollins.

Delpit, L. (1996). The politics of teaching literate discourse. In W. Ayers & P. Ford (Eds.), *City kids, city teachers: Reports from the front row* (pp. 194–208). New York: New Press.

Fraser, B. J. (1991). Two decades of classroom environment research. In B. J. Fraser & H. J. Walberg (Eds.), *Educational environments: Evaluation, antecedents, and consequences* (pp. 3–27). Oxford, UK: Pergamon.

Futrell, M. H. (1988). At-risk students: The economic implications, the moral challenge. In R. Yount & N. Magurn (Eds.), *School/college collaboration: Teaching at-risk youth* (pp. 31–36). Washington, DC: Council of Chief State School Officers.

Garmezy, N., & Masten, A. S. (1991). The protective role of competence indicators in children at risk. In E. M. Cummings, A. L. Greene, & K. H. Karraker (Eds.), *Life-span developmental psychology: Perspectives on stress and coping* (pp. 151–174). Mahwah, NJ: Erlbaum.

Garmezy, N., Masten A. S., & Tellegen, A. (1984). The study of stress and competence in children: A building block of developmental psychopathology. *Child Development, 55,* 97–111.

Gonzalez, R., & Padilla, A. M. (1997). The academic resilience of Mexican American high school students. *Hispanic Journal of Behavioral Sciences, 19,* 301–317.

Haberman, M. (1991). Pedagogy of poverty versus good teaching. *Phi Delta Kappan, 73,* 290–294.

Henderson, N., & Milstein, M. (1996). *Resiliency in schools.* Thousand Oaks, CA: Corwin.

Higgins, G. O. (1994). *Resilient adults: Overcoming a cruel past.* San Francisco: Jossey-Bass.

Kohn, A. (1993). Choices for children: Why and how to let students decide. *Phi Delta Kappan, 75*(1), 8–16.

Krovetz, M. L. (1999). *Fostering resiliency: Expecting all students to use their minds and hearts well.* Thousand Oaks, CA: Corwin.

Lee, V. E., Winfield, L. F., & Wilson, T. C. (1991). Academic behaviors among high-achieving African American students. *Education and Urban Society, 24,* 65–86.

Liddle, H (1994). Contextualizing resiliency. In M. C. Wang & E. Gorton (Eds.), *Educational resilience in inner city America: Challenges and prospects* (pp. 167–177). Hillsdale, NJ: Erlbaum.

Masten, A. S. (1994). Resilience in individual development: Successful adaptation despite risk and adversity. In M. C. Wang & E. W. Gordon (Eds.), *Educational resilience in inner-city America: Challenges and prospects* (pp. 3–25). Mahwah, NJ: Erlbaum.

Masten, A. S., Best, K. M., & Garmezy, N. (1990). Resilience and development: Contributions from the study of children who overcome adversity. *Development and Psychopathology, 2,* 425–444.

Maughan, B. (1988). School experiences as risk/protective factors. In M. Rutter (Ed.), *Studies of psychosocial risk* (pp. 200–220). New York: New York Press Syndicate of the University of Cambridge.

McClendon, C., Nettles, S. M., & Wigfield. A. (2000). Fostering resilience in high school classrooms: A study of the PASS Program (Promoting Achievement in School Through Sport). In M. G. Sanders (Ed.), *Schooling students placed at risk: Research, policy, and practice in the education of poor and minority adolescents* (pp. 289–307). Mahwah, NJ: Erlbaum.

McLaughlin, M., & Talbert, J. (1993). *Contexts that matter for teaching and learning.* Palo Alto, CA: Stanford University.

Meier, D. (1995). *The power of their ideas: Lessons for America from a small school in Harlem.* Boston: Beacon.

Nelson-LeGall, S., & Jones, E. (1991). Classroom help-seeking behavior of African American children. *Education and Urban Society, 24,* 27–40.

Nettles, S. M., Mucherach, W., & Jones, D. S. (2000). Understanding resilience: The role of social resources. *Journal of Education for Students Placed At Risk, 5,* 47–60.

North Central Regional Educational Laboratory. (1994). Resilience research: How can it help city schools. *Cityschools 1*(1), 11–18.

Nuthall, G., & Alton-Lee, A. (1990). Research on teaching and learning: Thirty years of change. *The Elementary School Journal, 90,* 546–570.

Padrón, Y. N., Waxman, H. C., & Huang, S. L. (1999). Classroom and instructional learning: Environment differences between resilient and nonresilient elementary school students. *Journal of Education for Students Placed at Risk, 4*(1), 63–81.

Padrón, Y. N., Waxman, H. C., Powers, R. A., & Brown, A. (2002). Evaluating the effects of the Pedagogy to Improve Resiliency Program on English language learners. In L. Minaya-Rowe (Ed.), *Teacher training and effective pedagogy in the context of student diversity* (pp. 211–238). Greenwich, CT: Information Age.

Pallas, A. M., Natriello, G., & McDill, E. L. (1989). The changing nature of the disadvantaged: Current dimensions and future trends. *Educational Researcher, 18*(5), 16–22.

Pianta, R. C., Steinberg, N., & Rollins, K. (1995). The first two years of school: Teacher-child relationships and deflections in childrens' classroom adjustment. *Development and Psychopathology, 7,* 295–312.

Pianta, R. C., & Walsh, D. J. (1996). *High-risk children in school: Constructing sustaining relationships.* New York: Routledge.

Read, L. (1999). Teachers' perceptions of effective instructional strategies for resilient and nonresilient students. *Teaching and Change, 7*(1), 33–52.

Reyes, O., & Jason, L. A. (1993). Pilot study examining factors associated with academic success forHispanic high school students. *Journal of Youth and Adolescence, 22,* 57–71.

Rutter, M. (1979). Protective factors in children's responses to stress and disadvantaged. In M. W. Kent & J. E. Rolf (Eds.), *Primary prevention of psychopathology: Social competence in children* (pp. 49–74). Oxford, UK: Blackwell.

Rutter, M. (1987). Psychosocial resilience and protective mechanisms. *American Journal of Orthopsychiatry, 57,* 316–331.

Seligman, M. (1995). *The optimistic child.* Boston: Houghton Mifflin.

Stallings, J. A., & Mohlman, G. G. (1988). Classroom observation techniques. In J. P. Keeves (Ed.), *Educational research, methodology, and measurement: An International handbook* (pp. 469–474). Oxford, UK: Pergamon.

Stephen, V. P., Varble, M. E., & Taitt, H. (1993). Instructional strategies for minority youth. *The Clearing House, 67,* 116–120.

Storer, J. H., Cychosz, C. M., & Licklider, B. L. (1995). Rural school personnel's perception and categorization of children at risk: A multi-methodological account. *Equity and Excellence in Education, 28*(2), 36–45.

Swanson, D. P., & Spencer, M. B. (1991). Youth policy, poverty, and African Americans: Implications for resilience. *Education and Urban Society, 24,* 148–161.

Travis, J. E. (1995). Alienation from learning: School effects on students. *Journal for a Just and Caring Education, 1,* 434–448.

Wang, M. C., Haertel, G. D., & Walberg, H. J. (1994). Educational resilience in inner cities. In M. C. Wang & E. W. Gordon (Eds.), *Educational resilience in inner-city America: Challenges and prospects* (pp. 45–72). Mahwah, NJ: Erlbaum.

Waxman, H. C. (1992). Reversing the cycle of educational failure for students in at-risk school environments. In H. C. Waxman, J. Walker de Felix, J. Anderson, & H. P. Baptiste (Eds.), *Students at risk in at-risk schools: Improving environments for learning* (pp. 1–9). Newbury Park, CA: Corwin.

Waxman, H. C. (1995). Classroom observations of effective teaching. In A. C. Ornstein (Ed.), *Teaching: Theory into practice* (pp. 76–93). Needham Heights, MA: Allyn & Bacon.

Waxman, H. C., & Huang, S. L. (1996). Motivation and learning environment differences between resilient and nonresilient inner-city middle school students. *Journal of Educational Research, 90,* 93–102.

Waxman, H. C., & Huang, S. L. (1997). Classroom instruction and learning environment differences between effective and ineffective urban elementary schools for African American students. *Urban Education, 32*(1), 7–44.

Waxman, H. C., Huang, S. L., & Padrón, Y. N. (1995). Investigating the pedagogy of poverty in inner-city middle level schools. *Research in Middle Level Education, 18*(2), 1–22.

Waxman, H. C., Huang, S. L., & Padrón, Y. N. (1997). Motivation and learning environment differences between resilient and non-resilient Latino middle school students. *Hispanic Journal of Behavioral Sciences, 19,* 137–155.

Waxman, H. C., Huang, S. L., & Wang, M. C. (1997). Investigating the multilevel classroom learning environment of resilient and nonresilient students from inner-city elementary schools. *International Journal of Educational Research, 27,* 343–353.

Waxman, H. C., Padrón, Y. N., & Arnold, K. A. (2001). Effective instructional practices for students placed at risk of failure. In G. D. Borman, S. C. Stringfield, & R. E. Slavin (Eds.), *Title I: Compensatory education at the crossroads* (pp. 137–170). Mahwah, NJ: Erlbaum.

Wehlage, G. G., Rutter, R. A., Smith, G. A., Lesko, N., & Fernandez, R. R. (1989). *Reducing the risk: Schools as communities of support.* London: Falmer.

Werner, E. E., & Smith, R. S. (1977). *Kauai's children come of age.* Honolulu: University of Hawaii Press.

Werner, E. E. & Smith, R. S. (1992). *Overcoming the odds: High risk children from birth to adulthood.* Ithaca, NY: Cornell University Press.

Wolin, S. J., & Wolin, S. (1993). *The resilient self: How survivors of troubled families rise above adversity.* New York: Villard.

CHAPTER 4

RESILIENCE RESEARCH AND PRACTICE

National Resilience Resource Center Bridging the Gap

Kathy M. Marshall
University of Minnesota

The notion of resilience has brought infectious hope to practitioners whom 10 years ago were experiencing tremendous professional burnout and frustration. This enthusiasm to some degree has dismayed classical resilience researchers who originally aimed to understand prevention of psychopathology.

As grassroots practitioners from multiple professions—youth development, substance abuse prevention, health and human services, and education—began to disseminate the hope of resilience, they created what they needed, drew on what they could find, and used published research as they understood it. Today, many practitioners widely promote the paradigm shift from risk to resilience.

In some ways, this burgeoning interest may seem to articulate a notion of resilience that disgraces the history of resilience research. In the classic resilience research designs, there is no resilience in the absence of risk. Resilience is defined in terms of adaptation or development (Masten,

---

Educational Resiliency: Student, Teacher, and School Perspectives, pages 63–84
Copyright © 2004 by Information Age Publishing
All rights of reproduction in any form reserved.

2002). Seminal classical studies examined how subjects responded to substantial risk and trauma. Researchers like Norm Garmezy, Emmy Werner, Michael Rutter, Ann Masten, and others pioneered the prospective developmental longitudinal studies. These are exactly the studies that captured the keen interest of both community-based prevention practitioners and research scientists.

Resilience legitimately became a popular term, a buzzword, and almost a movement in education, youth development, and prevention circles. Simply put, practitioners said it made common sense, felt better, and brought more positive outcomes to point youth to their health rather than to their weaknesses and problems. The research touched a chord. The draw of resilience has energized practice in many professional fields. Resilience is popular today partly because of enthusiastic practitioners.

Similarly, resilience research is growing and expanding in multiple arenas well beyond the traditional focus on psychopathology prevention. Researchers from youth development, family social science, community development, social work, medicine, and many other disciplines are making significant contributions. New terms like "strengths-based," "positive youth development," "health promotion," "brain-based learning," "mind–body," and more characterize rapidly growing explorations.

SEA CHANGE IN RESILIENCE RESEARCH

Our knowledge of resilience is evolving (Masten, 2002; Zimmerman & Arunkumar, 1994). In 1987, Michael Rutter distinguished *protective factors* and *protective mechanisms*. He said most researchers assumed vulnerability or protection "lies in the variable rather than the process. It does not and cannot.... It makes no sense to label variables.... It is the process or mechanism, not the variable, that determines the function" (p. 317). Rutter offered a critical bridge between resilience research and practice that warrants deeper exploration today. Prevention involves both the environment and the individual in dynamic interaction—*protective processes*.

Masten and Coatsworth (1998) suggest the newest, least understood but most promising prevention initiatives yet to be explored are process-focused. "We still lack data on specific effects.... We have little understanding of the process by which change and protection occur" (p. 215). Although the research team presents characteristics of resilient children and adolescents gleaned from the literature, Masten and Coatsworth say these qualities "are only known to be associated with resilience and are not necessarily causal influences. These attributes, in fact, could be consequences of success rather than causes of it" (p. 213).

Martin Seligman, past president of the American Psychological Association, articulates a sea change (Seligman & Csikszentmihalyi, 2000).

> What psychologists have learned over 50 years is that the disease model does not move psychology closer to the prevention of...serious problems.... Prevention researchers have discovered that there are human strengths that act as buffers against mental illness: courage, future mindedness, optimism, interpersonal skill, faith, work ethic, hope, honesty, perseverance, and the capacity for flow and insight, to name several. Much of the science of this new century will be to create a science of human strength whose mission will be to understand and learn how to foster these virtues in young people.... Psychologists need now to call for massive research on human strengths and virtues.... The major psychological theories have changed to undergird a new science of strength and resilience. (pp. 7–8)

Emmy Werner and Ruth Smith's 40-year, person-focused Kauai longitudinal study (2001) indicates extraordinary resilience and a capacity to recover from and overcome problems shaped the journey to midlife for most of the study's 489 participants.

> What lessons did we learn? Most of all...they were lessons that taught us a great deal of respect for the self-righting tendencies in human nature and for the capacity of most individuals who grew up in adverse circumstances to make a successful adaptation in adulthood. (p. 166)

Does this suggest that over time the capacity for resilience in every person, regardless of circumstances or degree of risk, may emerge? How can education and prevention efforts invite, support, and speed the process for most young people?

HOPEFUL DIRECTIONS FOR PRACTICE

The question emerging from the unfolding research is not "Nature or nurture?" or even "Who is resilient and who is not?" Practitioners need to ask, "Do I believe every child is innately 'at promise' rather than 'at risk'?" If we agree, then our work is cut out for us. "How can I help the young person learn to access natural common sense and capacity for health and well-being, for optimal outcomes, and positive behaviors?" There is something fundamental behind manifested "resilient" behaviors. "At promise" means children are just that—filled with capacity, realized or unrealized, for healthy transformation and change. This natural capacity for resilience is like a self-righting magnet that draws a person to health. What ignites the self-righting process?

It would be wrong and misleading to conclude that pronouncing children "at promise" is enough. Emmy Werner warns, "We don't accomplish this by fiat." Seeing the potential and positive capacity of every child is, however, essential. "I hope this comes shining through my research" (E. E. Werner, personal communication, June 6, 2002).

Prevention becomes a multifaceted initiative in light of these perspectives. Substance abuse prevention professionals have been historically advised by the U.S. Center for Substance Abuse Prevention (CSAP) to work with six essential external or phenomenological domains—information dissemination, education, alternative activities, identification and referral, community-based processes, and environmental strategies.

Such phenomenological external approaches to resilience alone are not enough and all too often lead to reductionist programs and initiatives. Resilience is an inside-out process—an existential process of every child and youth "being and becoming." This involves learning how the *protective mechanism* of healthy psychological functioning occurs. Thus resilience is both attributional and contextual—a dynamic inner and outer process that ignites self-righting. To the degree that practitioners can both foster the natural capacity for resilience—common sense and wisdom—found within every person, and create optimal societal conditions for youth to thrive in, efforts will be successful.

Effective practices must involve the *protective processes* of caring relationships, high expectations, and opportunities for meaningful participation and contribution well documented in resilience research summarized by Bonnie Benard (1991). These are transactional processes of person-in-environment. When we are engaged in this kind of work, we may choose to no longer think of our work as preventing difficulties, but rather as fostering individual human development in the context of community. "Moving to a resiliency approach requires a personal transformation of vision ... the lens through which we see our world. To make systemic changes ... depends on changing hearts and minds" (Benard, 1993, pp. 4–5).

The paradigm shift may need to occur within each of us. Are we fixing human problems or developing human resources? Is the epicenter of such work in the environment or in the individual, or, perhaps, in both? What we know—have come to intuitively understand about human capacity—matters immensely. The sources of knowing are both our common sense and scientific research. Quality research and practice are interdependent.

The pressures for practitioners and researchers are distinct. In simple terms, researchers must secure massive ongoing funding, meet clear scientific standards, and publish continually. Practitioners must make do with meager short-term funding, meet daily overwhelming youth needs, and specifically improve academic performance, prevent chemical use, and restore civility to earn their keep.

We have needed a functional bridge between the two worlds of research and practice for so long. The current interest in resilience invites us to build the bridge.

FRAMEWORK FOR TAPPING NATURAL RESILIENCE

After nearly a decade working in more than 20 states, Bonnie Benard and I recognized the need to assist practitioners in building a functional bridge between resilience research and practice. Work with the federally funded Western and Midwestern Regional Centers for Drug Free Schools and the North Central and Northwest Regional Educational Research Laboratories, as well as intermediate schools districts, individual school systems, and community agencies, clearly exposed the gap between research and practice. Interest in resilience was keen in almost every sector. Therefore, we conceptualized a simple framework to guide community-based youth prevention planning (Benard & Marshall, 1997; Marshall, 1998).

The lights went on for us one November morning in 1995. We knew the issue was deeper than prevention strategies. It involved what we knew intuitively about the capacity of kids and adults for healthy functioning, and what we learned scientifically from the evolving, broadly multidisciplinary resilience research. We needed a conceptual framework to link these *two ways of knowing* what works in order to bring out the best in kids. Thus the resilience operating philosophy emerged.

As illustrated in Figure 4.1, the essential planning steps examine individual and systemic beliefs, conditions of empowerment, program strategies, and evaluation of both individual and societal outcomes. There are key questions for each phase in the planning framework:

- **Belief:** Are all children, youth, and adults at promise even if they do not realize it?
- **Conditions of Empowerment:** What are the conditions of empowerment revealed by research and best practice?
- **Program Strategies:** What program strategies and approaches will create conditions that tap resilience?
- **Evaluation, Individual Outcomes:** What results can we realistically expect for children, youth, and adults when we tap resilience?
- **Evaluation, Societal Outcomes:** What happens at family, organizational, community, or societal levels?

Unlike most planning frameworks, which are based on problem-focused needs assessment and external strategies or solutions, the foundation for systems-change tapping resilience rests first on leaders' belief about human functioning and natural capacity for resilience. This framework empha-

Figure 4.1. Framework for tapping natural resilience (Benard & Marshall, 1995).

sizes the ordinary human capacity for healthy transformation and change. It forces planners to decide if there are "throw-away" children, or if there is hope for all regardless of risk factors. This innate capacity for resilience, when realized and tapped with effective evidence-based strategies, restores hope for healthy human development and societal progress across the board, including prevention of substance abuse and related high-risk behaviors, improved performance, relationships, and mental health. After decades of exploration, resilience researcher Ann Masten (2001) states:

> The great surprise of resilience research is the ordinariness of the phenomena.... Resilience does not come from rare and special qualities, but from ordinary everyday magic of ordinary, normative human resources in the minds, brains, and bodies of children, in their families and relationships, and in their communities. This has profound implications for promoting competence and human capital in individuals and society. (pp. 227, 235)

NATIONAL RESILIENCE RESOURCE CENTER: OPERATIONALIZING RESILIENCE

NRRC assists school, community, and organizational leaders in enhancing their capacity to tap natural, innate health or resilience of youth, families, communities, and systems. Belief in innate human capacity for well-being and the evidence from resilience research are the linchpins in this NRRC systems-change approach. (See Marshall, 1998, "Reculturing Systems with Resilience/Health" in a 1998 publication of The Carter Center, *Promoting*

Positive and Healthy Behaviors in Children. Call (404) 420-5165 for a free single copy.)

Tapping Resilience with Resilience/Health Realization

The primary NRRC strategy for tapping resilience has been developed from a best practice known as Health Realization. NRRC training programs and technical assistance promote full human development, enhance individual well-being, and improve program outcomes.

At the Center, we refer to a *resilience operating philosophy* grounded in more than 50 years of multidisciplinary international resilience research. This body of scientific study establishes the hopeful fact that people can and do *self-right*. Traditionally, this research focused on identifying people who overcame or adapted to severe stress and trauma. These studies, as summarized by Bonnie Benard (1991), point to three phenomenological *protective factors* that foster resilience: *caring and supportive relationships, encouraging high expectations,* and *meaningful opportunities for participation.* The research, however, does not tell us how to teach adults to become caring, encouraging, or inviting.

We looked for strategies that would increase the *health of the helper.* Michael Rutter (1987) indicates, "the protective function does not simply reside within the individual. Intrinsic qualities ... also influence other people's reactions. Because the protective mechanism lies in the interaction rather than in the individual attribute ... it can be used in interventions" (p. 327). Similarly, Don Crary, with one of the Annie E. Casey Foundation New Futures projects, reports:

> When there's improvement, it usually isn't that the services per se were different, it's about a change in the person who delivered the service, and the way they delivered it. It became clear systems change meant changing the interactions between people in all the systems...a very different and difficult agenda. (Walsh, 2000, p. 2)

Therefore, in planning services NRRC aimed to strengthen individual practitioner's well-being.

When adults are at their best, they extend protective factors naturally. Resilience/Health Realization, developed in both clinical and community settings in the last 25 years, teaches people how to tap their resilience or realize their natural innate mental health. This is an educational process (Mills & Spittle, 2001; Pransky, 1998; Stewart, 1993).

Health Realization is a principle-based understanding of how human beings function. Learning how they operate psychologically frees people of all ages and circumstances to tap their resilience—realize their innate mental health, common sense, wisdom, and well-being. In many ways, Health Realization develops the " 'steeling' qualities that derive from successful coping" Rutter (1987, p. 320) believes "warrant further investigation." In simple terms, the principles of Health Realization might be described below.

1. **We create our experience of life with our thinking.** Thought is the human ability to create meaning. There are two modes of thought: fresh insight and analytical, conditioned, memory-based thought. When we learn to use both insight and memory in a healthy, effective manner, *thought is a protective mechanism.* Wisdom traditions across cultures have recognized the importance and spiritual nature of calm, clear, reflective, present-moment thinking. Knowing we create life from the inside out with our thinking brings hope. It means the circumstances of our lives do not have control of us. In a clear-headed frame of reference, we can navigate life successfully. Every person is the *thinker* creating his own illusory experience moment-to-moment. Think of a juicy lemon and you will salivate. Shift your attention to blue whales and your feelings, mood, behavior, and experience changes. We create our personal reality with our own thinking. We often innocently and needlessly terrorize ourselves with our thinking! "What if? If only! I should have…." The result of this inside-out process for both youth and adults can create an insecure state of mind characterized by bad feelings and undesirable behaviors. With healthy functioning, the result is a secure state of mind. Without a doubt, this understanding holds promise for all practitioners attempting to bring out the best—tap resilience—in self or others.

2. **Every person has wisdom within.** At the very core, every person is whole. This inner spirit is every person's birthright. A Native American worldview, for example, acknowledges that we can live in balance—realize our inner spirit—if we attend carefully to the mental, emotional, physical, and spiritual aspects of our being. A person may or may not discover this secure state of mind (HeavyRunner & Morris, 1997). The healthy self is never destroyed and it can always be realized. We are part of something greater than we are. As reflective humans, we ponder the meaning of life, our place and purpose in this world. Fostering resilience addresses these questions. It is human nature to long for connection with others. This inner spirituality has many names across cultures—universal intelligence, life force, source, energy, God, Chi, Qi, and more. It is important to distinguish spirituality from religion. Religion is a private matter of

belief, worship, and affiliation. Spirituality is neutral, formless, an inner aspect of life common to all human beings.

The necessity of acknowledging the role of spirit and inner reflection in education is well documented in a recent issue of *Education Leadership* edited by Parker Palmer (1998–1999), by child psychiatrist Robert Coles in *The Spiritual Life of Children* (1990), and in *Paths of Learning* edited by Richard Prystowsky (2002). At the University of Minnesota, the National Resilience Resource Center, in collaboration with faculty from the School of Nursing, has offered the first course on Spirituality and Resilience for graduate credit through the Center for Spirituality and Healing. Emmy Werner notes psychologists and researchers have avoided this important subject for too long (E. E. Werner, personal communication, June 6, 2001).

Health Realization points to this spiritual nature and builds confidence in trusting the unknown, waiting and noticing fresh insights—out-of-the-blue "ahas." Each person is the *knower*. Everyone can learn to notice and tap this common sense. *The wisdom within every person is a protective mechanism and source of natural resilience.*

3. **Human beings have awareness, the ability to bring thought to life.** The third principle explaining human functioning is consciousness—the human ability to be aware. We recognize our thoughts and how thinking creates our individual experiences of life. We are more than our thinking, feelings, and behaviors. We are the "observer" who stands at "second attention" recognizing our thinking. Our five senses bring thought to life. You are the *noticer*.

These three principles explain how experience happens from the inside out. The principles, always in operation, make a life event or circumstance seem hopeful or hopeless, healthy or unhealthy, stressful or productive. The degree to which a young person or adult understands these three principles at work in their lives can be called *level of understanding*. People tap natural resilience to the degree they understand the three principles of how they function psychologically. These universal principles apply regardless of age, condition, circumstance, race, gender, or other defining characteristics. NRRC trainings amplify the principles by exploring related topics such as impact listening, rapport, insight, and memory-based thinking, separate realities, moods and feelings, standards of healthy functioning, and more.

According to Masten and Coatsworth (1998), the three most important human adaptive systems in fostering and protecting development in all environments are the quality of self-regulation of attention, emotion, and behavior; parent–child attachment relationships, and good cognitive development. Learning Health Realization principles directly enhance these adaptive systems.

Michael Rutter (1987) pointed to the fundamental role of personal thinking. "Most risk factors are not absolutes that are independent of the person's appraisal and cognitive processing" (p. 325) and protection resides "in the ways in which people deal with life changes and in what they do about their stressful or disadvantageous circumstances" (p. 329).

The NRRC process of tapping resilience is deeper than prevention strategies, wellness programs, community empowerment, collaboratives, youth development initiatives, innovative educational models or interventions such as traditional therapy. Tapping resilience is an undergirding inside-out process.

National Resilience Resource Center Outcomes

It has been NRRC's experience that when people increase understanding of how they function, their quality of life improves. These changes often include *increased personal reflection or spiritual development, enhanced personal well-being, better relationships with others,* and *greater work satisfaction.* A natural outgrowth is that adults are genuinely and naturally more caring for students and others. It is also easier to see students or colleagues as "at promise." Encouraging high expectations are a by-product. Finally, this improved vantage point is a catalyst to creating and offering meaningful opportunities for participation to others. By strengthening the *health of the helper,* the odds of an organization or individual extending protective factors to others are increased in a natural, effortless way.

NRRC's primary work has been with large-scale, ongoing systems change efforts in public school communities. These initiatives generally start modestly and grow to scale in a natural way. The following discussion of NRRC work in both St. Cloud, Minnesota, and Menomonie, Wisconsin, is based on NRRC semi-structured interviews, focus groups, school district records, and other information (Marshall, 2000).

What began as a simple interest in evaluating the St. Cloud, Minnesota, Safe and Drug Free Schools program in 1994 led to district-wide Student Assistance Team training, and a Resilience/Health Realization pilot training program with 35 team members from one junior high and the early childhood program. By 2003, initiative reached more than 2,500 persons from the full spectrum of public agencies and small nonprofits serving children, youth, and families. The same is true in rural Menomonie, Wisconsin, where more than 350 persons have participated since 1996. In both sites, the National Resilience Resource Center (NRRC) works on multiple fronts with a combination of training and technical assistance.

SCHOOL IMPROVEMENT: NORTH JUNIOR HIGH, ST. CLOUD, MINNESOTA

The NRRC resilience work with adults began at North Junior High in 1996. Instruction of 800 seventh- and eighth-grade students began in 1998–99. The preliminary results are impressive. The school climate changed in remarkable ways. By the third year, leaders at North believed they achieved a critical mass of faculty members whose insights into their innate health and resilience made a significant difference in the life of the school. It is also important to note that solid, effective school administration and a variety of sound activities contributed greatly to this success. Principal Pat Welter reported the school's experience (Marshall, 2000).

> *"Something is different this year!"*
> *"The staff is calmer—more relaxed."*
> *"The kids are respectful."*
> *"Our mood is lighter—things aren't as hectic."*
> *"Even the cafeteria is a fun place to be."*

It did not take more than 3 weeks into the school year for staff members to make comments such as, "This was the smoothest start to the school year that we have had." By October and November, a time when the staff is usually beginning to show signs of frustration and stress, teachers were still exclaiming, "We are having such a nice year." Staff members began telling stories of students who were able to "quiet their minds" and calm down with just a gentle reminder. Staff claimed, too, that being aware that their reality was "just thought" and they could "let thoughts go" made a significant difference in how well they could deal with the behaviors of middle-school students.

We arrived at February before we knew it, staff members were still feeling that the peace in the building was real! A cafeteria monitor exclaimed that even the lunch periods (of 150 students for 22-minute lunches) were the best in 5 years. A substitute custodian remarked that he could tell something was different in this building and he wanted us to be aware of it if we weren't. He said, "You're getting at something pretty powerful here!"

Discipline data, too, reveals significant change. Student behavior incidents had improved measurably at North Junior High. From school year 1997–98 to school year 1998–99, suspensions were 70% lower; fights were reduced by 63.8%; and incidents of violence dropped 65.1%.

Student Voices

North Junior High students in St. Cloud, Minnesota, learning Resilience/Health Realization, reported in District 742 focus groups what this has meant in their lives:

> "Me and my dad fight like cats and dogs. I'll start talking to him and he'll start yelling at me so I yell at him...I think our parents need to learn it the most...especially my dad 'cause he needs to learn how to cool down when he gets that way."

> "I got suspended before I found out some of this.... I actually punched a kid.... But then I found out it was a separate reality thing and it could've been stopped."

> "I used quiet mind because I didn't do any of my homework and I had a ton to do the next day. So I did it all in school. Just kind of calmed myself down at the end of the day and did a bunch. Got it all done. I was proud of myself."

> "[I used it in] dealing with anger with classmates...like to tell them to calm down. You get between them and try to calm them both down before you try to say anything or get them more mad at you."

Student and Teacher Survey Data

School improvement surveys of students and teachers at North also show that something important was happening. While annual comparative student data is not as meaningful as the staff data because the population of students changes, it is nevertheless interesting to note the trends:

- 13% increase in students who say students are generally respectful to each other
- 21% increase in students who say students are generally respectful to adults
- 9% increase in students who say the school is a friendly place
- 10% increase in students who say adults in this school are helpful

North faculty survey data documents these perceptual changes about North at that time:

- 21% increase in faculty believing there is good communication
- 27% increase in faculty believing they can participate in school-level decisions
- 19% increase in faculty believing North is a good place to work
- 24% increase in faculty believing students of different races get along well
- 34% increase in faculty believing students respect each other
- 44% increase in faculty believing students respect adults

- 40% increase in faculty believing positive interactions among students have increased
- 33.9% increase in faculty believing positive student-to-adult interactions increased

While this data is by no means conclusive, it does correspond to the anecdotal information North leaders received for the entire year. While it may be too soon to make definitive statements about the eventual impact of Resilience/Health Realization on students, it is not too soon to report that virtually all staff members who have been involved report significant change in their personal lives. Principle Pat Welter says, "For this we have a great deal of gratitude" (Marshall, 2000, p. 2). She goes on to say,

> The high-risk students we are most interested in reaching are those students whose support systems outside of school are virtually nonexistent. While these students are performing poorly academically, they have average or above-average intelligence. They tend to be impulsive, aggressive, and acting out, but they also have some internal emotional issues. Most of them have flirted with drugs, alcohol, sex, and gang activity; some have court involvement. They are seeking excitement, stimulation, and "highs" in their lives, but they also seem to be seeking safety, comfort, and security. While they may have some attendance problems, they keep coming to school; we believe this is partially due to their friends, but also because they know that there are adults here who do care and who provide some sense of safety and security.
>
> The most frustrating thing for adults who work with these students is to see the overwhelming potential they possess and to feel so helpless in our seeming inability to assist them to significantly change their lives. Our hope was that Resilience/Health Realization strategies might be a way to help them tap their own innate strength—resilience—and release their potential in spite of their external reality. Without some additional intervention, we believe that many of these students will end up in and out of the court. (Marshall, 2000, p. 4)

While serious budget cuts coupled with ongoing staff turn over have limited the St. Cloud school district's ability to maintain systemic efforts like those described at North Junior High, community agency progress with more than 34 organizations is documented. In 2003 NRRC reports Resilience/Health Realization training participants show improvements in the following areas after four days of training spread over three months:

- Statistical significance at .01
  - Decreased perception of "life is stressful"
  - Decreased feeling "I feel the way I do because things happen to me"
  - Decreased worrying
  - Increased contentment

- Statistical significance at .05
    - Decreased feeling that "I've got a lot on my mind"
    - Decreased frustration with failures
    - Increased sense of being "a happy person"
    - Increased "experience of well-being"
    - Decreased "arguments with others"

This enhanced "health of helpers" makes it easier and natural for trained adults to extend essential protective factors of caring and support, encouraging high expectations and meaningful opportunities for participation to students, families, clients, and other professionals. NRRC evaluation currently in progress continues to document this trend.

SYSTEMS CHANGE: MENOMONIE, WISCONSIN

A similar story unfolded in rural Wisconsin (Marshall, 2000). In October 1996, school social worker Gary Johnson invited staff of the School District of the Menomonie Area Pupil Services team to consider a paradigm shift from seeing students as "at risk" to "at promise." "We are aiming to look at what is right with kids rather that what is wrong. We know it makes a huge difference to see natural resilience—innate health—in everyone," Johnson says (p. 5).

Today, a system-wide change is underway with stakeholders from the school district, county public health and human services, treatment agencies, law enforcement, domestic abuse programs, and other organizations. More than 350 adults have begun a long-term training process facilitated by NRRC. Menomonie has a population of about 13,000 and 10% of the student body is Hmong.

A focus group conducted by Joan Patterson from the University of Minnesota Maternal and Child Health program, with school district staff trained in Resilience/Health Realization, documented personal progress. Changes were observed in three primary domains: the individual's relationship to him/herself, the individual's relationship to others, and the individual's outlook on life. In summary, these changes in the self could be described as:

- changed attitudes (especially related to a reduced need for personal control)
- new coping behaviors, particularly an appraisal coping strategy of thinking differently about a situation, which resulted in
- reduced feelings of distress and greater calmness

Changes observed in participants' relationships with others included:

- improved listening skills
- greater acceptance of others' divergent views
- belief in the ability of others to realize their own health
- increased support and cohesiveness among colleagues

Staff members also seemed to reflect a new way of looking at life, which could be characterized as a greater trust that things would work out in their own way and in their own time. This view is consistent with what Antonovsky (1979, 1987) has referred to as a "sense of coherence."

Educators' Improved Well-Being

Findings from the School District of the Menomonie Area's focus groups included these comments from a variety of school professionals with NRRC Resilience/Health Realization training:

> *"I don't go to bed and think about things that happened or might happen. I just go to sleep more quickly."*
>
> *"It makes me smile a lot more. What changes have occurred as a result of this training—my entire life! I just say that I feel like life is lighter now and [I notice] the peace that comes from just kind of trusting that things will be okay."*
>
> *"This can apply to absolutely every single, solitary person."*
>
> *"One of the biggest things for me is...if I just listen to them [my children] they will solve their problems.... It's seeing their resilience, knowing that they have it. It's the intuitive knowing that they have it."*
>
> *"It's just very clear with me, how well I am doing at home, how well I am relating to everyone."*
>
> *"Overall school improvement through this initiative and the commitment of the individuals trained over a long-term basis—this just doesn't happen in districts. It's incredible."*
>
> *"I work with a lot of kids I have thought of as victims...but I also believe that I see the strengths they have in them and I find myself going at that angle more."*
>
> *"With the staff.... It makes us feel like we are in this journey together. I just see it in the feel of the building."*
>
> *"No one can ever take this away from us. We have it within us—we really do."*
>
> *"When our team started training we drew a picture of ourselves squished under a rock. I wouldn't feel that way anymore. I think we are getting healthier and are better able to balance things. Maybe the rock will still be there, but we don't feel as squashed by it as we have been. We aren't taking it personally. We're recognizing what is not healthy much more quickly."*

In school-reform terms, these "voices of change" evidence what Michael Fullan (1998) describes as school reculturing from the inside out. He argues that systems change most easily when teachers communicate to students:

> "You've got it within you to succeed in life, to be happy and to be proud of yourself. No matter what anyone has told you, no matter what you believe right now, you've got it." When an individual teacher believes this, she can improve a life. When large numbers of teachers can come to believe it, they can do a whole world of good. Hope, optimism and self-belief among teachers are the vital wellsprings of successful learning and positive education change.... It is individuals who must hope, but it is institutions that create the climate and conditions which make people feel more hopeful—or less so. (pp. 1–2)

Fullan (1993) is known for probing the depths of educational reform: "When you go deeper you go different. What appears linear becomes a new world...by raising our consciousness and insights about the totality of educational change...we can do something about it.... We need a new mindset to go deeper" (pp. vii–ix).

The resilience mindset begins with personal change. "Many reformers still have to learn that teachers will not commit to change if they cannot see the point." Fullan (1998) says, "going deeper means getting clear and coming clean about purposes...to love and care, to serve, to empower, and of course, to learn" (pp. 29–30). The personal health and well-being of staff members governs how they see and serve students, parents, and colleagues.

Teachers from the Menomonie, Wisconsin, school system focus group at Downsville Elementary indicate both deep *intra*personal and *inter*personal change is happening:

> "I think I am just easier on myself. [Before] I would really take things to heart. Now I just think, 'Well, that's a thought. I'm going to go past that.' "

> "Knowing separate realities has really helped me with parents. I used to just get red and hot when some of the parents would come in the attack mode. I talked to a parent the other day and she was very confrontational. I just stayed as calm as I could be, and by the end of the conversation she had turned around and was agreeing with me without me having to say much."

> "We've gotten much closer as a staff. People listen to one another; they feel like they can go to one another. You can say, 'I don't know what to do. What should I say? How should I handle this?' You get support and get help and you get ideas."

> "Everybody here knows this is a long-haul thing, this is a life-long thing. This is not going to be done next year. I like that!"

A FINAL WORD

These stories offer part of the promising evidence inviting educational leaders to initiate school change as an inside-out process. This process of tapping and fostering resilience with Health Realization brings hope and restores energy. Findings from NRRC school community focus groups show individuals with one year of training experience these benefits:

- Increased personal reflection
- Enhanced sense of personal well-being (mental to physical) and reduced stress
- Improved relationships with others (partners, children, family, friends, colleagues)
- Increased satisfaction in the workplace

As understanding is deepened and the circle of trained persons grows, systems begin to shift toward common sense, health, and well-being—natural systemic resilience. There is a simpler way for organizations to be and it begins with the inside-out process of resilience-based systems change called Resilience/Health Realization. Protective factors—caring, encouraging high expectations, and meaningful opportunities for participation—are extended naturally as the *health of the helper* blossoms. Improved school climate and student outcomes are inevitable by-products. What was difficult and overwhelming becomes effortless and gratifying. As Parker Palmer (1998) notes, "The most practical thing we can achieve in any...work is insight into what is happening inside us as we do it. The more familiar we are with our inner terrain, the more surefooted our teaching—and living—becomes" (p. 5).

ACKNOWLEDGMENT

Special thanks to Dr. Pat Welter, Principal of North Junior High in St. Cloud, Minnesota, and to Alcohol and Other Drug Abuse Prevention Coordinator Gary Johnson of the School District of the Menomonie Area in Wisconsin, for assistance in developing their districts' stories; Joan Patterson, PhD, of the University of Minnesota Maternal and Child Health Program for evaluation assistance; Bonnie Benard for a decade of invaluable collaboration; dedicated NRRC facilitators; and leaders in the University of Minnesota College of Continuing Education for vision and commitment to excellence in innovative education. Finally, the University of Minnesota legacy of premiere resilience, school improvement, and prevention researchers including Emmy Werner, Norm Garmezy, Ann Masten, Michael Resnick, Robert Blum, John Romano, and Karen Seashore must be acknowledged.

REFERENCES

Antonovsky, A. (1979). *Health, stress, and coping.* San Francisco: Jossey-Bass.
Antonovsky, A. (1987). *Unraveling the mystery of health.* San Francisco: Jossey-Bass.
Benard, B. (1991). *Fostering resiliency in kids: protective factors in the family, school, and community.* Portland, OR: Northwest Regional Educational Laboratory.
Benard, B. (1993, March). Resiliency requires changing hearts and minds. *Western Center News, 6*(2), 4–5.
Benard, B., & Marshall, K. (1997). A framework for practice: Tapping innate resilience. *Research/Practice,* pp. 9–15.
Coles, R. (1990). *The spiritual life of children.* Boston: Houghton Mifflin.
Fullan, M. (1993). *Change forces: Probing the depths of educational reform.* New York: Falmer.
Fullan, M. (1998). *What's worth fighting for out there?* New York: Teachers College Press.
HeavyRunner, I., & Morris, J. (1997). Traditional native culture and resilience. *Research/Practice,* pp. 19–27.
Marshall, K. (1998, November). Reculturing systems with resilience/health realization. In *Promoting positive and healthy behaviors in children: Fourteenth Annual Rosalynn Carter Symposium on Mental Health Policy* (pp. 48–58). Atlanta, GA: The Carter Center.
Marshall, K. (2000). *Experiences implementing resilience/health realization in schools.* Unpublished manuscript, University of Minnesota, National Resilience Resource Center at Minneapolis.
Masten, A., (2001). Ordinary magic: Resilience processes in development. *American Psychologist, 56*(3), 1–12.
Masten, A. (2002). Resilience in development. In C. R. Snyder & S. J. Lopez (Eds), *Handbook of positive psychology* (pp. 74–88). London: Oxford University Press.
Masten, A., & Coatsworth, J. D. (1998.) The development of competence in favorable and unfavorable environments: Lessons from research on successful children. *American Psychologist, 53,* 205–220.
Mills, R., & Spittel, E. (2001). *The wisdom within.* Renton, WA: Lone Pine.
Palmer, P. (1998). *The courage to teach: Exploring the inner landscape of a teacher's life.* San Francisco: Jossey-Bass.
Palmer, P. J. (Ed.). (1998–1999). The spirit in education. *Education Leadership, 56*(4).
Pransky, G. (1998). *The renaissance of psychology.* New York: Sulzburger & Graham.
Prystowsky, R. (Ed.). (2002). Spirituality and education. *Paths of Learning, 12.*
Rutter, M. (1987). Psychosocial resilience and protective mechanisms. *American Orthopsychiatric Association, 57*(31), 316–329.
Seligman, M., & Csikszentmihalyi, M. (2000). Positive psychology: an introduction [Special issue]. *American Psychologist, 55*(1), 7–8.
Stewart, D. (1993). *Creating the teachable moment: Innovative approach to teaching and learning.* Blue Ridge Summit, PA: TAB Books.
Walsh, J. (2000). *The key insight. The eye of the storm: Ten years on the front lines of new futures* [Online]. Baltimore: The Annie E. Casey Foundation. Available: http://www.aecf.org

Werner, E., & Smith, R. (2001). *Journeys from childhood to midlife: Risk, resilience and recovery.* Ithaca, NY: Cornell University Press.

Zimmerman, M., & Arunkumar, R. (1994). Resilience research: Implications for schools and policy. *Society for Research in Child Development, VIII*(4), 1–17.

APPENDIX

National Resilience Resource Center: Guide to Application in Student Services

NRRC helps professionals discover the efficacy of moving from "risk" to "resilience," of seeing youth as "at promise" rather than "at risk." This profound shift is discussed in nearly every major profession – education, social work, health care, and more. George Pransky refers to a "renaissance in psychology" (Pransky, 1998) and Darlene Stewart (1993) describes "creating the teachable moment."

For educators and other helping professionals the philosophical shift ushers in a new kind of practice for working with youths one-on-one, in small groups and in classrooms. School and human service professionals—counselors, social workers, psychologists, support group facilitators, nurses, assistant principals responsible for discipline, and others make this shift to get better student outcomes. With the advent of Resilience/Health Realization, professional practice has been reinvented with a focus on the innate health of those we serve rather than on deficits, problems, and dysfunction. Richard Carlson (1995) calls it a "shortcut through therapy." Where there has been systemic application, general school climate and student behaviors improve greatly (Marshall, 2000).

Resilience/Health Realization can strengthen professional development programs, curriculum and instruction redesign, school policies and procedures, parent programming, and other aspects of school improvement. A sample discussion of the resilience operating philosophy applied to school-based student services follows because Emmy Werner indicates in the 40-year Kauai longitudinal study (Werner & Smith, 2001) there is room for improving counseling and social work practice:

> The men and women in this cohort consistently ranked mental health professionals (whether psychiatrists, psychologists, or social workers) much lower than the counsel and advice given by spouses, friends, members of the extended family, teachers, mentors, co-workers, members of church groups, or ministers. Their low opinion of the professional's help did not improve from the second to the third and fourth decade of life. This finding taught us a lesson in humility! (p. 169)

Student Services: Sample Application of Resilience/Health Realization

When we approach students for whom there are concerns—academic, behavioral, social, medical—consider the following Resilience/Health Realization guidelines when working with young people individually or in small groups:

Every student regardless of the presenting concern has innate mental health.
   Your job as a helping professional is to remember that at all times and to not be dissuaded by the student's behavior, feelings, appearance, or life circumstances. The student's innate health may be only briefly visible, persistently elusive, or cleverly disguised. You must be alert moment-to-moment. Seeing that health is an act of faith. You are on a treasure hunt. The certainty you have of the student's health is what brings the young person hope.

Your own "health as a helper"—grounding—is necessary if you are to reach the student.
   Health is contagious. Your own mental health speeds the helping process. If you are in a good feeling, the student will notice and be drawn to you. If you are insecure, uncertain of what to say or do, overwhelmed, unsure of your ability to meet student needs, the student will know and lose hope.

Your own level of understanding about Resilience/Health Realization is critical.
   Articulate what you know about resilience and healthy psychological functioning in a way that fits the student you are sitting across from. The teachable moment is fleeting. Once you are confident that you understand the three principles in operation, you will be naturally prepared for the turning points in individual and group sessions. You will trust your insights to guide you in an effortless way.

You may need to go beyond what you have learned.
   These guidelines may be in conflict with what you learned in graduate school. For starters, these may be obvious differences:

- *Delving into the full details of a student's past unacceptable behaviors, circumstances, incidents, diagnoses, labels, and problems will lower your mood and his.* A low mood is no place to solve a problem. George Pransky (1993) recommends getting just a "specimen," a taste of the situation, and spending most of your time building rapport, listening, and relying on your own insights to guide the student to a greater state of well-being. From that vantage point it is more likely that difficult situations can be addressed with fresh ideas and progress made by the student himself.

- *Listen for the feeling, not the content.* "Active listening," analyzing content, and identifying all the problems and options, takes you, the helper, off track, keeps you from hearing the student, and fills your head with busy analytical thoughts that block fresh, needed insights.
- *There are no problems except overly analytical thought.* It doesn't matter how you analyze a student's situation; the solution will always require common sense and well-being. Without those no amount of planning and services will fill the bill. A secure state of mind for both you and the student invites common sense answers and solutions to surface.
- *Educate; don't do therapy.* Notice what the student does not yet know about healthy human functioning. What can you teach about the Health Realization principles that relates directly to the student's current situation? Your job is relating and teaching, not fixing or labeling. Don't get swept away in the surface issues. Concentrate on teaching the student healthy psychological functioning. Stay with the student; teach what he needs to know, not everything you know.
- *Expect the student to do well, improve, and return to healthy functioning.* Understanding the principles in operation brings life-long improvement and impacts the student's quality of life. Give up the notion that 20% of the students in your system will always require 80% of your time. Why create an uphill battle for the students who need your encouragement the most? Focus on releasing their health rather than containing their behavior. Special education, alternative schools, labels, and diagnoses are not automatically permanent conditions.
- *Lighten up.* Humor is the sign of a light heart and common sense is not far behind. Nobody does well in an overly serious environment. Students learn better and you teach more effectively when you are relaxed.
- *Drop the past; forget the future; concentrate on being in the moment with the student.* This increases your chances of creating rapport, listening with impact, and inviting your own health and the student's to operate. What happened, why, future goals, and options all will be addressed by the student when he is in a healthy state. Until the student experiences increased well-being, nothing can change. The moments of good feeling, rapport, and health you create during direct contact with the student will be intriguing to the student. When he is curious, you can explain how this healthy functioning occurs. Such understanding will serve the student life-long in all situations.

Try as teachers or administrators might, a student will not be "fixed" by being sent from the classroom to the counselor. The total school building team approach with Resilience/Health Realization—everybody doing something in classrooms, halls, extracurriculars, the office, the PTA, the school board, and the community—is what makes the deep, lasting systemic difference. It does take healthy professionals in a healthy system to foster the resilience of a child.

part II

STUDIES OF STUDENTS' RESILIENCY

CHAPTER 5

A LONGITUDINAL LOOK AT THE LITERACY DEVELOPMENT OF CHILDREN PRENATALLY EXPOSED TO CRACK/COCAINE

Diane Barone
University of Nevada, Reno

Several years ago when I initiated a study to describe the literacy development of young children prenatally exposed to crack/cocaine, I was unsure that such children would learn to read or write successfully in mainstream classrooms. I entered the study with the images of these children as infants crying uncontrollably. Coupled with these images were the dire warnings that children prenatally exposed to crack/cocaine would be out of control in classrooms and impossible to teach (Millroy, 1989; Nachan, 1990). While not one of my central questions, I still wondered what teachers would do if such out-of-control children entered school. How would they cope?

However, after observing and talking to these children over 4 years at home and in their classrooms, I learned from them the meaning of resilience. Resilience is defined for this study as a person's ability to adjust or be adaptable and successful in an academic setting. This was not a term or concept with which I was familiar at the time, nor was the literacy community in general. To gather a better understanding, I studied Werner's (1992) work to learn about resiliency in individuals. She talked about the importance of a caring person in a child's life who fostered resilience. I then explored all the data to see if such a person existed for each child. In fact, a foster parent, teacher, or church leader most often served in this role. Moreover, it was frequently the child who secured these relationships, especially in school situations. I found that it was the synergistic relationship that was most important in fostering resiliency for these children.

While the result of resiliency might seem unusual in a study focused on literacy development, it will be further explained later in this chapter. Before exploring this result in more depth and other results, I present a theoretical background about prenatal crack/cocaine exposure and the details of this study.

A CLOSER LOOK AT ISSUES CENTRAL TO PRENATAL CRACK/COCAINE EXPOSURE INFLUENCE OF THE MEDIA

A child who has been prenatally exposed to crack/cocaine is often considered a "media star" (Neuspiel & Hamel, 1991, p. 61) because this child has drawn the attention of the media as well as that of educators, physicians, and politicians. The attention centered on these children began in the late 1980s and continued into the 2000s, although the images on television or in newspapers are not as frequent today. Nonetheless, while the images and stories are not as incessant, the misconceptions surrounding these children are still plentiful, especially in schools.

The myths about children prenatally exposed to crack/cocaine have been stubborn and resistant due in part to vivid media coverage. Most often reporters have only shared the worst-case scenarios as if they were the norm (Griffith, 1995). Embedded within the coverage is the notion that if a child was prenatally exposed to crack/cocaine, then only this exposure would be the reason that he or she might have difficulty in school. Other variables, like high poverty or minority status, are disregarded. Interestingly, there has been no discussion that a child with prenatal exposure could be successful in school.

MYTHS CENTERED ON PRENATAL CRACK/COCAINE EXPOSURE

This narrow view has contributed to many faulty perceptions of this drug and its effects. The myths about this drug's influence center on three basic assumptions. The first is that all children who have been prenatally exposed to crack/cocaine are severely affected. However, medical research has *never* documented a prototypical crack baby (Chasnoff, 1992). The second is that little can be done for these children so that they might be healthy and successful in school. The third myth is that all the medical, behavioral, and learning problems potentially exhibited by these children are caused directly by their exposure to crack/cocaine (Griffith, 1995).

Contrary to these myths, children prenatally exposed to crack/cocaine present a full continuum of physical and cognitive effects from their mother's use of drugs (Chasnoff, 1991; Cohen & Taharally, 1992; Villarreal, McKinney, & Quackenbush, 1991). Some children exhibit no effects while other children may demonstrate serious physical difficulties. The most consistent documented effects are lower birth weight and smaller head circumference (Bennett, 1992; Berlin, 1991; Brodkin & Zuckerman, 1992). However, low birth weight and small head circumferences in newborns are also reported to be the results of alcohol and cigarette use by mothers (Coles, Platzman, Smith, James, & Falek, 1992).

To complicate the picture further, beyond considering the possible insults that the mother might instill on the fetus and the ease or difficulty of the birth process, there are the effects of the early home experiences of the newborn to consider. Approximately 50 to 75% of these children return home with their mother or a relative (Williams & Howard, 1993). For example, if a newborn returns to the home of his or her mother who is still involved with drugs, he or she will suffer from passive exposure from inhalation of smoke or through breast milk (Chasnoff, Lewis, & Squires, 1987). Along with the presence of drugs, these homes tend to be disorganized, suffer from family violence, and are often socially isolated (Johnson, 1993). Beeghly and Tronick (1994) feel "that the long-term developmental outcome of infants prenatally exposed to cocaine is primarily determined by the quality of the affective-communicative mutually regulated system established by the cocaine-exposed infant and its caregiver" (p. 159).

It is immediately evident that the goal of moving from crack/cocaine exposure to direct results in a newborn is not possible. In addition to the mother's use of crack/cocaine, other events also cloud this picture. First, most drug-using pregnant women do not seek prenatal care (Schutter & Brinker, 1992). They are afraid that their doctor will report them to the authorities (Frank, Augustyn, Knight, Pell, & Zuckerman, 2001). As a result of limited or no prenatal care, many of these children are born premature. With prematurity comes a whole host of possible complications for a newborn. Premature children can display language delays, fine motor coordination delays, and delays in perceptual development (Gregorchik, 1992). Additionally, they can experience difficulties with socioemotional relationships, learning, and focusing attention (Bennett, 1992).

An interesting discovery made during most of the studies focused on these children is that they score in the normal range on individual intelligence tests (Cohen & Taharally, 1992; Frank et al., 2001; Rodning, Beckwith, & Howard, 1989). Additionally, Griffith (1992) discovered that the results on the Bayley Scales of Infant Development show little difference between cocaine/polydrug children from 3 to 24 months and nonexposed groups. There were also no differences for these groups of children on the Stanford Binet administered when they were 3 years of age.

While the results of these tests are very positive, it is important to remember that in addition to these children's prenatal drug exposure, many of them are living in poverty situations. As a result, there are numerous risks to the achievement of school success for these children. Clearly, environmental factors could contribute either alone or synergistically with a child's prenatal exposure. Work done by Padrón and Waxman (1999), Allington (1983), Hiebert (1991), Delpit (1988), among others, document the difficulty that poor, minority children have in achieving success in school. These issues must not be set aside when considering the school careers of most children identified with prenatal drug exposure.

Moreover, contributing to the persistence of the myths centered on these children is the first wave of studies about them. Few journals published or shared results that countered the early reports of calamitous outcomes for these children (Gonzalez & Campbell, 1994; Greider, 1995; Hutchings, 1993; Lester & Tronick, 1994). Frank and Zuckerman (1993) wrote about the first studies and the difficulties that resulted.

> The early reports of adverse effects of prenatal exposure to cocaine, including neurobehavioral dysfunction, a remarkably high rate of SIDS, and birth defects, were initial observations that constitute the legitimate first step in the scientific process. However, these unreplicated findings were uncritically accepted by scientists and lay media alike, not as preliminary, and possible unrepresentative case reports, but as "proven" facts. It is not easy to disseminate scientific data contrary to prevailing popular belief. (p. 299)

Extending on this earlier work, Frank and colleagues (2001) selected 36 studies that met their criteria for quality studies in the area of prenatal crack/cocaine exposure. From careful examination of these articles, they stated:

> Among children up to 6 years of age, there is no convincing evidence that prenatal cocaine exposure is associated with any developmental toxicity different in severity, scope, or kind from the sequelae of many other risk factors. Many findings once thought to be specific effects of in utero cocaine exposure can be explained in whole or in part by other factors, including prenatal

exposure to tobacco, marijuana, or alcohol and the quality of the child's environment. (pp. 1623–1624)

While these results were not known in the 1980s or 1990s, they certainly counter the misconceptions surrounding children and prenatal drug exposure. They document the many variables that can contribute to a child's academic development.

However, even with the strength of this research base, teachers hold on to their beliefs that children who were prenatally exposed to crack/cocaine will be out of control in their classrooms. When they see children enter their rooms who are having difficulty conforming to the established behavioral expectations, especially in high poverty schools, they are quick to surmise that they have been prenatally exposed to crack/cocaine or other drugs.

When teachers are asked if they are ready to work with students who have been exposed prenatally to crack/cocaine, or *crack babies* as the popular press labels them, they most often say no (Rist, 1990). Teachers as well as the lay public believe that school-age children who have been prenatally exposed to crack/cocaine will be difficult and perhaps impossible to teach.

From this research base, I began my study centered on the literacy development of children who had experienced prenatal crack/cocaine exposure (Barone, 1999). I knew as I entered the study that my beliefs were similar to those of classroom teachers about the limited academic and emotional expectations of such children. I was aware of this bias and explicitly reflected upon it as I recorded the day-to-day classroom and home literacy experiences of the children. My goal was to carefully craft the literacy stories of 26 children over 4 years to learn about their literacy learning and instruction at home and at school. These stories would either support or dispel the myths that were prevalent.

THE STUDY

The Design

I chose to narrow my research to literacy development because literacy is often considered to be the most important determining factor of success in elementary school (Allington & Walmsley, 1995; Bartoli, 1995; Hiebert & Taylor, 1994). I realized, based on my experiences as a classroom teacher, that this study needed to be longitudinal in scope. I did not want to form generalizations from the data based on short-term observations. As an elementary school teacher who worked with a single group of primary students over 3 years, I learned about the irregular rhythms of literacy development. By considering these children over 4 years, I felt I could provide a sound context to describe their literacy development.

I also chose a longitudinal multicase study design (Yin, 1994). I selected 26 children so that my research would present a picture of more than one child's development. I worried that if only one child had been chosen, a biased picture might result. For example, the child could be successful or not. If the child was successful, then criticism would be leveled that this child is not representative of other prenatally exposed children. A bigger concern for me was the opposite result, that is, if the child was not successful, then this result might be generalized to all children prenatally exposed. And I potentially might have harmed children. To mitigate these results, a large group of children were selected. Additionally, this design allowed for the exploration of literacy development without any overt manipulation of the home or school environments (Merriam, 1988; Yin, 1994).

To understand each child's literacy development, I observed them in their homes and schools. I visited each home once per year during summer vacation for children enrolled in school. For children not enrolled in school, I visited their homes monthly until they began school. During these visits, I engaged each child in talking, book reading, drawing, and writing. I brought materials to the homes because books and paper were inconsistently available. While the children were involved with these activities, I engaged the parents in an informal discussion about their child's literacy development. Because the parents and I shared a similar goal, learning about literacy development of children prenatally exposed to crack/cocaine, we each benefited from these discussions. I learned about their child's literacy development through their eyes and they in turn tasked me about the larger group of children. The parents were worried and concerned about the learning possibilities for their child because they had been influenced by the alarming media reports, so they often nudged me to share my overall findings to alleviate their anxiety.

The Children

The State Welfare Department identified the children that were included in the study. Children that were included met three criteria. First, a urine toxicology done shortly after birth showed that the child had been exposed prenatally to crack/cocaine and that the mother had used these drugs just previous to delivery. Second, the children were 3 or 4 years old. I later extended these ages to between 1 and 7 to increase the number of participants in the study. Third, the child had a stable home environment, meaning that a child was not expected to move to another foster care home in the near future.

The reason for the stable foster placement was that I did not want the study biased negatively because a child was adjusting to one home situation after another; a situation that could easily influence a child's literacy development. All of the children in this study lived with adoptive parents or foster parents. None of the children lived with their natural parents, although some visited their parents occasionally. Interestingly, 23 of the children's foster mothers did not work out of their home. They were full-time homemakers and foster care providers, resembling the type of family that is associated with the 1950s or 1960s.

Most of the children were full-term infants (17), most were boys (18), most were African American (15), and most were in foster homes (20). Many of the children had allergies or asthma (11) (although this is not unusual for children living in the city of the study), two had epilepsy, one had cerebral palsy, and one had AIDS. I found it interesting that so many of the children, particularly the 5-year-olds, were receiving special education support. In most schools, children as young as this rarely qualify for this support. Most of the children receiving this support qualified based on language delays. It is also important to know that this study is overrepresented with poor, minority children. This is because these children are more readily identified as being prenatally exposed and are more often in the state welfare system.

During the 4 years of the study, only six children left the study. Three of these children were adopted out of state and were therefore impossible to follow. Three other children left their original foster care homes and were moved among many homes over a short period of time. Because of this lack of stability, I discontinued the children from the study. During the second year of the study, one additional child, Sean, was added because he was the foster brother of a child already in the study and had been informally observed during the entire first year.

Data Collection: Observation, Interviews, and Artifact Collection

Each child was initially observed in his or her home. A caseworker from the state welfare department scheduled the initial appointments and accompanied me to each home. During this meeting, I explained the study and secured written permissions. I then talked to the parents about their child's early physical growth and literacy development. Following this discussion, I spent time with the child in informal reading and writing activities like book reading, name writing, and drawing.

After this meeting, I observed each child either at home or in school once per month. The monthly observations continued throughout the study. For children enrolled in school, I visited their homes only once each year during summer vacation; all other visits were at school. For children not enrolled in school, all of my monthly visits were at home.

While I interacted directly with children when I observed them in their homes, I acted as a participant-observer in their classrooms (Jorgensen, 1989). I only interacted with the children if the teacher or a child requested my participation; I quickly responded and then returned to my note taking.

During my observations, I recorded developmental literacy concepts that were easily documented and that represented a variety of reading and writing activities. These included drawing and name writing (Harste, Woodward, & Burke, 1984), concepts of print (Clay, 1985), storybook reading (Sulzby, 1985), concept-of-word in print (Morris, 1983), and orthographic knowledge (Henderson, 1990). These developmental literacy concepts allowed for comparisons to be made across children throughout the study. They provided a rich array of data, which represented a broad-based view of literacy acquisition.

I interviewed the parents at each meeting. Most often these interviews were informal conversations about their child's literacy. I interviewed each teacher once per year and then engaged in informal conversations during my visits to his or her classroom. The teachers updated me at each visit on any new or interesting development in literacy that they noted about the focal children. While I talked to the children about the literacy activities that we did when I observed them at home, I also asked them about being a reader and writer. As with the other interviews, these were most often informal and conversational.

During observations at school and at home, I collected work samples from the children. At least once per year, I engaged the children in informal assessment. For the assessment, I asked the children to spell words and write a story or informational piece, read a book or retell one, write their name, and draw a picture of themselves.

Making Sense of the Data

As I observed these children over time, I wanted to describe their literacy development using broad parameters, not grade-level achievements based on school expectations. This choice was particularly important in this study as the children were enrolled in schools that varied from middle class to high poverty. In each school, the grade-level expectations varied considerably even though all of the schools were in the same public school district. For instance, a child in a middle-class setting was expected to be able to independently read any picture book by the end of first grade. At a high poverty setting, the expectations for first grade centered more on alphabet and related sounds and on behavior than independent reading outcomes.

To facilitate this descriptive process, three broad literacy categories were developed. The first category included children who were *getting the idea of reading and writing*. These children were usually enrolled in preschool or kindergarten. They pretended to read using storytelling focused on illustrations. They were beginning to understand how books were constructed, although they rarely pointed out individual words. Their writing consisted of scribbles or random letters or numerals usually written with a linear orientation (Holdaway, 1979; Morrow, 1983; Taylor, 1983; Teale, 1984). If a focal child reached this level by the end of kindergarten, then he or she was considered to be at grade level. The second category included children who were considered *beginning readers and writers*. These children were usually in kindergarten or first grade. Their reading was often word-by-word as they discovered concept-of-word in print. They fully understood a book's structure and the role of illustrations and text. In writing, they included the appropriate initial and final consonants with some confusion about the vowel (Carver, 1992; Clarke, 1988). When writing to their own topic, they most often wrote narratives or created lists (Calkins, 1986). If children reached this level by the end of kindergarten, they were considered to be above grade level. They were classified as at grade level if this development was demonstrated by the end of first grade. The third category included children who were becoming *fluent readers and writers*. These children were most often in second to fifth grade. In both reading and writing, they were developing confidence and fluency in their choices of text and written compositions (Calkins, 1986; Carver, 1992; Henderson, 1990). They were able to write most single-syllable words without difficulty. In reading and writing, they moved among genres depending on their purpose or interest. Children who achieved this development during third or fourth grade were determined to be at grade level.

As data were collected, I created a literacy profile for each child. I shared these summaries with the teachers or parents so that they could validate my analysis. At this time, the parents or the teacher usually updated me on new literacy events that they had observed or they extended my reports of the literacy concepts I had observed previously. Periodically, I made cross comparisons among all of the children in the study to note similarities and differences in literacy development. These comparisons provided a frame from which to observe and discuss the individual children within the study.

WHAT DID I LEARN?

The study began with 26 children and ended after 4 years with 21 children. During this time, the children were enrolled in as few as 15 schools to as many as 20 schools. With the exception of one child whose parents chose to home-school, the children all entered public schools.

Many of the children received special education support before and during elementary school. The qualification for this support was most often cited as language delay. During the first year, 10 children received special education services (four in preschool, five in first grade, and one in second grade). At the conclusion of the study, seven children still received special education support; however, three of these children were no longer eligible for these services in the future. Furthermore, four children qualified for gifted and talented programs.

Throughout the study, the majority of the children were described as being within the literacy categories that were established. That is, they were considered to be at grade level as demonstrated through their literacy practices. In Table 5.1, yearly summaries of the children's literacy growth, grouped by the age of the child at the beginning of the study, are provided. This result of age-appropriate literacy development was described as being supported by the children's stable home situations (the children remained in the same home throughout the study), early intervention (speech or special education) for many of the children, and the resiliency of the children. These characteristics were selected by doing repetitive searches throughout the data and were informed by the work of others (Aylward, 1990; Griffith, 1995; Mayes, Granger, Bornstein, & Zuckerman, 1992). These children, unlike children prenatally exposed to drugs and still living in homes where their natural mother continued to use drugs, had a stable, predictable home environment. Aylward (1990) supports the importance of a home free of environmental risks (e.g., poor mother–child interaction or health care) and biologic risks (e.g., poor diet or passive drug exposure) in enhancing a child's resiliency. He goes on to say that environmental deficits and stressors impair cognitive and psychological development. Mayes and colleagues (1992) and Chasnoff (1988) concur that the home environment is an important contributor to the outcome of these children, more so than the prenatal drug exposure.

Although the issue of resiliency was unusual when I first used it to describe these children (Barone, 1993a, 1993b, 1994), there are numerous studies that documented the relationship between this characteristic and school success (Allen, Michalove, & Shockley, 1993; Griffith, 1995; Padrón, Waxman, Brown, & Powers, 2000; Werner, 1992; Wolin & Wolin, 1993). Griffith (1995) stated that when "major risk factors are reduced or eliminated and when early screening, diagnosis, and intervention are pro-

Table 5.1. Summaries of Literacy Development for Children Who Completed the Study (Organized by Age at Entry to Study)

Name and age of child at the beginning of study	Year of study	Drawing	Name writing	Concepts of print	Storybook reading	Concept of word-in-print	Orthographic knowledge
Twilea, Becky, Sean, Patrick (2)	1	Scribbles—difference between writing and drawing	No	None	Listens to stories (1) no story	No	Prephonemic
	2	Same as year 1	Initial letter	Front of book Turns pages Top/bottom	(2) forms story (3) storytelling and reading	No	Prephonemic
	3	Self portrait	Yes	Aware of book organization	(4) book language	No	Prephonemic
	4	Same as year 3	Yes	Same as year 3	(5) reads predictable text	No	Semiphonemic
Jamal, Jose, Anna, Billy, Jennifer, Mark (3)	1	Scribbles—difference between writing and drawing	No	Front of book Turns pages	(3) storytelling and reading (4) book language	No	Prephonemic
	2	Self portrait	Yes	Aware of book organization	(5) reads predictable text (5) refusal	Almost	Semiphonemic
	3	Self portrait	Yes + last name	Full understanding	Same as year 2	Yes	Semiphonemic
	4	Self portrait	Yes + last name	Full understanding	Independent reader Word × word	Yes	Letter name

Table 5.1. Summaries of Literacy Development for Children Who Completed the Study (Organized by Age at Entry to Study) (Cont.)

Name and age of child at the beginning of study	Year of study	Drawing	Name writing	Concepts of print	Storybook reading	Concept of word-in-print	Orthographic knowledge
Mario, Ray, Curtis, Melisha, Josh, Melina (4)	1	Self portrait	Yes	Front of book Turns pages Top/bottom	(3) storytelling and reading (4) book language	No	Prephonemic
	2	Self portrait	Yes + last name	Aware of book organization	(5) reads predictable text (5) refusal	Almost	Semiphonemic
	3	Self portrait	Yes + last name	Full understanding	Independent reader Word × word	Yes	Letter name
	4	Self portrait	Yes + last name	Full understanding	Independent reader/fluent	Yes	Within word pattern
Lakisha, Danny, Dontay, Kevin (5)	1	Self portrait	Yes + last name	Full understanding	(3) storytelling and reading (4) book language (5) reads predictable text	Yes	Semiphonemic
	2	Self portrait	Yes + last name	Full understanding	Independent reader Word × word	Yes	Letter name
	3	Self portrait	Yes + last name	Full understanding	Same as Year 2	Yes	Letter name
	4	Self portrait	Yes + last name	Full understanding	Independent reader/fluent	Yes	Within word and syllable juncture
Loren (7)	1	Self portrait	Yes + last name	Full understanding	Independent reader Word × word	Yes	Within word pattern
	2	Self portrait	Yes + last name	Full understanding	Independent reader/developing fluency	Yes	Syllable juncture

Table 5.1. Summaries of Literacy Development for Children Who Completed the Study (Organized by Age at Entry to Study) (Cont.)

Name and age of child at the beginning of study	Year of study	Drawing	Name writing	Concepts of print	Storybook reading	Concept of word-in-print	Orthographic knowledge
	3	Self portrait	Yes + last name	Full understanding	Independent reader/fluent	Yes	Syllable juncture
	4	Self portrait	Yes + last name	Full understanding	Independent reader/fluent	Yes	Syllable juncture

Key:

Storytelling and reading

(1) no story—child retells story illustration by illustration, no story is formed
(2) forms story—child retells story illustration by illustration, a story is formed
(3) retelling and reading—child retells story using oral tradition and book language
(4) book language—child retells story using book language
(5) reads predictable text—child reads a memorized predictable text
(5) refusal—child refuses to read

independent reader/ word × word—child reads text independently at a slow pace
independent reader/fluent—child reads text fluently, in phrases rather than word groups

Orthographic knowledge

Prephonemic—no relationship between writing and sounds/letters in word represented
Semiphonemic—initial and perhaps final consonants are represented, no vowels
Letter name—most phonemes are represented, vowels included but often confused (e.g., BAD for bed, DRIV for drive)
Within word pattern—long vowel patterns are represented in single-syllable words but often confused (e.g., DRIEV for drive)
Syllable juncture—single-syllable words are generally spelled correctly, child is confused about the addition of affixes (e.g., POPING for popping)

vided...the majority of drug-exposed children seem to have the resilience to recover from the effects of prenatal drug exposure" (p. 91).

Throughout this study, I learned how important supportive parents and teachers were to these children as well as to the others in their care. The majority of the parents were concerned about their children's progress in school. They valued reading and writing knowledge. They trusted schools to be responsible for teaching their child. They helped their child at home with school tasks. Perhaps, more importantly, they enjoyed reading to their children.

I found new respect for teachers of children in high-poverty schools. Despite the current press, most were successful with the teaching and learning of all of the children who filled their classrooms. They found ways to set aside expectations and labels and to focus on teaching and learning. They let their students know in formal and informal ways that they believed in them and expected them to learn. They used the families of these children for support in their work in school.

Finally, the children made the labels attached to them meaningless. They were always inquisitive about learning. The majority consistently demonstrated that they were at grade level or above in literacy development. Additionally, they were able to accommodate the expectations for behavior and learning shared by their teachers. They adjusted and demonstrated their resiliency (Novick, 1998).

While the majority of children were successful literacy learners, five children experienced difficulty achieving age-appropriate literacy development at various times over the course of the study. Three children who experienced difficulty had an emotional or physical occurrence such as Sotos syndrome or physical/sexual abuse that helped to explain their slower rate of growth. Melisha, a 5-year-old, was diagnosed with Sotos syndrome, which results in rapid growth and moderate to severe mental deficiency, among other characteristics (Jones, 1988). Josh, a 5-year-old, was moved to a new school as a result of a school-busing dispute. Josh had a difficult time adjusting to his new school and frequently acted out in inappropriate ways. Because of his behavior and his parents' concerns, Josh moved to three other school sites during the year. Dontay, a 6-year-old, was moved to a program for emotionally disturbed youngsters after he was attacked by another child on a school bus. He had difficulty with schoolwork for about 6 months after this incident and then he rebounded.

The remaining two children experienced problems because of the rigid or limited instruction provided to them. Jamal had great difficulty adjusting to his kindergarten class and qualified for special education support. When he was tested for this placement, his intelligence, as measured by an individual intelligence test, placed him in the above-average range. He, however, was not able to handle the limited movement allowed in his classroom and he became frustrated with many of his teacher's academic expectations. For example, Jamal did not yet know how to write his name independently and his teacher became very upset when he would whine about this inability. She expected that all entering kindergartners were able to write their first name correctly. And one other child, Lakisha, had a special education teacher who provided instruction in phonics, but never provided time for reading anything beyond worksheets. Unfortunately, the worksheets focused on singular skills, infrequently understood by Lakisha (e.g., marking the words that had short vowels when Lakisha was just beginning to understand initial consonants). As a result, Lakisha was still not very proficient at reading or writing in second grade. By third grade, through the efforts of a new teacher, Lakisha became a reader and writer and tested out of special education support. At the end of the study, Lakisha was the only child not to have achieved age-appropriate literacy development.

Occasionally, a child experienced difficulty in school, but over time, the child, with the support of parents and teachers, moved beyond it. The success of these students was also surprising because, in addition to prenatal drug exposure, many of these children came from minority backgrounds and were living in economically poor circumstances. The stable home circumstances where a mother and often a father were present and the children were sure of continuity in the home, although most might be considered impoverished, supported the children's emotional as well as academic growth.

As I began the study, my focus was clearly on the literacy development of children prenatally exposed to crack/cocaine. However, as the study developed, I found that their prenatal exposure to crack/cocaine moved to the background of my concern. The children that I observed did not stand out as being different from the other children in their classrooms. Often, teachers suggested that I observe someone else who was presenting more of a challenge to them. As I visited the homes and schools of these youngsters, I found that the lesson I was learning was about how poor, minority children are supported or hindered in their education. I discovered parents who set aside time each day to work with their children on homework and reading. I found teachers who met with children before and after school just to talk to them. I learned that children, despite their birth circumstances, can be successful in school. I learned what it means to develop resilience through the support of caring adults.

To really understand resilience, it is necessary to share the literacy journey of one child, Danny. Through this close look, it becomes easier to understand the overall success of this group of children, although this success does not always include a straightforward explanation. In Danny's case, his teachers were critical to his success in school. His parents, most frequently his foster mother, had doubts about Danny that she constantly expressed to him, creating a home that would not be considered nourishing to a young child. Danny had been identified for special education support during preschool for language delay. Because of this, he received special education support during his early years in school.

DANNY

Danny, a biracial child, was 5 years old when I first met him. He lived with his foster mother and father in a large trailer. They had one adopted older son with developmental difficulties. They also had additional foster children who came and went as the study progressed. These parents were professional foster parents as they were retired from previous employment. Their days centered on the needs of their foster children. All of the children in their care were considered high need because of developmental issues, or drug or alcohol prenatal exposure.

Danny had lived with this family since he was age 2. His mother had abandoned him soon after he was born and he had been placed in numerous protective situations until he arrived here. When he first came, his foster parents were concerned with his behavior. His mother said, "He didn't know how to eat with silverware. He only used his hands. He didn't know how to sit at a table. He would hit and bite. We had a lot to do to make him behave." After talking about behavior, she shared information about his literacy knowledge. Danny knew the letters of the alphabet, he could write letters, and he enjoyed looking at books. They did not read to him and indicated that his teachers were responsible to teach him to read. In her final description of him, she said that "he is hyper and a slow learner."

After I talked to Danny's parents, Danny and I interacted with paper and books. As I shared the books that I had brought, Danny was quick to identify the illustrations. He did not make connections from one illustration to another. He also drew a self-portrait and wrote his name. He talked about himself as he drew. He shared his love of soccer and of books.

Kindergarten

When I first visited his kindergarten room, Danny was busy with alphabet work and story reading and writing. His kindergarten teacher grouped her students into small groups for some instruction. She had adult leaders, most often parents, for each group of students. When Danny worked with her, they began by identifying letters of the alphabet. The teacher held up a card and asked, "What's that?" A child was called on and he or she said the name of the letter and the sound it makes. Then they moved to a rereading of a predictable text. The children all read a little bit behind the teacher. After the rereading, the teacher asked the children to find words in the book. Danny was asked to find the word "cry." He did this easily and did not even need to read the text to get to the word.

His kindergarten classroom was filled with books. His teacher moved between skills-based instruction like the alphabet work to more meaning-based activities centered on books. She provided time for children to discuss stories and to reread them for fluency.

In the afternoon, Danny worked with his special education teacher on language-based activities. This teacher coordinated her instruction with that of the kindergarten teacher. In most ways, the instruction in the morning and afternoon were similar. In fact, in the afternoon, the special education teacher spent time in Danny's kindergarten room and Danny accompanied her.

As I talked to Danny's kindergarten teacher, she was pleased with his development in literacy. She said that "he is well on his way to becoming a reader." At the end of this year, Danny knew the alphabet and the corresponding sounds of the letters. He wrote words easily by using the appropriate initial and consonants and guessing at the vowel. He was able to read predictable text and decode CVC words fluently. He could find words in the text without relying on surrounding text and therefore had full concept of word-in-print. Danny was a beginning reader and writer at the end of kindergarten and considered to be above grade level in his literacy understandings. He also no longer qualified for special education support.

First Grade

Danny moved to a new school for first grade. This was a brand new elementary school that was grounded in multiage philosophy. The principal hired teachers for this school who valued teaching to students' strengths rather than to grade-level expectations. Children were taught as individuals and not as a class of students. They also utilized a writing and reading workshop with skills-based instruction where necessary. Additionally, most teachers organized their instruction around year-long themes.

This school served one of the most high-risk populations of students in the city. Approximately 40% of the children were homeless and 80% of the students qualified for free or reduced-price meals. The majority of children in this school were not of minority status and few children were learning English as a new language, however.

Danny was enrolled in a class that had first and second graders in it. The expectation was that the first graders would stay with this teacher for 2 years. Only new first graders entered the room each year. All primary classrooms in the state had reduced class size expectations so there were only 17 children in his room.

Danny's first grade teacher had a similar curriculum in literacy to the one he was exposed to in kindergarten. The only major difference was that the teacher encouraged the children to write in journals and to create stories on a daily basis. She encouraged children to work together, allowing them freedom to move within the room as long as they were engaged in an instructional activity. She most often moved around the room and interacted with children privately.

While David developed as a reader and was considered to be at grade level at the end of the year, his biggest literacy learning seemed to occur in his writing. He became a confident writer as the year developed. One example of this is his writing about a squid. His teacher had brought in a squid for the children to explore. She had read books about squids and other sea creatures as well. Following this exploration, the children were asked to write about the squid. This is what Danny wrote:

The New Squid

You hav to put him in watr or he wont breth [breathe] he cant swim if you don't kep him in watr or he wil di [die]. If he dosnt have fins he cant swim if he dint et [eat] he wod di he is cut [cute]

While there are spelling errors in this piece, Danny was able to produce it in about 10 minutes without support. There is no punctuation in this rough draft, but there are ideas that hold together. He has focused on meaning for his first draft and he has included his personal thoughts about the squid—"he is cut." And in his writing, it is clear that he knows how to represent initial and final consonants, and he provides good attempts at representing short vowels. He is using the vowel name (e.g., "kep" for "keep") for long vowel words.

At the end of the year, Danny's teacher was pleased with his literacy knowledge and felt that he was at grade level. He was able to read most picture books without help and he could easily write for his own purposes as well as satisfy classroom assignments. He accomplished this without any special education support. Unlike his teacher, his foster mother was concerned about Danny. When I visited her, Danny was grounded for leaving the yard. She considered him to be "irresponsible." However, with respect to literacy, she noted that "He likes to look at books. He is always finding one to look at."

This visit was at an emotionally troubled time for the family. Two of the foster children had just left as they were adopted, and she thought that Danny would be adopted soon as well. She cried throughout most of this visit due to the loss of the foster children. Although Danny enjoyed looking at my books, writing, and drawing during my visits, he would not leave his mother's side nor was he engaged with any of the materials that I had brought on this day. He appeared to need the security of being close to his foster mother because so much change occurred in his home.

Second Grade

Danny continued at his school but his first grade teacher retired. Because of her retirement, he, along with his classmates, had a brand new teacher. This teacher brought with her a similar philosophy as that of Danny's first grade teacher. She began each day with a writing workshop and then the children had time for silent sustained reading. Following these activities, she broke the children into groups for reading instruction. When children were not working with her, they wrote in journals or completed activities centered on the book they were reading. The room was wonderful to visit as it was filled with books and children's work was displayed everywhere. It was rare to see a child not engaged with a book or an exploration activity related to a book.

Danny's journals were interesting to view throughout the year. He began the year by writing one sentence each day. His teacher wrote back to him each night and tried to encourage him to extend his writing. By the end of the year, he discovered a strategy that satisfied him and pleased his teacher. He used a stem like, I like, and then produced lists. In this way, he found it quite easy to fill a journal page. In April Danny wrote:

I hate peas and rainy days.
I hate slime.
I hate to be handsome.
I hate school.
I hate writing.
I hate romance.
I hate rules.

The list continued with 30 things that Danny hated. His teacher responded with, "I think that you dislike some interesting things. How about writing about what you like?"

Danny maintained grade-level expectations through this year. He started to read simple chapter books by the end of the year and he enjoyed talking about them. As in previous years, Danny thrived at school, but home was a different story. His foster mother now felt that Danny had fetal alcohol syndrome. She told me, "He is going to be a sociopath and I want him to move to another house. I am talking to the social worker to have him moved." I asked if he had done anything for her to think that he was going to be a sociopath. She said, "No, I just know that is what happens to kids who have fetal alcohol symptoms." This was my last visit to Danny's home as his mother said that I should not come back. She confided that "Danny thinks he is important after you leave and I have to punish him. It is better for you just to see him at school."

This visit clearly showed the lack of emotional stability for Danny at home. His mother escalated from telling him that he would be adopted to saying that she wanted him out of the house because he was going to be a "sociopath." While this unstable atmosphere developed at home, Danny was building personal relationships at school. His teacher from first grade, who was now retired, visited him each and every time she came to school. She made it a point to talk to him and ask how he was doing. His current teacher wrote personal notes to him everyday in his journal. Danny also tried to find reasons to stay in during recess to work with his teacher. He decided that he "needed to be the helper."

Third Grade

Contrary to his foster mother's wishes, Danny remained with her throughout his third grade year. He entered a third-, fourth-, and fifth-grade classroom. His teacher organized her room similarly to his previous teachers. The only major difference was in reading instruction. The teacher grouped the students for book club discussions. The teacher shared the choice of books with her students. On some occasions, she chose the books and they were targeted to themes that the children were studying. On other occasions, the children were able to pick the books that they wanted to read. The children were expected to write about their books in a log each day and she wrote responses back.

During this year, Danny extended his meaning-making around books. He engaged in conversations with students and he made personal connections to stories in his log. He often used a double entry draft format for writing. For this format, students copy part of the text and then they write why this part was chosen. Early in the year Danny wrote about Ramona (Cleary, 1969). Following are a few of his entries:

> I remember when I was in second grade and my teacher said. I'll get a present but she didn't get me one and I was mad like Ramona.
>
> DED
>
> | Ramona was going up and down The street saying yah, yah. I'm the baddest witch in town. | I was going up and down the street saying something also. Ramona didn't like the mask at all. Ramona said which witch is which. |

These connections allowed Danny to build a personal connection with the teacher. He was able to share his experiences in and out of school and as a result, she was able to make his instruction personally meaningful to him. In addition to the personal connections that Danny made about books, he began to write stories to engage his fellow classmates. He often interviewed students to find out what kinds of stories they wanted to hear and then he wrote them. His journal entries changed drastically. He engaged in ongoing conversation with his teacher about his life outside of school. In August Danny wrote:

> One of the teachers is going to be a principal.
>
> Teacher's response—Do you want to be a principal?
>
> A little bit but not that much. It might be fun to boss the kids around and take them on a field trip. I love to give you a big goodbye.
>
> Teacher's response—I like your big goodbyes.

Not surprisingly, Danny finished the year at grade level. Beyond this limited description of his development, he was able to comfortably read complex stories and build personal connections, he saw real reasons for writing and the importance of audience, and he used his literacy knowledge to build connections with students and his teacher. When I asked him how he had become such a good reader, he laughed and said, "by reading." He was one of a few students in the study that did not say by learning how to sound out words. His instructional contexts, particularly the consistency of them, helped him understand that reading was more than pronouncing words.

At the end of the year, Danny left his foster parents' home and moved in with relatives of his natural mother and father. He was to be enrolled in a new school for his fourth and fifth grade experiences. This was a change that Danny had conflicting feelings about. On some days he bragged about the move and on other days he worried about his new home and school.

Danny's story both reveals and conceals his resiliency. Typically, it would be expected that his resiliency would be grounded in his home. Certainly, the consistency of physical care for Danny helped him, but he did not live in a home that supported him as a worthwhile individual. His foster mother constantly saw him as troubled and when he was in second and third grade, she actively sought to have him out of her house. Danny did not participate in out-of-school or in church-related activities so he did not have the support of such groups.

Danny moved beyond these obstacles as demonstrated in his in-school success. He had the ability to build relationships with teachers. Whenever I mentioned Danny's name to a teacher, they smiled and talked about him in detail. They often mentioned spending time with him during recess or

before or after school. And he had a special relationship with the principal of his elementary school. She often just visited him to see how he was doing. Danny's story demonstrates the power of teachers in supporting children's emotional and academic growth. Moreover, it describes the respectful curriculum that Rose (1995) detailed. This is a curriculum that is grounded in high expectations and builds on individual students' potential while simultaneously engaging students in authentic literacy activities.
In each of Danny's primary-grade experiences and even in his special education experiences, his teachers encouraged meaning-making, knowledge of fundamental skills, and the use of students as well as the teacher for scaffolding or mediation for what students needed in order to develop. Unlike numerous children, Danny qualified out of special education support and was able to maintain his teachers' grade-level expectations. In Danny's case, the school environment and his teachers and principal helped him to develop resilience. These people were the keys to understanding his resilience as an individual and as a learner.

The majority of children in this study had emotional and intellectual support both at home and at school. While Danny did not experience this consistency in support, he was one of the few children who had consistency of instruction through the primary grades. Most of the children entered classrooms each year that only resembled one another because of the desks and chairs that were present. They spent considerable time learning the teachers' expectations for behavior and academic performance. For example, in some classrooms, children were not allowed to talk to one another and their days were filled with completing worksheets, while in other classrooms, collaborative work was expected. This coherence in instruction and expectations certainly simplified Danny's adjustments to his teachers and their expectations. Because he did not have to adjust to new expectations each year, he could focus on building personal relationships with the adults in his school environment. Thus, he secured an identity for himself as a student who was successful in school.

FINAL THOUGHTS

When this study began, I had no idea if the children I observed would be successful in literacy learning or if they would experience great difficulty. In fact, when I reflected on my beliefs when I started the study, I really did not expect that so many would be at grade level or above in literacy development and I never anticipated that four of the children would qualify into gifted and talented programs. As can be seen by narrowing the focus to Danny, he was no different than other children in trying to meet the expectations of his teachers as he learned to read and write. More importantly, his reading and writing and the connections that he built with teachers and other students through it, supported his development of resilience. His school was the critical environment for him, not his home. If teachers had not supported him and if he was not able to build personal connections with his teachers and peers, Danny's story would likely not be one of resilience.

It will be important for teachers and others involved with children's learning to remain open to the academic possibilities for children prenatally exposed to crack/cocaine. While the images represented in the popular press are difficult to move beyond, it is the responsibility of educators to consider these children as individuals. Prenatal drug exposure does not lead to any specific emotional or academic outcome (Cohen & Taharally, 1992; Frank et al., 2001; Rodning et al., 1989). The complexities of the child's home and school situation and the interactions between these two are important to consider. It is also important to ponder the emotional and learning implications for children, beyond those who are prenatally exposed to crack/cocaine, who remain in foster care until they are age 18.

After observing and interacting with these children, their parents, and their teachers for over 4 years, I am optimistic about their futures. I am hopeful that their resilience will continue because resilience is a process, not a static state. The children's stable homes, their churches, their ability to read and write, and their teachers, among others, will help them expand the resilience that they now have. Hearing that others believe in them is key to future success. This study helps teachers and parents move beyond a singular consideration of a child's prenatal drug exposure to a view in which the child appears to be more like non-drug-exposed children than different. This is the message that I hope is taken from this study.

REFERENCES

Allen, J., Michalove, B., & Shockley, B. (1993). *Engaging children: Community and chaos in the lives of young literacy learners.* Portsmouth, NH: Heinemann.

Allington, R. (1983). The reading instruction provided readers of different reading abilities. *Elementary School Journal, 83,* 549–559.

Allington, R., & Walmsley, S. (Eds.). (1995). *No quick fix: Rethinking literacy programs in America's elementary schools.* New York: Teachers College Press.

Aylward, G. (1990). Environmental influences on the developmental outcomes of children at risk. *Infants and Young Children, 2,* 1–9.

Barone, D. (1993a). Dispelling the myths: Focusing on the literacy development of children prenatally exposed to crack/cocaine. In D. Leu & C. Kinzer (Eds.), *Examining central issues in literacy research, theory, and practice: Forty-second yearbook of the National Reading Conference,* (pp. 197–206). Chicago: National Reading Conference.

Barone, D. (1993b). Wednesday's child: Literacy development of children prenatally exposed to crack or cocaine. *Research in the Teaching of English, 27*(1), 7–45.

Barone, D. (1994). The importance of classroom context: Literacy development of children prenatally exposed to crack/cocaine—Year two. *Research in the Teaching of English, 28*(3), 286–312.

Barone, D. (1999). *Resilient children: Stories of poverty, drug exposure, and literacy development.* Newark, DE: IRA.

Bartoli, J. (Ed.). (1995). *Unequal opportunity: Learning to read in the U.S.A.* New York: Teachers College Press.

Beeghly, M., & Tronick, E. (1994). Effects of prenatal exposrue to cocaine in early infancy: Toxic effects on the process of mutual regulation. *Infant Mental Health Journal, 15,* 158–175.

Bennett, F. (1992). Recent advances in developmental intervention for biologically vulnerable infants. *Infants and Young Children, 3,* 33–40.

Berlin, C. (1991). Effects of drugs on the fetus. *Pediatrics In Review, 12*(9), 282–287.

Brodkin, A., & Zuckerman, B. (1992). Are crack babies doomed to school failure? *Instructor, 101*(7). 16–17.

Calkins, L. (1986). *The art of teaching writing.* Portsmouth, NH: Heinemann.

Carver, R. (1992). *Reading rate: A review of research and theory.* New York: Academic Press.

Chasnoff, I. (1988). Drug use in pregnancy: Parameters of risk. *The Pediatric Clinics of North America, 35,* 1403–1412.

Chasnoff, I. (1991). Drugs, alcohol, pregnancy, and the neonate. *Journal of the American Medical Association, 266*(11), 1567–1568.

Chasnoff, I. (1992). President's message. *Perinatal Addiction Research and Education Update,* pp. 2–3.

Chasnoff, I., Lewis, D., & Squires, L. (1987). Cocaine intoxication in a breast-fed infant. *Pediatrics, 80*(6), 836–838.

Clarke, L. (1988). Invented versus traditional spelling in first graders' writings: Effects on learning to spell and read. *Research in the Teaching of English, 22,* 281–309.

Clay, M. (1985). *The early detection of reading difficulties* (3rd ed.). Portsmouth, NH: Heinemann.

Cleary, B. (1969). *Ramona the pest.* New York: Dell.

Cohen, S., & Taharally, C. (1992). Getting ready for young children with prenatal drug exposure. *Childhood Education, 69*(1), 5–9.

Coles, C., Platzman, K., Smith, I., James, M., & Falek, A. (1992). Effects of cocaine and alcohol use in pregnancy on neonatal growth and neurobehavioral status. *Neurotoxicology and Teratology, 14*(1), 23–33.

Delpit, L. (1988). The silenced dialogue: Power and pedagogy in educating other people's children. *Harvard Educational Review, 58,* 280–298.

Frank, D., Augustyn, M., Knight, W., Pell, T., & Zuckerman, B. (2001). Growth, development, and behavior in early childhood following prenatal cocaine exposure: A systematic review. *Journal of the American Medical Association, 285,* 1613–1625.

Frank, D., & Zuckerman, B. (1993). Children exposed to cocaine prenatally: Pieces of the puzzle. *Neurotoxicology and Teratology, 15,* 298–300.

Gonzalez, N., & Campbell, M. (1994). Cocaine babies: Does prenatal exposure to cocaine affect development? *Journal of the American Academy of Child and Adolescent Psychiatry, 33,* 16–19.

Gregorchik, L. (1992). The cocaine-exposed children are here. *Phi Delta Kappan, 73*(9), 709–711.

Greider, K. (1995). Crackpot ideas. *Mother Jones, 20,* 52–56.

Griffith, D. (1992). Prenatal exposure to cocaine and other drugs: Developmental and educational prognoses. *Phi Delta Kappan, 74*(1), 30–34.

Griffith, D. (1995). Prenatal exposure to cocaine and other drugs: Developmental and educational prognoses. *Juvenile and Family Court Journal, 46,* 83–92.

Harste, J., Woodward, V., & Burke, C. (1984). *Language stories and literacy lessons.* Portsmouth, NH: Heinemann.

Henderson, E. (1990). *Teaching spelling* (2nd ed.). Boston: Houghton Mifflin.

Hiebert, E. (Ed.). (1991). *Literacy for a diverse society: Perspectives, practices, and policies.* New York: Teachers College Press.

Hiebert, E., & Taylor, B. (Eds.). (1994). *Getting reading right from the start.* Boston: Allyn & Bacon.

Holdaway, D. (1979). *The foundations of literacy.* Sydney: Ashton Scholastic.

Hutchings, D. (1993). Response to commentaries. *Neurotoxicology and Teratology, 15,* 311–312.

Johnson, H. (1993). Prenatal exposure to drugs and early development. *Early Child Development and Care, 84,* 81–89.

Jones, K. (1988). *Smith's recognizable patterns of human malformation* (4th ed.). Philadelphia: W.B. Saunders.

Jorgensen, D. (1989). *Participant observation: A methodology for human studies.* Newbury Park, CA: Sage.

Lester, B., & Tronick, E. (1994). The effects of prenatal cocaine exposure and child outcome [Special issue: Prenatal drug exposure and child outcome]. *Infant Mental Health Journal, 15,* 107–120.

Mayes, L., Granger, R., Bornstein, M., & Zuckerman, B. (1992). The problem of prenatal cocaine exposure. *Journal of the American Medical Association, 267*(3), 406–408.

Merriam, S. (1988). *Case study research in education: A qualitative approach.* San Francisco: Jossey-Bass.

Millroy, C. (1989, September 17). A time bomb in cocaine babies. *Washington Post,* p. B3.

Morris, D. (1983). Concept of word and phoneme awareness in the beginning reader. *Research in the Teaching of English, 17,* 359–373.

Morrow, L. (1983). Home and school correlates of early interest in literature. *Journal of Educational Research, 75,* 339–344.

Nachan, J. (Ed.). (1990, May 8-11). Children of the damned. (Special report). *New York Post.*

Padrón, Y., & Waxman, H. (1999). Effective instructional practices for English language learners. In H. Waxman & H. Walberg (Eds.), *New directions for teaching practice and research* (pp. 171–203). Berkeley, CA: McCutchan.

Padrón, Y., Waxman, H., Brown, A., & Powers, R. (2000). *Improving classroom instruction and student learning for resilient and non-resilient English language learners.*

Washington, DC, and Santa Cruz, CA: Center for Research on Education, Diversity and Excellence.

Rist, M. (1990). The shadow children: Preparing for the arrival of crack babies in school. *Phi Delta Kappan: Research Bulletin, 9,* 1–6.

Rodning, C., Beckwith, L., & Howard, J. (1989). Characteristics of attachment organization and play organization in prenatally drug-exposed toddlers. *Development and Psychopathology, 1,* 277–289.

Rose, M. (1995). *Possible lives: The promise of public education in America.* New York: Penguin.

Schutter, L., & Brinker, R. (1992). Conjuring a new category of disability from prenatal cocaine exposure: Are the infants unique biological or caretaking casualties? *Topics in Early Childhood Special Education, 11*(4), 84–111.

Sulzby, E. (1985). Children's emergent reading of favorite storybooks: A developmental study. *Reading Research Quarterly, 21,* 360–406.

Taylor, D. (1983). *Family literacy.* Exeter, NH: Heinemann.

Teale, W. (1984). Reading to young children: Its significance for literacy development. In H. Goelman, A. Oberg, & F. Smith (Eds.), *Awakening to literacy* (pp. 110–121). Exeter, NH: Heinemann.

Villarreal, S. F., McKinney, L. E., & Quackenbush, M. (1991). *Handle with care: Helping children prenatally exposed to drugs and alcohol.* Santa Cruz, CA: ETR Associates.

Werner, E. (1992). *Overcoming the odds: High risk children from birth to adulthood.* Ithaca, NY: Cornell University Press.

Williams, B., & Howard, V. (1993). Children exposed to cocaine: Characteristics and implications for research and intervention. *Journal of Early Intervention, 17,* 61–72.

Wolin, A., & Wolin, S. (1993). *The resilient self: How survivors of troubled families rise above adversity.* New York: Random House.

Yin, K. (1994). *Case study research: Design and methods* (2nd ed.). Thousand Oaks, CA; Sage.

CHAPTER 6

ACHIEVING SUCCESS

An Agentic Model of Resiliency

Ruth Silva
University of North Texas

Judy Radigan
University of Houston

> *"It is a necessary feature of action that, at any point in time, the agent could have acted otherwise."*
> —Giddens (1979)

One of the consistent themes in the literature on the educational progress of immigrant students within the host system is the thesis that these students will face difficulties, and that these difficulties will more often than not lead to a failure by the majority of the immigrant students to meet the demands of the system. Similarly, Portes and MacLeod (1996), queried whether the children of immigrants would be able to work their way upward into the "middle-class mainstream" or whether they would be blocked in this ascent based on their migrant status, and become part of a "multiethnic underclass or join an expanded multiethnic underclass." Suarez-Orozco (1995) extended this perspective and highlighted the implicit viewpoint within which this query was nested. He foregrounded the domination of sensationalism and myth in discussions of the "natural process" of assimilation of minorities.

In much the same way, attempting to separate the myth from fact, Trueba (1999), along with a growing number of educational anthropologists, pointed out that although predicting and explaining failure of some immigrant youth was by and large a favored topic in educational research dealing with minority youth, whereas "explaining success where failure is expected is a bit more intriguing"(p. 3). His [Trueba's] statement echoed Foley's 1997 observation that "school studies of minority youth tended to focus on why these youth failed in mainstream schools," thereby tending to underemphasize the factors leading to success and empowerment (p. 124).

These initial attempts to shift the critical discourse term from *failure* to *success* influenced a small, but growing body of anthropologists and educational researchers studying minority education from a sociolinguistic perspective, and within a pedagogical setting, respectively, to refocus their studies. The locus now shifted to an emphasis to those "underemphasized factors leading to success and empowerment" that Foley (1997) had called attention to.

The research study presented in this chapter is grounded within this new discourse of *success*. It explores and examines the ways in which immigrant students achieve and manage success on par, and sometimes above that of their Anglo counterparts. The success achieved by these immigrant students is examined against the background of a system that foregrounds the possibilities of their failure through the use of terms such as *at risk*, *deficit*, and *low socioeconomic status* as adjectival referents attached to the noun *immigrant*.

We present and analyze a case study of successful high school students who formed part of a larger study researching success among Latino, Asian, and Anglo high school students. The focus of our analysis of success will be on the concept of *agency* and its expression by the students in their daily dealings with their cultural peers, Anglo peers, and system authorities—that is, their actions as a result of the exercise of their *agentic* role. The discussion is centered on the students' own descriptions of how they act, react, and/or proact within the prevailing socioeducational culture in their school. The analysis will include a problematization of the definitions of the traditionally used term to describe these students as at risk per se, and application of the adjective *resilient* to describe them if they are successful. The discussion of our findings also focuses on the nascent process of identity construction by the students in the study. To explain and analyze the agentic role of the students, we utilize a theoretical model based on Giddens's (1994) concept of foundational agency. The agentic role of the individual student will be juxtaposed with the role and primacy of protective factors as explanations of resiliency-based success in current theory and research.

RESILIENCE: INDIVIDUAL EFFORT OR SYSTEM INTERVENTION?

The pioneering work of Rutter (1995), Garmezy (1991, 1993), and Werner (1993), amongst others, heralded the growth of the study of resiliency as a construct in explaining success where success was not predicted but achieved despite adverse circumstances. Garmezy's research, for example, centered on examining why some disadvantaged children turned out socially competent and did not display any behavioral problems, while similar others did not do so. This leads to the key question in resiliency research: Why was it that some [disadvantaged children] were able to beat the odds against them?

Continuing from this introductory work, resiliency research then focused on how young people acquired resiliency traits that had been identified in the first wave of resiliency research. Richardson (1995) described this as a process and experience of adapting to disruptive, challenging, and stressful situations and discovering ways to adapt that provide the individual with skills and knowledge they did not have before.

It is within this general field of resiliency research that current studies of resiliency among specified population groups are based. For example, research studies in the adaptive mechanisms of Latino and Asian American students in particular are beginning to grow in number. Alva (1991); Gordon, Padilla, Ford, and Thoresen (1994); Gonzalez and Padilla (1997); Suarez-Orozco and Suarez-Orozco (1995, 2000); and Trueba and Bartolome (2000) are among the many studies that have specifically explored Latino adaptive issues. Whilst some of these studies specifically use the term *resilience* to explain positive and successful behaviors, others, while not using the term specifically, nonetheless referred to the behaviors subsumed under the concept of resilience.

Defining Resilience

Masten (1994) defined resilience "in an individual" as referring "to successful adaptation despite risk and adversity." Garmezy, Masten, and Tellegen (1984) operationalized resilience as "manifestations of competence in children despite exposure to stressful events." Rutter (1995) defined resilience as facing "stress at a time in a way that allows self-confidence and social competence to increase through mastery and appropriate responsibility." Gordon (1995) defined it as "the ability to thrive, mature, and increase competence in the face of adverse circumstances." Sagor (1996) defined it "as a set of attributes that provides people with the strength and fortitude to confront the overwhelming obstacles they are bound to face in life." Winfield (1994) operationalized the definition for educational purposes by tying the definition of resilience to the doing or fostering of resilience by educational authorities. In all of these definitions both implicitly and explicitly, the presence of risk is at the center of the definition. Risk is the catalyst that leads to the "variations in the ways that people deal with threat and challenge." (Rutter, 1990, p.182). They either adapt positively and are termed resilient, or negatively, and are then termed nonresilient. Grotberg (1996) however, pointed out that "Recognizing features of resilience did not mean there was agreement on what resilience is, or on how to define it." "Defining resilience" she emphasized "is a continuing problem" (p. 2).

As one of the researchers (Silva) ruminated on these definitional issues, specifically, Rutter's use of the phrase "variations in the ways…" they raised a number of problematics. For example, was achieving or being resilient a *threshold* phenomenon (Radke-Yarrow & Sherman, 1990)? Therefore, was it an either/or phenomenon? Or is it an issue of successive mastery over difficulties? Apposite to this discussion, if it was a threshold phenomenon, did this imply some sort of "inborn higher threshold of sensitivity to stress" in the resilient individuals? "Is invulnerability a general trait, or are there specific invulnerabilities, just as there are specific vulnerabilities?" (Anthony, 1974).

Was the failure of immigrant/minority students predicated simply on the fact that they were a subject culture within the dominant host culture? Is *immigrantness* a specific vulnerablitiy? Thus implicitly providing support to the *deficit thinking* construct—that a minority group was by definition lacking or deficient and, therefore, vulnerable to failure in the superior ways of the dominant host and required restitution into operating normative structures to achieve success. Was restitution to be accomplished by the system putting into place the umbrella of *protective factors* that corrected the deficits in the student? In other words, was the system the *active agency*, and students the *passive recipients*? Applied to the students in this study, these definitions seemed somewhat inadequate and conceptually problematical.

Rutter's (1990) use of the phrase "variations in the ways…" seemed fundamental in defining the resiliency manifested by these students. Murphy (1962; Murphy & Moriarty, 1976) had drawn attention to the importance of the "variations in the ways" people deal with threat and challenge. Rutter (1990) seemed implicitly to amplify Murphy's comment by reiterating the essential nature of the "emphasis on the *active* role of the individual" (p. 182, italics added). Both of these studies provided some of the key issues undergirding our analysis—the *challenges* facing these students and the *active* role they played in dealing with these instances as challenges rather than as threats.

Finally, Foley, Levinson, and Hurtig (2001) posited that the answer to immigrant success may lie not in conforming to the dominant host's structures, but in "student agency" in dealing with these structures. These researchers suggest that this agency can be found by "studying the small everyday cultural practices of ethnic students" (p. 59). They suggest ethnographers study the way students of color use their communities, families, and peers as cultural resources. They also suggest a study of the way these students deploy expressive identity practices to succeed in school.

Resiliency, therefore, as we began to see it in the data before us, resulted not merely because of the existence and/or the operation of protective factors, but rather needed "to focus on protective mechanisms and processes" (Rutter, 1990, p. 183). Resiliency was the result of the manner or process "of *negotiating* risk situations" (Rutter, 1990, p. 182). Viewed from this definitional perspective it allowed us to foreground the students' actions as active responses to the umbrella of protective factors.

In the manner of Fink-Eitel (1992), this study describes how resilience operates in everyday life from the "frog's perspective." The "frog's perspective" is an approach that begins where the activity takes place, rather than in the Olympian heights of policymaking discussions. For this study the "frog's perspective" begins by asking the successful students in our study to reflect upon the following questions:

- If in terms of the current literature they possess an attribute termed resiliency, how exactly did they acquire this attribute?
- Why do they succeed?
- What enables them to maintain that success?
- What practices do these students create on their journey to success?
- And, finally, why do some acquire resilience and others in similar situations presented with similar support and options, not acquire it?

These are by no means new questions, rather a new perspective from which to examine the concept of achieving success and the role of resiliency in this process.

Current Paradigm

"Definitions," contended Winfield (1999), "have practical applications" (p. 1). From another perspective the definitions generally decide how the research is conducted and is ultimately used by the practitioner. Current models have focused on the provision of contexts, educational and social, that foster resiliency in youth deemed to be *at risk*. A key underlying premise in most of the current models is that educational resilience can be fostered through interventions that enhance student learning, develop their talents, and provide buffers against environmental adversities (Wang, Haertel, & Walberg, 1997). If successful these models will produce students who are socially competent, resourceful, autonomous, and have a sense of purpose.

There can be no argument that the qualities stated above are and should be the aims of all educational programs. In this chapter, however, we would like to present an alternative lens to view the processes used by the students in our study to achieve and maintain success. It is a lens firmly focused on how the students explain what they did in any given situation. It probes how each student used the available system supports and scaffolds. It analyzes the students' explanations of the prior circumstances, and current actions in achieving a desired state of affairs. Desired, primarily by them, and maybe coincidentally by the system. While it is not within the bounds of this chapter to detail the nuances of the term *success*, it is perhaps necessary to state that the conventional definition of success in terms of high GPAs was not the only one in use by these students. Success, particularly in its *socially competent* guise, was problematized by these students in terms of which society, and hence what was socially competent in this society.

Thus, to a certain extent it seems that admirable in intent though they are, current models have the potential to essentialize and generalize student behavior and solutions and thereby lead to schools developing paste-up strategies that continue the domination of the system with its assimilationist pedagogies. This potential exists when the research and practice lens is focused on the activities of the system rather than on the individual process of negotiating problematic situations. Everyday activities of immigrant students present issues of complexity that call for a new discourse in the form of models of agency that this study offers based on Giddens's (1997) foundational notion of agency.

AN AGENTIC MODEL OF RESILIENCY DEVELOPMENT

The Concept of Agency

The concept of agency as advocated by Giddens (1997) involves "intervention in a potentially malleable object world" (p. 56). Agency refers to more than just discrete actions, or even a series of discrete actions, it refers "to a continuous flow of conduct" (p. 55). In more specific terms Giddens delineated the role of what he termed the *acting subject involved in action or agency*. "An adequate account of human agency," he stated, "must, first be connected to a theory of acting subject; and second, must situate action in time and space as a continuous flow of conduct" (p. 2). He elaborated on the concept of the acting subject by explaining the choice of the agent at any point in time to decide between available courses of action. This Giddens termed *foundational agency*. Giddens presented in his theory the intentionality feature of human conduct, meaning that the acting subject consciously has definite goals in mind during the course of action, and that purposeful monitoring of action follows the action and motivation to act rather than preceding it. He termed this the reflexive monitoring of action. The ability to reflexively monitor action, he further explained, is possible because of the "capabilities of human agents to explain why they act as they do by giving reasons for their conduct" (p. 57). Giddens argued that this reflexive monitoring of action was the distinguishing feature of human action as compared to the behavior of animals.

In summary, one always has agency, and this means one always has the ability to act in one way as opposed to another way. But the degree of ability one has varies and the degree of voice one has also varies in relation to the situation within which agentic ability operates. Ultimately, however, regardless of the situation, the theoretical concept of agency in Giddens's thesis supports the notion of an active agentic role in human action, the presence of choice to act otherwise at any point in time in the process of events taking place. Thus, the picture of an intentionally acting subject achieving intended results is given textured levels of dimension.

The Agentic Model

The Agentic Model we use to analyze the actions of the students in our study is based on Giddens's (1997) notion of the "acting subject" possessing foundational agency as a "continuous flow of conduct" (p.2). However, it also takes into account the agency conferred on students within a discursive situation created by the school. The discursive situation is presented to the student in the form of the support structures based on protective factors. These two concepts provided the conceptual basis for the construction of a model based on the agentic role of subject within which we explain the success achieved by the students in our study. The model is a three-stage model moving from a *primitive process* to a *fully agentic process,* where success is the result of each individual student taking steps in a time–space interaction. To briefly reiterate the concept of agency as Giddens explains it, it refers to the intervention in a potentially malleable object world by an acting subject (the student-as-agent), who at any point in time could have acted otherwise.

THE STEPS TO BUILDING THE THREE-STAGE MODEL

Model #1—Homoestatic Causal Loop

Action taken by the student within the homeostatic causal loop operates at the most primitive level. It is a functionalist explanation of action based on the interdependence of system parts usually interpreted as homeostasis and involves the operation of causal loops—that is, circular causal relations, when a change in one item leads to a sequence of change, which ultimately returns to affect the original item and bring it back to the original state. It resembles a physiological or mechanical model incorporating the deterministic or mechanical notion of events, where the forces operate almost "blindly" (Giddens, 1997, p. 78).

Illustrating it with issues faced by students in our study, the homeostatic risk cycle would operate as below:

- At-risk student faced with a situation with hazard
- Leads to engaging in risky behavior
- Leads to trouble in school—low grades, lack of motivation, poor attendance, etc. (nonresilient behavior)
- Reverts to or continues to be an at-risk student

In the process above there is no controlling filter in the cycle that acts to affect the actions of the student. Although the student acts, the action is almost a mechanical reaction (not fully agentic) to the operation of the system—nothing is being considered outside the causal loop. The at-risk label is not questioned either, the system assumes that immigrantness is a hazard that will inevitably lead to risk behavior.

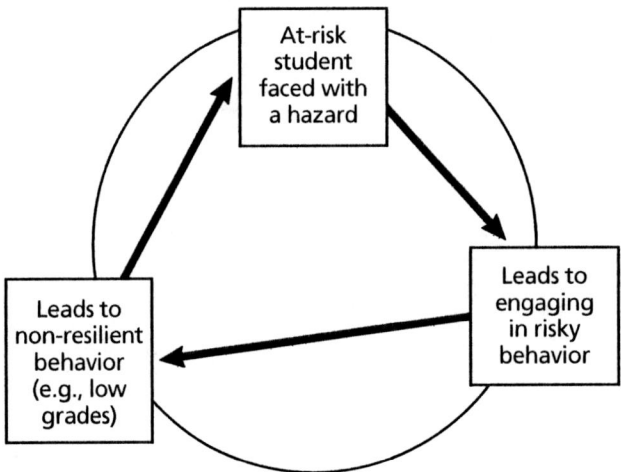

Figure 6.1. Homeostatic risk cycle.

Model #2—Self-Regulation through Feedback: An Institutional Analysis of Action

In this model an intervention is put in place, which acts as the controlling/crucial filter on the other elements in the cycle. In examples in our study, an intervention is activated by the parent, teacher, administrator, and/or the school district at the system level to deal with the students labeled " at risk."

- At-risk student faced with a hazardous situation.
- Engages in risky behavior (does not do homework, is disruptive in class, poor peer interactions, etc.).
- Intervention by the system (controlling/crucial filter): remediation, retention, counseling, in traditional models the protective factors.
- Leads to the student improving grades, attendance, punctuality, etc. In other words, develops acceptable behavior—resilient behavior.
- Becomes a not "at-risk" student.

In the model above the student has changed during this process. The critical questions, however, should be whether this change will last. In other words, is this resilient behavior according to the accepted definitions of resiliency? Change has been brought about by feedback from the system to the student through the intervention. The message is that risky behavior will not be accepted, the message may be punitive or it may be punitive. The student is acted upon rather than acting voluntarily. The critical question remains, however, is whether removal of the intervention will lead to a return to the original behavior and put the homeostatic causal loop into

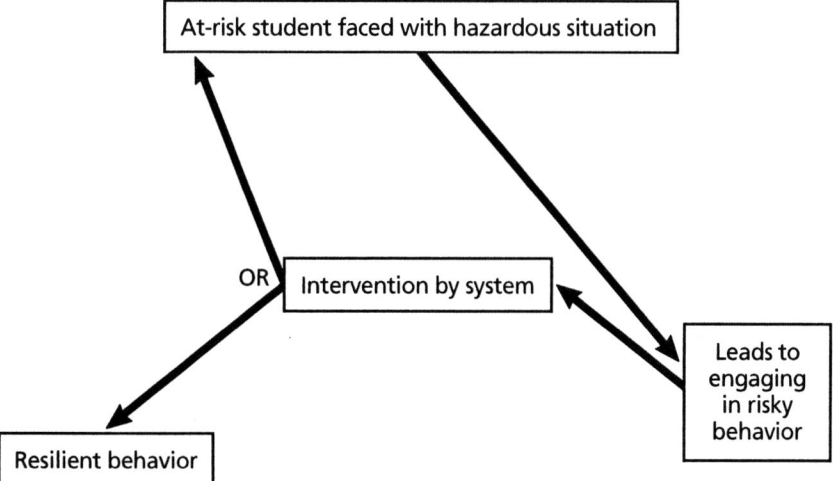

Figure 6.2. Self-regulation through feedback. An institutional analysis of action.

play once more. Did the student make this choice voluntarily as an acting subject exercising his/her foundational agency? Or was it the situation that forced the student to make the choice? These are issues that require the acting subject to explain his/her actions.

Model #3—Analysis of Strategic Conduct Based on Reflexive Self-Regulation by the Subject

This model examines, along with the method used in making choices by the student, the ecology of action situations. In the resilience literature, these are the support systems or the protective factors that enable the student to develop resiliency. The Agentic Model posits that the critical factor in developing resiliency is not the existence of the support systems per se, nor their actions, but rather how the student uses these systems in the process of negotiating risk situations. In other words not, merely the event, but the sequence of events will be analyzed.

Although the feedback system operates (as in Model #2), the distinguishing feature at this level is that the action taken belongs to a higher order involving self-regulation by the subject (student). Furthermore, the system in operation is examined not from the vantage of the system in action, but rather through an analysis of the strategic conduct of the agent. This model examines the students' use of the structural elements of school and schooling to achieve and maintain success, within the normative definition of school success. Giddens's notion of "could have acted otherwise" is a necessary feature of action at this stage.

The at-risk student faces situational hazards, which have the intrinsic ability to cause adverse effects. The student as agent (acting subject) has to make a choice. The choice made is based not merely on the presence of system intervention (existence of protective factors), but also on his/her knowledge of the social situation, and monitoring of the setting and of the interaction.

- At-risk student faced with a hazardous situation
- Choice is made based on their knowledge of the social situation—monitoring of the setting and of the interaction.
- As competent social agents   As incompetent social agents
        ↓   ↓
    make positive choices   make negative choices

It is critical to note that the working of the model at this third stage involves an analysis of the choice-making process within the ecology of the

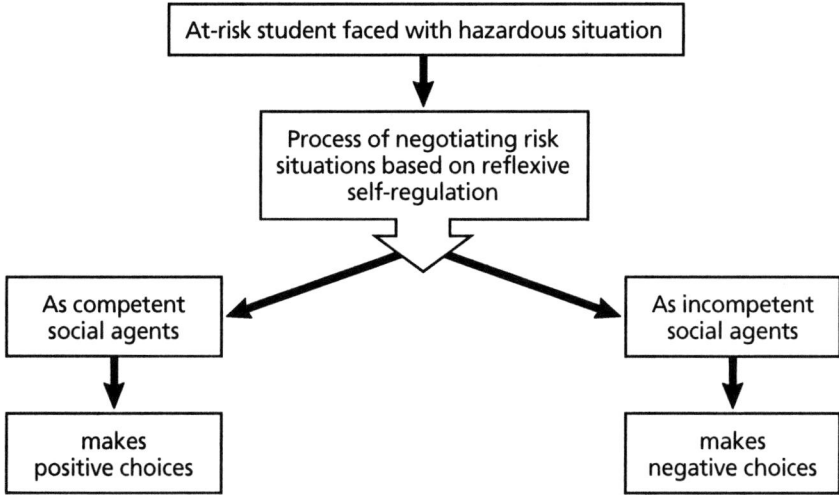

Figure 6.3. Analysis of strategic conduct based on reflexive self-regulation.

action situation. Finally, at this stage the homeostatic loop as well as the institutional intervention (simple feedback loop) is broken. The Agentic Model does not promote stasis nor merely institutionally controlled directed change, but rather a self-regulated, directional change that is made by the student-agent with knowledge of the situation and the process of interaction. Our data provides us with examples of such student-directed agentic action in dealing with the school and the system. An important point to be made at this point is that both resilient and nonresilient behavior must be analyzed within the social interaction in which it is meshed—as reflexively monitored conduct—that is, reflexive self-regulation by an acting subject. Resilient or nonresilient behavior is the result of the student making a definite choice at stage 3 through the manner in which the risk situation is negotiated within the context of the protective mechanisms. The next sections analyze the students' actions within the context of the three-stage Agentic Model.

THE COMMUNITY OF STUDENTS

The Community

Ricetown High School is the only high school in its district that serves two small suburban towns. The school's population of 3,500 breaks down into 64.9% Anglo, 29.8% Hispanic, 2.2% Asian, and 2.9% African American. The high school reports 28.5% students on free and reduced-price lunches while the district reports 50% in the same category (Texas Education Agency, 2000). Historically, Alston has been a Ku Klux Klan stronghold that boasted a sign until the 1960s that read, "No Niggers Allowed in Town after Sundown." The African American population has always been limited. Until the 1960s, the Mexican American students were schooled separately in their barrio that was "on the wrong side" of the railroad tracks.

Ricetown was noted for its rice production. A major flood in 1979 and a subsequent buyout of the rice farms by a large Arab conglomerate limited rice production and entrepreneurship. Two years before the rice production decreased, Folsom Oil Field ended its production. It had been the Ricetown School District's major source of income and provided teachers with the highest salaries in the area. The loss of the Folsom Oil Field coupled with the rice buyout caused Ricetown to be declared a blighted area in 1980. These events also stymied Ricetown's growth until recent years. The 1990s marked a rapid change in the population and in the economy of the area. Cheap land and no zoning have contributed to a community that now has a minority population of low-income families, most of them Latino, that is not completely reflected in the district's official breakdown. There has also been an influx of Asian students, recently from Pakistan and 10 years ago from Cambodia. The school board has a majority of members that reflect the pre-1960s era view of what the schools should be. As a result, there is no current program in the school district to improve the status of the low-income Latino and immigrant students. These two groups of students account for more than half of the low attendance, attrition rate, standardized test failure rate, and discipline problems at Ricetown High School.

Method of Analysis and Data Construction

Participants in this 3-year study included 30 Latino first- and second-generation immigrants, 15 Asian first- and second-generation immigrants, 15 Latino first- and second-generation immigrants, and 20 mainstream students from Ricetown High School. All of the students were academically successful in their studies and ranked in the top 10% of their class. The method of investigation included in-depth interviews with the academically successful immigrant students during the first and third years of the study. These tape-recorded interviews were transcribed and combined with field notes. During the second year of the longitudinal study, the Anglo students completed surveys modeled after the interview protocols used in the first year of the study. Informal interviews continued with the some of the Anglo students, immigrant students, and their teachers. During the final year of the study, focus group interviews were conducted with Anglo and immigrant students who had participated during the first two years of the study. Selected immigrant students were observed in class and some of those teachers were interviewed in-depth.

Portraits of Complexity

The Trickster

Ricardo was a ninth-grade student in an English class who was a first-generation immigrant from Mexico. His actions in school show a movement through the three models of agency. Throughout his schooling, sitting still in a classroom has been a hazard that exacerbated the at-risk label he gained due to his immigrant status. The homeostatic causal loop seemed to influence Ricardo's behavior when he has been forced to sit still for too long. He has reacted by talking, laughing, and clowning, thus initiating and completing a sequence of activities that return him to the original state.

When the system tried to intervene with discipline to induce model #2, self-regulation through feedback, Ricardo maintained his risk-taking behavior of acting out. Continual feedback in the form of "little talking notes" were sent home to his parents from kindergarten through sixth grade. These "talking notes" became a hazard that sent Ricardo back through the causal loop of clowning and reprimands.

These feedback attempts from model #2 did not affect Ricardo in his first 6 years of schooling. Instead of acting under the umbrella of either models #1 or #2, Ricardo's choice to continue his risky behavior is an example of model #3. He chose to continue his talking, laughing, and clowning, and even became more strategic as he chose when to demonstrate these socially unacceptable activities. Ricardo volunteered examples of this agency he used to invert the role of the dutiful student sitting at his desk.

> I can't stand desks the whole day. Sometimes I just break my pencil, so I can get up and sharpen it. That's how I can get out of my desk and come back. In sixth grade, I had a very strict teacher.... Like I'd walk in and give her a hug just to play around. And she'd look at me weird and want to send me to the office.

As Ricardo moved into high school his actions became even more strategic as he refined his agentic role. He had used his clowning to fit in with his peers in elementary school and middle school classes. He had reacted to the hazards of sitting still and discipline with more clowning, continuing the agentic model with challenging actions or subterfuge that held Ricardo in the role of an at-risk student with unruly behavior. When Ricardo recounted the reason, he finally decided to pay attention in math class in high school, his description replicated the second model with the feedback loop of the institutional classroom guiding Ricardo's response to his teacher. The protective factor of school decorum that required a student to maintain a silent demeanor and pay attention to the teacher was one that finally had taken hold on Ricardo. The hazardous situation of failing math caused Ricardo to heed the feedback of a teacher who only talked to the students who were "paying attention."

> I have trouble with math. I guess they don't understand. In my class, there's a lot of failures, and most of the people who are failing are always talking. And the teacher got tired of yelling, so she just doesn't get their attention anymore and let's them do their own thing. She only talks to the people who are paying attention.

Ricardo made conscious choices in most of his classes to regulate his actions. While institutional feedback, that paying attention brings teacher help and subsequent good grades, figure into his choice-making process, it his method and timing of negotiating these mechanisms (viz. his explanations) that are foregrounded in the process.

Role of agentic model in identity formation

High school also brought changes to Ricardo's clowning behavior. These changes involve strategic action in defense of his Mexican culture and a complete turn to model #3. His clowning became strategic action to confront biases against Latinos exhibited by his teachers and other students. Ricardo noted his reflexive self-regulation of his clowning as he "started to figure out when to do it and when not to do it."

Ricardo began to use his clowning ability to make controversial points. He offered an example of the way he confronted the stereotype of Mexico and South America as the only drug-producing areas in his social studies class. Ricardo explained that he realized if he wanted to disagree with a teacher or make a point in a classroom he could tell a joke. As he explained, "If I blurt it out the teacher will take it offensive."

Ricardo noted the way his teacher and his textbook claimed that most of the drugs came in from Mexico and South America. So Ricardo "made a joke about drugs in the Middle East and everyone laughed."

Ricardo's concern for the portrayal of the Latino was still strong when this researcher (Radigan) observed his antics in his English class. His class had just watched a video of Shakespeare's *Romeo and Juliet* with the Capulets as Latinos and the Montagues as whites. Some of the students had trouble with Leonardo Di Caprio's portrayal of Romeo. The teacher asked the students to explain their reaction to Di Caprio.

Field Note Excerpt: An Interactive Sequence on *Romeo and Juliet*

O'Dell: The Montagues. You didn't think they were all that—
Joaquin: The guys didn't look all that like fighting. DiCaprio. Ready to bust a cappio.
(*Talking at the same time*)
O'Dell: Bust a cappio? What does that mean?
Valentin: Just like—
Rebecca: It means—run.
O'Dell: Is that what it means, Valentin, to bust a cap in you?
(*Talking at the same time*)
Ricardo: Bust a cap e yo.
O'Dell: Shane, "What does bust a cap, yo" mean?
Shane: It means want to get your guts blown.
[*Quiet fills the room as Shane has raised his voice in response.*]
Ricardo: A white guy's shootin', so you better run, Mexican.
[*Ricardo stands up and performs a fast mime run down an aisle between Shane and the researcher (Radigan), and the class laughs.*]

There was a tacit rivalry in that class between the white boys and the Latinos. When Joaquin expressed his dislike of Di Caprio's Romeo and his wish *"to bust a cappio"* or do away with the actor, his meaning was questioned by the teacher. Tension began to rise as the students volunteered responses. Shane's response moved away from the Latino fun-making of Di Caprio to the act of violence. Ricardo, who was sitting in front of Shane, quickly rose and performed his mime run slightly in front of Shane as he proclaimed, "A white guy's shootin', so you better run, Mexican." Ricardo's unexpected response that drew from Rebecca's "run" and Shane's voice raised in protest even brought Shane's laugh. Ricardo had broken the tension by pulling up a stereotype that recognized Shane's tacit challenge to the Latinos and the role of the Mexican as subservient to Shane's "white man challenge."

There was no discussion about the position of the Latinos versus whites in the classroom, but Ricardo's sense of agency took an ironic turn as he acted out the school's cultural stereotype, as he seemed to understand a tacit claim that Shane was making. Ricardo offered a dramatically clownish challenge to cultural beliefs about Anglos oppressing Latinos. Ricardo was an example of Murillo's (2001) borderized "trickster" who awakened the class with his *movidas* (maneuverings). Ricardo also had advanced beyond the homeostatic model of reacting to hazards with a causal loop that carried him back to his at-risk position through elementary and middle school classes. His protective factor had moved beyond the institutional "pay attention" to the clever *movidas* of his trickster identity. His agentic action in his ninth-grade English class demonstrated the self-regulated and strategic action of a Latino defending his culture.

A student trapped in the hyphen of success and identity. Leonora, a second-generation Mexican, has spent most of her academic life trapped in the hyphen of Mexican and/or American, success and identity. These two arenas are interwined as success comes with being American. Yet Mexican is an undeniable part of who she is. She lived in the model #2 with the feedback loop of the white institution governing her successful academic life and the feedback loop of her Mexican parents governing her home life. Even though Spanish has always been spoken at home, Leonora *"never picked up on it."* The hazard of being in the regular track in school was avoided by listening to the tacit message, "Learn English only and be on the academic, gifted, and talented track," thereby overcoming the risks inherent in the hazard. Leonora explains this simply, *"People do not think Mexicans are smart."* The feedback that whites are smart translates to Leonora as *"Speak only English. Be an American."* With this feedback she can be successful in school and discard the at-risk label. So, one might ask if this feedback relating success to speaking English and being American is removed, will she revert to being Mexican?

Leonora admitted that she had a difficult time talking about Mexican culture. It was only when she asked a white friend about family food that Leonora realized she ate Mexican food four out of seven days. In her sophomore and junior years she responded to the feedback loop of the call of her father and Mexican friends to "be a Mexican." These conflicting feedback loops made Leonora's high school years difficult as home life and academic life intersected with conflicting identities. The protective factor that kept Leonora from resolving this conflict was success she experienced as an American speaking English and foregoing her Mexican identity at school. This same protective factor kept Leonora from achieving the reflexive self-regulation required to move her to exercising full agency as envisaged in model #3.

A cultural broker

Paulo was a first-generation immigrant who began his high school years governed by the second model with the institutional feedback loop of "Speak only English" and "Pay attention." However, his personal life was governed by the feedback loop of "Trust only your own kind." Paulo distinguished between these two loops in our (Radigan's) first interview as he displayed how self-conscious his immigrant status and his communication skills in English made him feel.

> In my classes I don't speak a lot because they are American teachers, and I am not very good in English. And so the only thing I do is pay attention and

do what they say. I pretty much focus on what they say to do, tell me to do. It's not like I'm like other students.

Paulo's response to "Trust your own kind" was to be the protective factor in the feedback loop that maintained his exclusive friendship with other immigrants:

There is always a limit. How do I say this? With other students [non-Latino, nonimmigrants] I don't feel comfortable, because I don't feel like they are my friends or that I won't be accepted whenever I talk, and I feel afraid of talking to them because they might say something about me.

It was as if in the 3 years he had been in high school, Paulo had learned to be a cultural broker who realized the tacit prejudices of the mainstream students and the teachers in the high school, and the power they wielded. Paulo's science teacher, who taught him during his freshman and junior years, was open in her expression of the dominant group's view.

They [the immigrants] need to learn English. The parents are not pushing the kids, and they don't have the language.... The students who come in dressed appropriately are the ones I am going to appreciate the most. They are the "preppies." They follow the rules. It's your natural bias to give them more attention.

This science teacher's view carries the institutional bias and tacit protective factor of preferring the "preppies" and the sociolinguistic bias of "the kids who don't have the language" and don't dress appropriately that Foley (1997) explains is part of the response to the deficit thinking model. Paulo's use of the agentic model expressed itself in the way he chose to dress. Rather than following the feedback loop of dressing like a prep (a college preparatory student wearing button-down shirts, blue jeans, and sneakers), Paulo chose to dress like a young man on a white-collar job search. A pale yellow short-sleeved shirt covered a white undershirt. Tailored black-pleated pants were finished with a slim belt of the same color. Black dress shoes with dress socks complete his look.

Even though Paulo's dress code was more formal than the "preppies," he still garnered the teacher's attention with his neat attire. This science teacher had taught Paulo during his freshman year when he did not talk to her or to the mainstream students in the class. She was surprised and pleased to see the change in his behavior in 2 years. She explained, "Last course he stayed with the Hispanic students and was very quiet. This course he hung out with 'the guys.' [The 'guys' are the preps and the jocks most of the teachers seem to like.] He talked this year." Paulo did make a choice (displaying the agentic model) in all of the classes I visited to sit among the

American students even when there were other immigrants or Mexican American students in his classes. He had learned the way to please his teacher and broker for a strong position in class among his fellow students. This is a young man who had chosen to walk the walk and talk the talk of the new culture as he retained his Mexican heritage and practiced it with his family and friends outside of the classroom.

Two protective factors were at work in the scenes depicted here. The institutional protective factor of dressing like, talking like, and being with students whom the teachers found acceptable was guiding Paulo's behavior in class. Paulo had also held on to the protective factor of "trusting his own kind" as he maintained his Mexican friendships and family ties outside of the classroom. Paulo had successfully translated his agentic role through reflexive action according to the context of the situation at hand. This agentic role was a contrast to the previous portrait of Leonora who remained conflicted by similar protective factors and feedback loops. Leonora and Paulo together seem a good example of complex differences in the agentic journey of identity formation.

TWO EXAMPLES OF AGENTIC POSITIONALITY IN IDENTITY FORMATION AND ACHIEVING SUCCESS

The next two students follow the path of the agentic model as they assume strong positions in defense of their cultures. This positionality operates "by critiquing the relationships between particular stories and broader interpretive frameworks" (Maher & Tetreault, 1994, p. 210). These two students critique the stories of others from the position of their culture and their rights. The stories of these two first-generation immigrant students, Lubna, from Pakistan, and Anita, from Nicaragua, exemplify students who assume the agentic role in their actions through taking a definite and stated position to defend their culture and their identity.

A comparison of the story told by Lubna in her freshman interview and in a later focus interview with another immigrant student 2 years later are worth considering for the change from the role of victim to that of assuming a positionality from which she could defend her home culture. Note the bolded words in both stories.

Interview Excerpt: A Comparison of a Similar Story Told in Freshman and Junior Year

Freshman Year

    L: We studied my country in world geography, and all the children were laughing at me that people make houses out of mud, and I didn't say anything. I just ignored

Junior Year

> them. My father wants me to ignore everybody. He tells it like that. So, I don't say anything.... If I, like, say something, then all the class will be all around me. And I'm just going to be one to a lot of students.
>
> *L:* Once, one of the students he was doing a project over our country, and he brought the books and he said, "Look this is your country." And that book was from 1960. (Laugh) He said, "Look, you guys make houses from mud and blah, blah, blah. (Laughter again) I said, "That's not true. He said, "Oh, yes it is. Those are the books." So I brought him a picture of my house because it wasn't made of mud. It was made of bricks and everything.

Lubna explained that the second story happened in her sophomore year. Whether the second story is a retelling of the same story or a new story, there is a definite change in agency. In the earlier story Lubna responds to the feedback of the student laughter with silence in a demonstration of the second model with its institutional feedback making fun of her inferior culture. There is a reinforcing loop of following her father's admonition "to ignore everybody." In the story told 2 years later, Lubna "acts" to disprove one student's report by bringing a picture of her house, which refutes the student's report on "houses of mud." The agentic model freed her from the institutional and parental feedback loops so that she could affirm her culture. For Lubna, the institutional protective factor of following the dominant culture and the reinforcing home protective factor of "ignoring cultural references and remaining silent" had proved to be obstacles in her agentic movement.

Anita, the other first-generation immigrant, discusses the reason why it is difficult to have a discussion about opposing cultural beliefs in regular classes. Anita characterizes a scene comparable to the one described by Lubna. The dominant Anglo students in this depiction restrict their discussion to normative claims about generalized cultural stereotypes and are not interested in an open discussion that could challenge their cemented cultural beliefs.

> If I were to go to like a world geography class where it's all kinds of people not just the higher educated people, they're not nice conversations. Well, I don't know, they're racist you know. They're not educated conversations. They're like yeah, "Well, Mexicans this, or black people this, and white people that," instead of explaining and trying to understand what's going on. They just put each other down, and so it's like, you know, I keep my mouth shut then.

The dilemma of mainstream students' closed beliefs is exacerbated by teachers with similar beliefs. Teachers, too, can cement themselves tacitly in pragmatic infrastructures reflecting closed cultural beliefs. This is a positionality that is difficult for an immigrant to overcome and often forces the immigrant student to respond to model #2's institutional feedback loop of stereotypical racism with silence. Invariant cultural positions are fueled by various claims like, "Speakers of other languages are rude because they use their language to talk about English-only people right in front of us." This tacit claim may have caused a teacher's reaction to Anita in a speech class. Nonetheless, Anita unabashedly negotiated a change in her speech class to open this language class to the prejudice in the community. Rather than activate model #2, Anita activates the agentic model of reflexive action as she assumes a positionality in defense of her native language. The discussion of this negotiated change with one of us (Silva) began with Anita's assertion that there is no one knowledge authority.

Interview Excerpt with Silva and Anita

Silva: If a teacher said to you I have proof and the proof is something in a book?
Anita: I don't do really good with authority. I don't accept anything unless it can be proven thoroughly.... I've been told twice now in the 3 years that I've been at school that I'm not allowed to speak Spanish in the classroom..... And me being told I can't speak my own language. I said, "No I don't think so," and she was like, "Yes, you're not allowed to speak Spanish,"... I went to the assistant principal and I said, "Hey, you know, she's telling me I can't speak Spanish. There's no rule in the school that says I cannot speak Spanish." And he said, "You're correct." I was like, "Will you please write me a letter so I can show it to her. Therefore, she can never tell me that." And he wrote it and I said, "Here you go. I'd like you to read this. I'm sorry if I was rude." And she's like, "I'm sorry, go ahead."

Not only did Anita confront her teacher about the unfairness of the speak-only-English class rule, she sought support from a school authority for a change in the classroom rule. Here, agency and positionality sparked action to bring equity for a minority group.

DISCUSSION

These portraits of complexity revealed both agency and identity development, but neither of these processes can be essentialized into prescriptive strategies for institutional practice. Leonora and Paulo together seem a good example of complex differences in the agentic journey of identity formation. Suárez-Orozco and Suárez-Orozco (2000) maintain that as the immigrant migrates from home to school, she makes use of multiple identities to deal with obstacles and obtain success in school. For these two students identity formation difficulties related to their agentic action as they negotiated their migration between home and school. Leonora wrestled with school and parental causal loops and conflicting messages: the feedback of "be an American" from school and "be a Mexican" from home. Her Mexican and American identities intersected as she had to choose the friends with whom she would run and select among school activities. Paulo was receiving the same feedback, but he chose to activate his American identity at school and his Mexican identity at home and with his friends. Leonora seemed to be a victim of circumstances, living in the hyphen, acted upon by school and family, whereas Paulo negotiated his way through the school day as a cultural broker using his adopted Americanness to gain success in his academic work and his Mexicanness with his friends.

For all of these students, school and parents provided tacit protective factors that sometimes proved to be obstacles to success rather than secure paths. Tacit feedback about language and clothes other than those accepted by the institution becomes an oppressive obstacle to the agency development and identity formation for these successful students. Students who chose to face these obstacles like Lubna and Anita take a position that exposes and thematizes the negative feedback. These students also realize their own positionality in the agentic model and the resources and rules they can garner to support their position. The unregulated trickster *movidas* of Ricardo became strategic actions that demonstrated his ability to be a barometer in the classroom for tacit biases and prejudices that were not easily exposed.

IMPLICATIONS

In the resilience literature, there are support systems or protective factors that enable the student to develop resiliency. The Agentic Model posits that the critical factor in developing resiliency is not the existence of the support systems, nor their actions, but rather how the student negotiates potentially hazardous situations. For the students in this study, the system's tacit support of Anglo speech and dress and interpretation of academic knowledge proved to be obstacles that the students reacted to or used for academic success or to make points about their culture. In the homostatic model the student is ignored. His immigrantness seems to be a problem over which the student has no control because the system operates "blindly" and the student remains at risk. In the self-regulation through feedback model, students receive an intervention as a stimulus to get the desired academic or behavioral response, but there is no guarantee that the response will be repeated if the stimulus disappears. In the first two models, the student's agency is either nonexistent or limited. It is our belief that an Agentic Model based on reflexive self-regulation frees students to make positive choices as competent social agents or to make negative choices as incompetent social agents. These choices, however, are not made in a vacuum. They are made in conjunction with the protective factors put in place by the school, home, and community. The key point, as stated earlier, and that requires reiteration is that it is the process of negotiating risk situations by the student, within the ecology of the protective factors, that is central in the Agentic Model. Finally, it was our choice to find students who made positive choices, but the trickster, Ricardo, turned his negative comedic action into cultural comments with reflexive self-regulation.

As we analyse the actions of students who demonstrate positive agentic action as they form multiple identities in their journey from home to school to work, we begin to move away from essentializing theories that omit the complexities of students' everyday interactions and negotiations. The immigrant is no longer inherently at risk but is equally at promise. Nonetheless, the myths persist. Our study of the academically successful immigrant student carries the generalization that these students are not the norm and Anglo students are. Their successes are considered isolated moments in the academic process. We are suggesting however, that the current interventionist discourse of Resiliency with its emphasis on the active role of protective facts on passive, unmotivated, immigrant students be replaced with a new discourse of Resiliency based on the concept of an active student agency using and manipulating the environment.

REFERENCES

Alva, S. A. (1991). Academic invulnerability among Mexican-American students: The importance of protective resources and appraisals. *Hispanic Journal of Behavioral Sciences, 13*, 18–34.

Anthony, E. J. (1987). Risk, vulnerability, and resilience: An overview. In E.J. Anthony & B.J. Cohler (Eds.), *The invulnerable child* (pp. 3–48). New York: Guilford.

Fink-Eitel, H. (1992). *Foucault: An introduction.* Pennbridge Books.

Foley, D. E. (1997). Deficit thinking models based on culture: The anthropological protest. In R. R. Valencia (Ed.), *The evolution of deficit thinking: Educational thought and practice* (pp. 113–131). London: Falmer.

Foley, D. A., Levinson, B. A., & Hurtig, J. (2001) Anthropology goes inside: The new educational ethnography of ethnicity and gender. *Review of Research in Education, 25*, 37–98.

Garmezy, N. (1991). Resiliency and vulnerability to adverse developmental outcomes associated with poverty. *American Behavioral Scientist, 34*, 416–430.

Garmezy, N. (1993). Children in poverty: Resiliency despite risk. *Psychiatry, 56*, 127–136.

Garmezy, N., Masten, A. S., & Tellegen, A. (1984). The study of stress and competence in children: A building block for developmental psychopathology. *Child Development, 55*, 97–111.

Giddens, A. (1979). *Central problems in social theory: Action, structure and contradiction in social analysis.* Berkeley: University of California Press.

Gordon, K. A. (1995). The self-concept and motivational patterns of resilient African American high school students. *Journal of Black Psychology, 21*, 239–255.

Gordon, K. A., Padilla, A. M., Ford, M., & Thoresen, C. (1994). *Resilient students beliefs about their schooling environment: a possible role in developing goals and motivation.* Paper presented at the annual conference of the American Educational Research Association, New Orleans, LA.

Grotberg, E.H. (1995, September 27–30). The international resilience project: Research, application and policy. Paper presented at the Symposio Internacional, Stress e Violencia. Lisbon, Portugal.

Maher, F. A., & Tetreault, M. K. (1994). *The feminist classroom: An inside look at how professors and students are transforming higher education for a diverse society.* New York: Basic Books.

Masten, A. (1994). Resilience in individual development: Successful adaptation despite risk and adversity. In M. Wang & E. Gordon (Eds.), *Educational resilience in inner-city America.* Hillsdale, NJ: Erlbaum.

Murillo, E. V. (2001). Education in the new Latino diaspora: Policy and the politics of identity. In S. Wortham, E. V. Murillo, & E. Haman (Eds.), *Sociological studies in educational policy formation and appropriation* (pp. 1–16).Westport, CT: Ablex.

Murphy, L. & Moriarty, D. (1976). *Vulnerability, coping, and growth.* Yale University Press.

Portes, A., & MacLeod, D. (1996). Educational progress of children of immigrants: The roles of class, ethnicity, and school context. *Sociology of Education, 69*, 255–275.

Radke-Yarrow, M., & Sherman, T. (1990). Hard growing: Children who survive. In J. Rolf, D. Masten, K. Chicchetti, H. Nuechterlein, & S. Weintraub (Eds.), *Risk and protective factors in the development of pyschopathology* (pp. 97–119). New York: Cambridge University Press.

Richardson, G. E. (1995). *The resiliency training manual.* Dubuque, IA: Brown & Benchmark.

Richardson, G. E., & Nixon, C. J. (1997). A curriculum for resiliency. *Principal 77*, 26–28.

Rutter, M. (1985). Family and school influences on cognitive development. *Journal of Child Psychology and Psychiatry, 26,* 683–704.

Rutter, M. (1990). Psychosocial resilience and protective mechanisms. In S. Weintraub (Ed.), *Risk and protective factors in the development of psychopathology* (pp. 181–214). New York: Cambridge University Press.

Rutter, M. (1995). Psychosocial adversity: Risk resilience and recovery. *Southern African Journal of Child and Adolescent Psychiatry, 7,* 75–88.

Sagor, R. (1996). Building resiliency in students. *Educational Leadership, 54*(1), 38–43.

Suárez-Orozco, C., & Suárez-Orozco, M. M. (1995). *Transformations: Family life and achievement motivation among Latino youth.* Palo Alto, CA: Stanford University Press.

Suárez-Orozco, C., & Suárez-Orozco, M. M. (2000). Some conceptual considerations in the interdisciplinary study of immigrant children. In E. T. Trueba & L. I. Bartolome (Eds.), *Immigrant voices: In search of educational equity* (pp. 17–36). Lanham, MD: Rowman & Littlefield.

Trueba, E. T. (1999). High achievement high school students in Houston: A study of learning environments and strategies across languages and cultures. Proposal presented to the Spencer Foundation.

Trueba, E. T., & Bartolome, L. I. (Eds.). (2000). *Immigrant voices: In search of educational equity.* Lanham, MD: Rowman & Littlefield.

Wang, M., Haertel, G., & Walberg, H. (1997). Fostering resilience: What do we know? *Principal, 77,* 18–20.

Werner, E. (1993). Risk, resilience, and recovery: Perspectives from the Kauai longitudinal study. *Development and Psychopathology, 5,* 505–515.

Winfield, L. (1991). Resilience, schooling, and development in African-American youth. *Education and Urban Society, 24*(1), 5–14.

Winfield, L. (1994). Developing resilience in urban youth (NCREL monograph, NCREL, Urban Education Program). Available: http://ncrel.org/sdrs/areas/issues/educatrs/leadershp/le0win.htm.

CHAPTER 7

MATHEMATICS LEARNING ENVIRONMENT DIFFERENCES BETWEEN RESILIENT, AVERAGE, AND NONRESILIENT ELEMENTARY STUDENTS

Hui-Li Chang
University of Houston

One of the core beliefs and visions for education is to assist *all* children, especially at a young age, to reach their potential in becoming autonomous, lifelong learners (National Association for the Education of Young Children, 1987). Lifelong learning has become an important attribute for success within our society (State Education and Environment Roundtable, 2002). In particular, to fully function in our society, proficiency in mathematics has become extremely important. The National Council of Teachers of Mathematics (NCTM) has long realized the importance of mathematics in a changing world and the need for continuous improvement of mathematics education. The "Principles and Standards for School Mathematics" reflects the NCTM's vision to reach excellence in mathematics education by having high expectations of and providing strong support for all students.

Within the mathematics community, we are far short of attaining the vision of equity in mathematics education. Because of long-standing inequities, there are serious educational challenges currently facing our society in the area of mathematics education. One of the more telling symptoms of these challenges lies in the observed gap between high and low achievers in mathematics. There is ample evidence for this mathematics achievement gap. The National Assessment of Educational Progress (NAEP), for example, examined mathematics scores for white students and found that they were significantly higher than corresponding mathematics scores of African American and Hispanic students, indicating the existence of a gap between high and low achievers at three levels of mathematics (ages 9, 13, and 17).

The gap can be considered as a symptom showing that not all children are reaching their potential. The desire to provide equal opportunity for every student and to narrow the gap are the main motivations for this study. Therefore, how do educators begin to close the achievement gap and provide high-quality effective mathematics education for all students?

AN APPROACH TO THE PROBLEM

These serious and important challenges that educators face will require sustained effort and contributions from all levels of our educational system. In an effort to improve the situation in mathematics education, this study draws on two educational frameworks: educational resilience and the classroom learning environment. The intent of this study is to draw on the solid base of knowledge about the classroom learning environment and to apply it to the mathematics classroom, especially in light of the constructivist approach advanced by the NCTM. By comparing and contrasting resilient (academic high achieving, high motivation, and high attendance) and nonresilient (academic low achieving, low motivation, and low attendance) elementary school students, this study intends to identify important factors that can be provided within the classroom and that may raise the academic outcomes of mathematics students.

REVIEW OF RESEARCH

Recently, researchers have recognized the importance of a quality classroom learning environment for encouraging students at risk of academic failure to succeed (Waxman, 1992; Waxman & Huang, 1998; Waxman & Padrón, 1995). Fostering and maintaining a positive classroom learning environment has become a means for enabling students to achieve in school (Pierce, 1994). In order to gain insight as to why some students are able to overcome difficult circumstances (resilient) while other students (nonresilient) with similar backgrounds are not able to do so, this research draws upon two distinct and emerging theoretical frameworks. First, educational resilience: "The heightened likelihood of success in school and other life accomplishments despite environmental adversities brought about by early traits, conditions and experiences" (Wang, Haertel, & Walberg, 1994). Second, the classroom learning environment: "The relationship and interaction between the environment and the personal variables which have shown to be highly effective in research on classroom learning environment and how it [the learning environment] induces change and stability in students" (Moos, 1979).

The core assumptions of this research are the beliefs that (a) all students are capable of learning and have untapped potential, and (b) every student has the capability to overcome adversity if relevant protective factors are present in that student's life (Krovetz, 1999). As an application of research, Alva (1991) suggested that educational policies needed to be focused on expanding protective resources and improving students' perception of their learning environment. Unlike socioeconomic status, for example, which educators can do little about, equity in the learning environment (e.g., appropriate participation, satisfaction, working conditions) is something educators can provide.

Teachers as a Protective Factor

Resilient students tend to have a meaningful relationship with someone who functions as a mentor or guide, such as a teacher or parent. In particular, that caring adult can be the student's teacher, who can give a student the motivation to succeed (Noddings, 1988). Most resilient children have at least one strong relationship with an adult, who is not always a parent. The impact of a caring teacher on an at-risk of academic failure student can be significant. Teachers can play an important role in serving as an external support and protective mechanism that can help students cope with stress.

To advance resiliency, educators can enhance the classroom learning environment to give the best chance of promoting student outcomes. Students ultimately respond to what they perceive is important (Chavez, 1984; Schultz, 1979). One of the differences between resilient and nonresilient students that were found in previous studies (Waxman, Huang, & Padrón, 1997; Waxman, Huang, & Wang, 1997) was in their perceptions of the learning environment. Findings indicated that resilient students had a significantly higher social self-concept, achievement motivation, satisfaction, feedback, and academic self-concept than nonresilient students. There were numerous studies that correlated academic outcomes with perceptions of the learning environment (Pierce, 1994; Wang, Haertel, & Walberg, 1993). Thus, understanding the perceptions of the students' learning environment is critical to providing the optimum setting within the classroom (Fraser, 1990). The approach of this research, therefore, is to find specific ways for educators to provide the optimum classroom learning environment for all students to learn via a study of resilient students' perceptions of the mathematics classroom learning environment.

In addition to guiding academic content knowledge, acquiring, and mastering skills, teachers can also provide protective factors. To help students develop the values and attitudes needed to persevere in the classroom and to achieve a high level of academic performance, teachers may play a critical role in fostering resiliency. Literature has suggested that an effective teacher should: (a) promote self-confidence, (b) encourage self-responsibility (Wang & Palincsar, 1989), (c) provide empathetic support (Benard, 1995), (d) help students set realistic goals (Wang et al., 1994), (e) present a caring attitude, (f) develop values necessary for achieving high grades, (g) cultivate personal relationships between teacher and student (Coleman & Hoffer, 1987), (h) provide opportunities for participation (Benard, 1995), and (i) promote the positive use of time (McMillan & Reed, 1994) in the classroom instruction in order to promote learning success of students.

Effective instruction is a means to assist students in constructing their own learning (Waxman & Huang, 1997). Among the most important goals of effective teaching is to provide learning experiences that are in concert with the needs of the students, giving them the best chance to achieve academic competence and enhance their development (Wang et al., 1994). By studying how resilient students in a classroom setting have overcome adversity, research may provide educators with guidelines to create classroom learning environments that foster resiliency for all students.

NEED FOR THE CURRENT STUDY

The literature on resiliency forms a foundation for our research. However, many studies have not examined important psychosocial behaviors that significantly influence students' cognitive and affective outcomes, such as achievement motivation and academic self-concept. Furthermore, it is crucial to include students' motivation and aspirations as scales within a complete study because they have been found to be highly related to both students' academic achievement and the classroom learning environment (Cheng, 1994; Knight & Waxman, 1990; Uguroglu & Walberg, 1986). Student motivation and classroom learning environments have been studied and discussed separately. However, they are closely related within the topic of resiliency and should be included within the same survey to obtain a comprehensive view (Knight & Waxman, 1990). In addition, interviews with students may be a rich source of additional complementary information to understand students' personal experiences and interaction with teachers and other students in the classroom environment. These are the shortcomings of existing studies that are to be addressed in the present study.

By providing protective factors within the classroom learning environment, educators may foster resiliency in students. The aim of the present research study is to identify which factors educators can provide through the mathematics classroom learning environment to promote resiliency. This study examines high and low achievers, students by ethnicity, and resilient and nonresilient students. Based on the literature review, survey items were carefully selected to be included on 11 scales to accommodate the time limit set by school officials and the attention span of the participants. This research extends prior research in four ways:

1. This research focuses on elementary school mathematics instead of middle or high school because it is important to foster resiliency as early as possible.
2. The data used in this research were collected from a rural area where more than half of the students are from an economically disadvantaged background, unlike most of the previous researches that were administered at urban or inner-city schools.
3. The majority of the participants in the first study are white whereas previous research focused on African American, Asian American, or Latino students.
4. This research includes semi-structured interview results to supplement quantitative data.

PURPOSE OF THE STUDY

The purpose of this study is to first compare resilient, average, and nonresilient elementary grade students' perceptions of their mathematics learning environment. Second, mathematics classroom learning environment factors reported as being important to resilient students in overcoming their adversities and leading toward their academic success will be identified. If key factors responsible for resiliency in mathematics learning can be identified, changes can be recommended in the mathematics classroom learning environment to enable all students to achieve the NCTM vision of success and equity in mathematics. Knowledge of different perceptions of the learning environment and classroom behavior between resilient and nonresilient students may allow educators to modify the classroom learning environment in order to narrow the gap between high-achieving students and those students at risk of academic failure who have not done well academically.

RESEARCH QUESTIONS

The present study proposes the following research questions:
1. Are there significant differences by group (i.e., resilient, average, and nonresilient) and ethnicity (i.e., minority and white students) on elementary students' perceptions of their mathematics classroom learning environment?
2. To what extent do reported differences occur between resilient, average, and nonresilient students' attitudes toward school experiences, parent involvement, aspirations, and academic self-concept?

To help answer the research questions, the present studies combined the results of two quantitative surveys with data taken from a set of semi-structured interviews, supplementing the written response with viewpoints articulated by the students. The combined results are used to provide a comprehensive insight into how resilient, average, and nonresilient students' perceptions of their classroom learning environments differ.

METHODS

Self-reported survey data and semi-structured interview information were conducted to enhance the understanding of resiliency in elementary school students. In the self-reported survey portion, there were two separate but related studies. Both survey studies used similar research designs, methods, and data analysis procedures. According to the reliabilities of the scales from Study 1, the survey instrument used in Study 1 was moderately revised before it was administered to participants in Study 2. Detailed personal experiences were systematically collected through semi-structured interviews in the areas of (a) school experiences, (b) parent involvement, (c) student aspirations, and (d) academic self-concept.

Research Design for Study 1

To gain insight as to why some students were able to overcome difficult circumstances (resilient) while other students with similar backgrounds have not (nonresilient), Study 1 compares third-, fourth-, and fifth-grade resilient (academic high achieving), average, and nonresilient (academic low achieving) students' perceptions and attitudes toward their mathematics classroom learning environment. A causal-comparative research design was used to examine students' perceptions of their mathematics learning environment in (a) cohesion, (b) competition, (c) difficulty, (d) friction, (e) satisfaction, (f) academic self-concept, (g) parent involvement, (h) student aspirations, (i) feedback, (j) equity, and (k) teacher support. This study used these 11 dependant variables to see if they were contingent upon the independent variables of group (resilient, average, and nonresilient) and ethnicity (African American or white).

Method for Study 1

Survey Participants

A total of 160 third-, fourth- and fifth-grade students from nine mathematics classrooms (three classes from each grade level) from an elementary school in a rural setting near a major metropolitan area in the south central region of the United States participated in this study. There were nearly equal distributions (35%) of third- and fourth-grade students, while 30% were fifth grade students, among which boys and girls were equally distributed (50%). The majority of the participants were white (77.5%), and about 22.5% were African American.

Teachers from the participating school were asked to identify approximately three resilient (i.e., high-achieving students on both standardized achievement tests and daily school work, very motivated, with excellent attendance) (Padrón, Waxman, & Huang, 1999; Waxman, Huang, & Wang, 1997) and approximately three nonresilient students (i.e., low-achieving students on both standardized achievement tests and daily schoolwork, not motivated, with poor attendance) in their class. The remaining students were classified as average for the purposes of this study.

Survey Instrument

The survey used in this study was comprised of selected portions of five existing student survey instruments that specifically dealt with the classroom learning environment:

1. My Class Inventory (MCI) (Dryden & Fraser, 1996; Fraser & O'Brien, 1985; Padrón et al., 1999; Waxman, Huang, & Wang, 1997)
2. Multidimensional Motivation Instrument (MMI) (Uguroglu & Walberg, 1986; Waxman & Huang, 1996; Waxman, Huang, & Padrón, 1997)

3. Instructional Learning Environment Questionnaire (ILEQ) (Knight & Waxman, 1990; Waxman & Huang, 1996; Waxman, Huang, & Padrón, 1997)
4. What is Happening in This Class (WIHIC) (Aldridge, Fraser, & Huang, 1998; Fraser, Fisher, & McRobbie, 1996; Rawnsley & Fisher, 1997)
5. Classroom Environment Scale (CES) (Huang & Waxman, 1996; Waxman & Huang, 1996; Waxman, Huang, & Padrón, 1997)

These questionnaires have been used in a wide variety of studies aiming to measure students' perceptions of their environment, including relationships with other students and teachers. Seventy-four items that were selected from the five existing surveys were rephrased to measure students' perceptions of their mathematics classes instead of their general impressions of school. Students circled either "Yes" or "No" in response to statements read to them about their mathematics class.

Validity of the survey. The instruments used in this study have previously been found to be reliable and valid in a number of different school settings and have been identified as being particularly applicable for elementary school students (Fraser, Anderson, & Walberg, 1982; Hardwick, 1996; Huang & Waxman, 1997; Padrón et al., 1999; Waxman, Huang, & Wang, 1997). The Cronbach's alpha reliability analyses were carried out to test the internal consistency, yielding a range of reliability coefficients from .59 to .84. This indicated that the scales in the survey have adequate reliability for this type of instrument (Waxman & Huang, 1997). The results of the discriminant validity statistics indicated that the mean correlation coefficient of a scale with each of the other scales ranged from .00 to .68, with an average of .24, which showed that items from different scales were essentially unrelated. In addition, an ANOVA with class as the main factor was conducted to determine the effect of their classroom learning environment on students' perceptions. An eta^2 analysis was used to interpret the proportion of the total variability of the dependent variable (11 scales) that was accounted for by variation of the class. Students from various classrooms had very different perceptions of their classrooms with regard to five scales. The mean eta^2 value of the 11 scales was .10, indicating that about 10% of the variance in students' classroom learning environment scales was accounted for by class membership. Thus, all 11 scales used in this study were able to differentiate significantly between classrooms. The results discussed above establish the validity of the survey used for the present research.

Survey Procedure
Near the end of the school year, all the third-, fourth-, and fifth-grade students in the participating schools completed the self-reported survey.

Trained researchers from the Center for Research on Education, Diversity, and Excellence (CREDE) read the survey items to all students so that reading and language difficulties would not interfere with students' ability to answer the questions. The students were informed by the researchers that the instruments were not tests and that the completed questionnaires would not be seen by their teachers or other school personnel. Each survey took an average of 25 minutes to finish.

Survey Data Analysis

A 3 (group) × 2 (ethnicity) multivariate analyses of variance (MANOVA) was used to compare the student groups and ethnicity of students' perceptions of their mathematics classroom learning environment. The results from this analysis enabled us to determine if there were significant differences among the group perceptions of their classroom environments and allow identification of which scales were important. The Tukey post hoc test with multiple comparisons was used to determine where the differences originate.

Research Design for Study 2

Like the Study 1, the purpose of the second study was to compare fourth- and fifth- grade resilient (academic high achieving), average, and nonresilient (academic low achieving) students' perceptions and attitudes toward their mathematics classroom learning environment. A causal-comparative research design was used to investigate elementary fourth- and fifth-grade students' perception of their mathematics classroom learning environment. Study 2 used 10 dependent variables, (a) cohesion, (b) competition, (c) difficulty, (d) satisfaction, (e) academic self-concept, (f) parent involvement, (g) student aspirations, (h) equity, (i) teacher support, and (j) achievement motivation, to examine if they are contingent upon the independent variables of group (resilient, average, and nonresilient) and ethnicity (Latino and Other ethnic groups).

A total of 146 elementary school students (Grade 4, 49.3%, and Grade 5, 50.7%) from eight mathematics classrooms (four classes from each grade level) from a large, public elementary school located in the vicinity of a metropolitan city in the south central region of the United States participated in the Study 2. There were 121 Latino students and 25 students categorized as "Others" in the study, among which boys and girls were equally distributed (50%).

Survey Instrument

According to the instrument reliability results from Study 1, revisions of the survey used in Study 1 were made for Study 2. The revised survey also comprised of selected portions of five existing student survey instruments that specifically dealt with the classroom learning environment, the same as those listed in Study 1.

Validity of the Survey

Cronbach's alpha reliability analyses yielded a range of reliability coefficients from .64 to .76, which indicates that the majority of the scales in the survey have adequate reliability for this type of instrument. An average correlation coefficient of .25 showed that the scales have adequate discriminant validity, although several of the scales in the instrument may be correlated to some degree. The mean eta^2 value of the 10 scales was .10, indicating that about 10% of the variance in students' classroom learning environment scales was accounted for by class membership. Thus, all 10 scales used in this study were able to differentiate significantly between classrooms.

Procedure and Data Analysis

The procedures and data analysis for Study 2 were very similar to Study 1.

Interviews

Eighteen resilient, seven average, and 14 nonresilient students from the fourth- and fifth-grade survey participants from Study 1 were randomly selected to be interviewed by two trained researchers. The semi-structured interview instrument used in the present study was adapted from interview schedules from existing studies (Brown & Padrón, 2001; Richardson, Casanova, Placier, & Guilfoyle, 1989; Wang, Freiberg, & Waxman, 1994) to collect students' background information, as well as students' (a) school experiences, (b) parent involvement, (c) student aspirations, and (d) academic self-concept. The semi-structured interview questions were open-ended yet specific in intent, allowing individual responses.

Students were taken out of their study period to be interviewed and were given adequate time to answer questions. In the event that the students did not understand the interviewer's question, the questions were restated. The semi-structured interviews were audio-taped with permission. Each interview lasted about 25 minutes. The audiotapes were transcribed and rigorously coded to look for trends. The results then were quantified in percentages.

RESULTS

Learning Environment Results

Study 1 Results

Overall descriptive statistics are used to report the means and standard deviations of students' perceptions of their classroom learning environment scales. The mean values for each scale range from 1 to 2. A mean scale score close to the value of 2 indicates that students agreed with all the items on the scale for the most part, whereas a mean score of close to 1 indicates that all the students generally disagreed with the items on the scale. Overall, the results indicated that students in this school had positive perceptions of their classroom learning environments. The scale with the highest average mean was student aspirations ($M = 1.96$, $SD = .15$), followed by parent involvement ($M = 1.84$, $SD = .24$) and teacher support ($M = 1.82$, $SD = .27$). The feedback ($M = 1.72$, $SD = .26$), equity ($M = 1.71$, $SD = .31$), competition ($M = 1.71$, $SD = .34$), and satisfaction ($M = 1.70$, $SD = .34$) scales had similar mean values that were also high. The scales with the lowest mean value was difficulty ($M = 1.35$, $SD = .34$), followed by friction ($M = 1.51$, $SD = .32$), academic self-concept ($M = 1.58$, $SD = .35$), and cohesion ($M = 1.60$, $SD = .30$).

A 3×2 GLM MANOVA was used to determine if there were significant main effects by group (resilient, average, and nonresilient) or by ethnicity (African American and white non-Hispanic), and if there was a significant interaction by group × ethnicity on the 11 scales of survey. The MANOVA result revealed an overall significant multivariate effect by group, $F(2, 154) = 2.17$, $p = .001$, on the 11 scales. There was no statistically significant multivariate effect by ethnicity, $F(1, 154) = .54$, $p = .894$, and there was no significant interaction by group × ethnicity, $F(2, 154) = .98$, $p = .503$. The Tukey *post hoc* test revealed that there were significant differences among resilient, average, and nonresilient students on five scales: difficulty, $F(2, 154) = 7.97$, $p = .001$; friction, $F(2, 154) = 3.70$, $p < .05$; satisfaction, $F(2, 154) = 4.15$, $p < .05$; academic self-concept, $F(2, 154) = 19.81$, $p < .01$; and student aspirations, $F(2, 154) = 3.47$, $p < .05$.

The results indicate that resilient students have significantly higher perceptions of satisfaction, academic self-concept, and student aspirations than the nonresilient students. Nonresilient students reported higher means on difficulty and friction scales than the resilient students. There were no differences between nonresilient and average students, and there were no differences between average and resilient students on the difficulty and friction scales.

Study 2 Results

The results for study 2 indicated that students in this school also had generally positive perceptions of their classroom learning environments. In Study 2, the scales with the highest average means are student aspirations ($M = 1.94$, $SD = .18$), followed by achievement motivation ($M = 1.90$, $SD = .23$), teacher support ($M = 1.83$, $SD = .27$), cohesion ($M = 1.82$, $SD = .25$), satisfaction ($M = 1.82$, $SD = .25$), competition ($M = 1.79$, $SD = .28$), equity ($M = 1.77$, $SD = .26$), and parent involvement ($M = 1.73$, $SD = .29$). The scales with the lowest mean values in Study 2 are difficulty ($M = 1.30$, $SD = .29$) followed by academic self-concept ($M = 1.63$, $SD = .32$).

The 3×2 MANOVA results revealed that there was an overall significant multivariate effect by group, $F(2, 140) = 2.32$, $p = .001$, on the 10 scales. There was no significant multivariate effect by ethnicity, $F(1, 140) = 1.63$, $p = .106$, and no significant interaction by group × ethnicity, $F(2, 140) = .71$, $p = .820$, on the 10 scales. The Tukey *post hoc* test revealed that there were significant differences among resilient, average, and nonresilient students on three scales: difficulty, $F(2, 140) = 12.51$, $p < .01$; satisfaction, $F(2, 140) = 5.60$, $p < .01$; and academic self-concept, $F(2, 140) = 10.13$, $p < .01$.

The Tukey post hoc results indicated that resilient students had significantly higher perceptions of satisfaction and academic self-concept than the nonresilient students. Nonresilient students reported higher means on the difficulty scale than the resilient and average students. There were no significant differences among resilient, average, and nonresilient students on the cohesion, competition, parent involvement, student aspirations, equity, teacher support, and achievement motivation scales.

Student Interview Results

The semi-structured interviews included questions about the students' (a) school experiences, (b) parent involvement, (c) student aspirations, and (d) academic self-concept, as well as general background information. The results of the semi-structured interviews revealed that these resilient, average, and nonresilient groups differed significantly from each other in their attitudes toward their mathematics classroom learning environment. In general, resilient students were found to have a positive school experience, better achievement, higher aspirations, and higher academic self-concept than the average and nonresilient students. There were no differences among these three groups on their parents' involvement.

In general, most of the students felt positive about school, but agreed that academically related work was the most difficult area for them about school. When they encountered problems, resilient students tended to seek help from their families, while average and nonresilient students had the tendency to ask their teachers for help. A greater percentage of resilient students liked mathematics than average and nonresilient students. On the other hand, percentage-wise more average and nonresilient preferred Language Arts than resilient students.

In addition to classroom learning, the interviews inquired about other modes of learning. Most of the students reported that their parents have been to their school for school events, parties, or school plays. More students indicated that they have been to recreational places, the zoo, museums, or the circus with their families than with their school. Almost all the students indicated that their parents provide reading materials, books, magazines, and newspapers; however, only few of the resilient students said that they had access to encyclopedias or dictionaries at home.

Most of the resilient students reported that they have the confidence to finish their education, but nearly a quarter of the nonresilient students were not sure about their ability to finish. From the interview results, it seemed that more of the resilient students had extrinsic motivation than their average and nonresilient peers. Nonresilient students worried a lot about how they are doing in school compared to their classmates. Twice the fraction of resilient versus nonresilient students thought academic success is the most important reason for being successful in school.

Almost twice the percentage of resilient than nonresilient students said that they liked mathematics, but more than a third of the nonresilient group were vague about this topic. Only resilient students expressed that their fondness of mathematics was due to the challenge of understanding the subject. Resilient students reported that they were more confident about their mathematics abilities than their average and nonresilient peers.

DISCUSSION

The results from both survey studies indicated that nonresilient students, in general, perceived more difficulty mastering the work assigned in mathematics class than resilient students. Nonresilient students also perceived significantly higher friction in the classroom (the amount of tension and quarreling among students) than resilient students. On the other hand, resilient students perceived higher satisfaction, academic self-concept, and student aspirations than nonresilient students. Neither a statistically significant main effect for ethnicity (Latino and other ethnic groups), nor a statistically significant interaction group × ethnicity was found in either study.

Such findings corroborate results of previous studies that also found that resilient elementary school mathematics students expressed more satisfaction with their classroom learning environment than nonresilient students (Dellinger, Daniel, Stuhlmann, & Ellett, 1999; Padrón et al., 1999;

Waxman, Huang, & Wang, 1997). This should not be surprising given that nonresilient students have more difficulty mastering the work assigned in their mathematics classroom than average and resilient students (Padrón et al., 1999).

The observed differences in the friction scale (i.e., the amount of tension and quarreling among students), however, had not been found as a significant factor in previous studies (Padrón et al., 1999). This addition to the literature certainly bears further examination by other researchers in this area. In this study, it was also found that resilient students have higher academic self-concept and student aspirations than do average and nonresilient students. This finding lends support to other studies (Waxman, Huang, & Padrón, 1997; Waxman, Huang, & Wang, 1997) with similar findings. In the present research, the resilient, average, and nonresilient students were found to have statistically different sets of student aspirations, in agreement with a previous research study (Waxman & Huang, 1997).

Surprisingly, there was no statistically significant difference between resilient and nonresilient students in terms of their mathematics teachers' responses to their performance and classroom feedback levels. This conflicts with previous research results (Waxman, Huang, & Wang, 1997), which found that resilient students perceived stronger feedback from teachers than did nonresilient students. This is surprising because feedback was found to be an important aspect of student learning (Benard, 1995; Waxman & Huang, 1996). Research also suggests that teacher support is a significant variable that influenced student outcomes. Students should feel that they can approach their teachers for discussions about personal issues (Alva, 1991). The findings from the present studies, however, showed that there were no significant differences among resilient, average, and nonresilient students' perceptions about teacher support (the teacher can help the student directly and the teacher takes a personal interest in them). One possible explanation is that teachers in both studies were doing a satisfactory job providing feedback and support to all students. In other words, students perceived these two factors, teachers' support and feedback, were important, but there was little difference in the students' responses among groups. Furthermore, unlike previous research, the results of the present studies did not yield an overall main effect for ethnicity (African American and white), nor an interaction by group × ethnicity. This seemed to indicate that the students from the participating schools felt that their teachers were successful in providing equal educational opportunities.

From examining the series of semi-structured student interviews, it appeared that academic success was more important for these resilient students than their nonresilient colleagues when used as a criterion for their success in school. These results also indicated a larger percentage of resilient students were reporting intentions to attend and succeed in high school. This carried over into a stated desire by the resilient students to continue education beyond high school, a desire that was nowhere near as strongly stated by the nonresilient students. Furthermore, the resilient students seemed to better appreciate the roles teacher support and classroom environment played in determining success or failure in school. The nonresilient students, on the other hand, seemed to believe personal traits (laziness or smartness) were more responsible in explaining their school failure. Moreover, the nonresilient students reported that they were significantly more worried about school than resilient students.

Mathematics was found to be the favorite subject for a larger percentage of resilient students than for nonresilient students. The results could indicate that nonresilient students were given easier and less work in the mathematics classroom while resilient students received more challenging problems and a greater number of problems. The present studies also revealed that "grades" were considered as the sole criterion in mathematics learning assessment for both resilient and nonresilient students.

Resilient students reported possessing higher academic self-concepts and believing that they are better problem solvers than nonresilient students. Nonresilient students said that giving correct answers was the only indicator of being a good problem-solver. This result may indicate that teachers were focusing on the correct answers instead of the learning process or understanding as the pursuit of mathematics knowledge. Although nonresilient students reported using computers in the classroom, they were using them for test preparation, not for the intellectual instruction.

Equal Opportunity for All Students to Learn

Research has shown a strong correlation between opportunities to learn and student achievement (Grouws & Cebulla, 2000). Although there are no statistically significant differences on students' perceptions on the teachers' feedback and support scales, the fact that resilient students reported (during the interviews) receiving a greater amount of challenging work than the nonresilient students suggests that teachers do not provide equal opportunities to all students and expect less from the nonresilient students. According to the NCTM (2000), equity does not mean that every student receives identical instruction, but requires reasonable and appropriate attempts to promote access and opportunity for all students. Excellence in mathematics education requires teachers to have high expectations and strong support for all students. Thus, teachers should expect the best effort from all students, independent of the student's academic status.

Constructivist Teaching and Cooperative Learning

Because educational resilience, the heightened likelihood of success in school, and other life accomplishments despite environmental adversities brought about by early traits, conditions, and experiences (Wang et al., 1994) focuses on students' positive traits, teachers may want to understand the concept of resiliency and to draw upon and implement appropriate interventions to foster resiliency, especially among students at-risk of academic failure students. Professional developments can be an avenue to promote the understanding of resilience issues for preservice and in-service teachers.

Once teachers are aware of resiliency issues, they can promote resiliency in a number of ways. One of the most important ways by which teachers can foster resiliency is to mobilize protective processes (Masten, 1994). Building self-esteem and promoting enjoyment in mathematics learning are important factors that teachers can provide to foster resiliency. A risk-free classroom environment (Krovetz, 1999) that would support self-esteem and satisfaction in mathematics learning would not allow students to feel ashamed or inferior for making mistakes, but instead reward students for effort and progress (Cobb, Yackel, Wood, Wheatley, & Merkel, 1988). To help nonresilient students, who have difficulty doing mathematics, achieve and learn more effectively, teachers should find the students' window of understanding, select material that overlaps with their existing understanding, and then extend beyond it (Vygotsky, 1978). Teachers need to know how to ask questions that reveal what students already understand. If a student has difficulty answering a question or starting a problem, the teacher can ask leading questions to guide the student, with the intent on facilitating thinking instead of seeking the correct answer. Teachers can guide classroom discourse, providing support for developing student thinking, asking leading and nonleading (open-ended) questions (such as Why is the circumference important?), eliciting responses, and probing for interest (Cobb, 1995; Krummheuer, 1995; Wood, 1995; Yackel, 1995). As the teacher begins to understand the thinking of the students, the teacher's beliefs and practices will adjust and change, resulting in more effective student learning.

ACKNOWLEDGMENT

This research was supported in part by a U. S. Department of Education, Office of Educational Research and Improvement grant from the National Center for Research on Education, Diversity, and Excellence. The opinions expressed in this article do not necessarily reflect the position, policy, or endorsement of the granting agency.

REFERENCES

Aldridge, J. M., Fraser, B. J., & Huang, T. C. I. (1998, April). *A cross-national study of perceived classroom environments in Taiwan and Australia*. Paper presented at the annual convention of the American Educational Research Association, San Diego, CA.

Alva, S. A. (1991). Academic invulnerability among Mexican-American students: The importance of protective resources and appraisals. *Hispanic Journal of Behavioral Sciences, 13*, 18–34.

Benard, B. (1995). *Fostering resilience in children*. Urbana, IL: ERIC Clearinghouse on Elementary and Early Childhood Education.

Brown, A. P., & Padrón, Y. N. (2001). *Portraits of fourth- and fifth- grade resilient and non-resilient Latino students*. Paper presented at the annual convention of the American Educational Research Association, Seattle, WA.

Chavez, R. C. (1984). The use of high-inference measures to study classroom climates: A review. *Review of Educational Research, 54*, 237–261.

Cheng, Y. C. (1994). Classroom environment and student affective performance: An effective profile. *Journal of Experimental Education, 62*, 221–239.

Cobb, P. (1995). Mathematical learning and small-group interaction: Four case studies. In H. Bauersfeld (Ed.), *The emergence of mathematical meaning: Interaction in classroom cultures* (pp. 25–129). Mahwah, NJ: Erlbaum.

Cobb, P., Yackel, E., Wood, T., Wheatley, G., & Merkel, G. (1988). Creating a problem-solving atmosphere. *Arithmetic Teacher, 36*, 46–47.

Coleman, J. S., & Hoffer, T. (1987). *Public and private high schools: The impact of communities*. New York: Basic Books.

Dellinger, A. B., Daniel, C. S., Stuhlmann, J., & Ellett, C. D. (1999, January). *Triangulating multiple perspectives on classroom learning environments for disabled students*. Paper presented at the annual meeting of the Southwest Educational Research Association, San Antonio, TX.

Dryden, M., & Fraser, B. J. (1996, April). *Evaluating urban systematic reform using classroom learning environment instruments*. Paper presented at the annual convention of the American Educational Research Association, New York.

Fraser, B. J. (1990). Students' perceptions of their classroom environments. In K. Tobin, J. B. Kahle & B. J. Fraser (Eds.), *Windows into science classrooms: Problems associated with higher-level cognitive learning* (pp. 199–221). Bristol, PA: Falmer.

Fraser, B. J., Anderson, G. J., & Walberg, H. J. (1982). *Assessment of learning environments: Manual for Learning Environment Inventory (LEI) and My Class Inventory (MCI)*. Perth, Australia: Western Australian Institute of Technology.

Fraser, B. J., Fisher, D. L., & McRobbie, C. J. (1996, April). *Development, validation, and use of personal and class forms of a new classroom environment instrument*. Paper presented at the annual convention of the American Educational Research Association, New York.

Fraser, B. J., & O'Brien, P. (1985). Student and teacher perceptions of the environment of elementary school classrooms. *Elementary School Journal, 85*, 567–580.

Grouws, D. A., & Cebulla, K. J. (2000). *Improving student achievement in mathematics* [Online]. International Academy of Education. Retrieved March, 15, 2002, from the World Wide Web at: http://www.ibe.unesco.org/International/Publications/EducationalPractices/EducationalPracticesSeriesPdf/prac04e.pdf

Hardwick, J. M. J. (1996, April). *A three year study of motivation (MMI) and learning environments (ILEQ) as per TAAS scores of high, middle, and low performing students*. Paper presented at the annual convention of the American Educational Research Association, New York.

Huang, S.-Y. L., & Waxman, H. C. (1996, April). *Learning environment differences between high- and low- achieving minority students in urban middle school*. Paper presented at the annual convention of the American Educational Research Association, New York.

Huang, S.-Y. L., & Waxman, H. C. (1997, March). *Classroom behaviors of Asian American students in mathematics*. Paper presented at the annual convention of the American Educational Research Association, Chicago.

Knight, S. L., & Waxman, H. C. (1990). Investigating the effects of the classroom learning environment on students' motivation in social studies. *Journal of Social Studies Research, 14*(1), 1–12.

Krovetz, M. L. (1999). Fostering resiliency. *Thrust for Educational Leadership, 28*(5), 28–31.

Krummheuer, G. (1995). The ethnography of argumentation. In H. Bauersfeld (Ed.), *The emergence of mathematical meaning: Interaction in classroom cultures* (pp. 229–269). Hillsdale, NJ: Erlbaum.

Masten, A. S. (1994). Resilience in individual development: Successful adaptation despite risk and adversity. In M. C. Wang & E. W. Gordon (Eds.), *Educational resilience in inner-city America: Challenges and prospects* (pp. 3–26). Hillsdale: NJ: Erlbaum.

McMillan, J. H., & Reed, D. F. (1994). At-risk students and resiliency: Factors contributing to academic success. *The Clearing House, 67*, 137–140.

Moos, R. H. (1979). *Evaluating educational environments*. San Francisco: Jossey-Bass.

National Association for the Education of Young Children. (1987, July, 1996). *Mission, philosophy, and goals* [Online]. Retrieved February, 14, 2002, from the World Wide Web at: http://www.naeyc.org/about/mission_statement.htm

National Council of Teachers of Mathematics. (2000). *Principles and standards for school mathematics*. Reston, VA: Author.

Noddings, N. (1988, December 7). Schools face crisis in caring. *Education Week*.

Padrón, Y. N., Waxman, H. C., & Huang, S.-Y. L. (1999). Classroom behavior and learning environment differences between resilient and nonresilient elementary school students. *Journal of Education for Students Placed at Risk, 4,* 63–81.

Pierce, C. (1994). Importance of classroom climate for at-risk learners. *Journal of Educational Research, 88,* 37–42.

Rawnsley, D., & Fisher, D. L. (1997). *Using personal forms of a learning environment questionnaire in mathematics education.* Paper presented at the International Conference on Science and Mathematics and Technology Education, Hanoi, Vietnam.

Richardson, V., Casanova, U., Placier, P., & Guilfoyle, K. (1989). *School children at risk.* Philadelphia: Falmer.

Schultz, R. A. (1979). Student importance ratings as an indicator of the structure of actual and ideal sociopsychological climates. *Journal of Educational Psychology, 71,* 827–839.

State Education and Environment Roundtable. (2002, September 12, 1997). *Lifelong Learners: The result of a good education* [Online]. Retrieved February 14, 2002, from the World Wide Web at: http://www.seer.org/pages/lifelern.html

Uguroglu, M. E., & Walberg, H. J. (1986). Predicting achievement and motivation. *Journal of Research and Development in Education, 19*(3), 1–12.

Vygotsky, L. S. (1978). *Mind in society: The development of higher psychological processes.* Cambridge, MA: Harvard University Press.

Wang, M. C., Freiberg, H. J., & Waxman, H. C. (1994). *Case studies of inner-city schools (Interim report).* Philadelphia: National Center on Education in the Inner Cities.

Wang, M. C., Haertel, G. D., & Walberg, H. J. (1993). Toward a knowledge base for school learning. *Review of Educational Research, 63,* 249–294.

Wang, M. C., Haertel, G. D., & Walberg, H. J. (1994). Educational resilience in inner cities. In M. C. Wang & E. W. Gordon (Eds.), *Educational resilience in inner-city America: Challenges and prospects* (pp. 45–72). Hillsdale, NJ: Erlbaum.

Wang, M. C., & Palincscar, A. S. (1989). Teaching students to assume an active role in their learning. In M. C. Reynolds (Ed.), *Knowledge base for the beginning teacher* (pp. 71–84). Oxford: Pergamon.

Waxman, H. C. (1992). Reversing the cycle of educational failure for students in at-risk school environments. In H. C. Waxman, J. W. d. Felix, J. Anderson, & H. P. Baptiste (Eds.), *Students at risk in at-risk schools: Improving environments for learning* (pp. 1–9). Newbury Park, CA: Corwin.

Waxman, H. C., & Huang, S.-Y. L. (1996). Motivation and learning environment differences in inner-city middle school students. *Journal of Educational Research, 90,* 93–102.

Waxman, H. C., & Huang, S.-Y. L. (1997). Classroom instruction and learning environment differences between effective and ineffective urban elementary schools for African American students. *Urban Education, 32,* 7–44.

Waxman, H. C., & Huang, S.-Y. L. (1998). Classroom learning environments in urban elementary, middle, and high schools. *Learning Environments Research, 1,* 95–113.

Waxman, H. C., Huang, S.-Y. L., & Padrón, Y. N. (1997). Motivation and learning environment differences between resilient and nonresilient Latino middle school students. *Hispanic Journal of Behavioral Sciences, 19,* 137–155.

Waxman, H. C., Huang, S.-Y. L., & Wang, M. C. (1997). Investigating the classroom learning environment of resilient and non-resilient students from inner-city elementary schools. *International Journal of Educational Research, 27,* 343–353.

Waxman, H. C., & Padrón, Y. N. (1995). Improving the quality of classroom instruction for students at risk of failure in urban schools. *Peabody Journal of Education, 70*(2), 44–65.

Wood, T. (1995). An emerging practice of teaching. In H. Bauersfeld (Ed.), *The emergence of mathematical meaning: Interaction in classroom cultures* (pp. 203–227). Hillsdale, NJ: Erlbaum.

Yackel, E. (1995). Children's talk in inquiry mathematics classrooms. In H. Bauersfeld (Ed.), *The emergence of mathematical meaning: Interaction in classroom cultures* (pp. 131–161). Hillsdale, NJ: Erlbaum.

CHAPTER 8

THE STUDENT–TEACHER AXIS

Idiosyncratic Credit and Cutting the Slack

Sue McGinty
James Cook University, Australia

In the 1990s I conducted a 2-year project in a Midwestern high school in Illinois. The aim of the research was to uncover some of the patterns of behavior of resilient young women who had stayed in school rather than dropped out. What made these young women different from their peers? This question of resilient behavior had always fascinated me. In the 1980s I taught in remote areas of Australia where I saw young people with many talents and possibilities turn away from education and drop out of school, creating shattered lives often affected by teen pregnancy, drugs, and alcohol. What interested me most were the students who did not do this. They came from similar backgrounds, had similar talents, and yet they persisted with their education and went on to live lives that were productive for themselves and others.

The opportunity to examine this issue in a systematic way came about when I was offered a scholarship to the University of Illinois at Urbana-Champaign. Under the expert tutelage of Alan Peshkin, I began my apprenticeship as a researcher-in-training in a Midwestern high school. Here, I was expected to become immersed in the daily life of the school for a whole year before actually commencing data collection for the project.

By the time I was ready for that phase I was familiar with the school in a way that made acquiring permission to do the research and access to staff and students a natural progression.

After interviewing over 40 young women, five were chosen for in-depth study. They agreed to be part of the project, which was conducted in their senior year of schooling. Each of these young women had lived with stressors such as poverty, family disruption, substance abuse, and antisocial behaviors for the greater part of their young lives—stressors that are usually regarded as nonconducive to school success. Before this research was begun, two of the young women had attempted or threatened suicide; all five were troubled by substance abuse in their immediate families; three were victims of physical abuse; and one was a victim of sexual abuse as a child. Only one described herself as middle class, whereas the others, in their own words, were "on welfare," "very poor," "poor," or "average." Despite these commonly accepted barriers to academic success, these young women excelled in school.

This chapter examines the schooling behavior of the five young women. It begins with a brief outline of each student's school experience, examining the nature of their relationships with teachers. The chapter concludes with an analysis of the student–teacher relationships that enabled students to establish "idiosyncratic credit" and teachers to "cut the slack." (For the full study, see McGinty, 1999.)

THE YOUNG WOMEN

Jackie: Exemplary Teacher Support and Understanding

Jackie came from a family that was engulfed in illness and unemployment. She was the youngest of six children and the only girl. She worked 40 hours a week to support her parents when they didn't have work or were too ill to work. After school she pumped gas at the local gas station from 3:00 PM to midnight most nights. This meant that homework was done after midnight or during school. Jackie often missed the first period of the school day because she was too tired to get to school on time. She had few friends at school and very little social life outside of school.

The protective factors (Garmezy, 1991; Garmezy & Rutter, 1983; Howard, Dryden, & Johnson, 1999) that assisted Jackie in becoming a successful student were found within her stressed family and within the school, among teachers who cut her some slack and in the advanced-level courses, which gave her an opportunity to express her talents as a writer. In her senior year, she used her credit with her teachers to take off more days than any other student in this study—44 full days and an additional 15 partial days—without negative repercussions.

The value Jackie placed on education came from her home, through the influence of her mother, who believed strongly that education was a way to overcome the limitations of social class (Connell, Ashenden, Kessler, & Dowsett, 1982). The support she received from teachers, both emotional and educational (Frame, 1982), upholds McCaslin and Good's (1992) point that structural support can make all the difference in enabling students with potential to make educational progress. There was a connection between Jackie's understandings of success and her methods of achieving it—a strange contradictory mix of independent action and dependency. The meaning she gave to success was "learning more and feeling good about it. And having the teachers positive toward you." Her focus was on the future and the freedom she sought in going to a private college, a place removed from her family (Benard, 1992). While this vision for the future kept her motivated during her studies, it was not realized once she graduated.

Strangely, the very factors that supported Jackie were those that, at the same time, put boundaries and limitations on her success. Her mother's illness kept her away from school for extended periods of time. During this time, however, she engaged in intellectual discussions and read, activities that enabled her to write well and comprehend issues at a level beyond that of most other high school students. Her long hours at the gas station left her little time for extracurricular activities, which were highly regarded by the school and by the prestigious college she aspired to attend. In fact, after completing high school, she enrolled in a liberal arts course at the local state university but withdrew during her sophomore year to take up full-time employment "to support her family."

Alexis: Success Through Identity

Alexis was a tall, thin African American woman who graduated from the school in 1992 with the highest GPA (3.9) of the 16 African American girls in the senior class. Alexis was an outstanding and successful student in many ways, and her vibrant personality and leadership qualities helped give her a prominent public image. Her activities revolved around the presentation of herself as a "leader" of the other African American students, a situation most of the black students were wise to. An intelligent girl but with a great deal of insecurity, Alexis put her energy into high-profile extracurricular activities rather than classwork. Alexis resisted more than any of the other girls in the study, however, being singled out as a successful student.

Alexis's earliest memories of school were of being bussed to school in the third grade. She spoke about being picked out as a student with potential:

> The kids hated me. I tried to get along with them, but then I realized: they don't need me. Anyway, they are not going anywhere now. My mom says I was a perceptive little kid. I ran away once on my tricycle with an empty brown-paper bag. I liked elementary school, and in grade 5 I had a black teacher who paid a lot of attention to me. I guess she did this because I had a lot of potential. I was in school not just to joke and play around. I wanted to do something with my life and not be in the ghetto all my life. I think teachers know just by watching a student—if they do their homework and are not fighting. Basically, they know who wants to be in school and who doesn't. Those who have been in the profession a long time can pick out those students.

Alexis also spoke of an elementary school teacher who knew a great deal about black history, and this impressed her. But what inspired her to learn the most were teachers with "energy." They were the ones who "wanted you to learn, and made you want to learn." In high school, Alexis had the affection and attention of the five African American teachers and several others as well. She said, "What's been good for me? Well, teachers' care. I'm noticed around here basically by most teachers and administrators. I don't know how that came to be."

Alexis was a leader. She was visible as president of the African American Club, cheerleading captain, and a spokesperson for African American students. She was chosen to introduce the Reverend Jesse Jackson, Jr., at a school assembly when he visited the school. She eagerly sought these leadership opportunities, and they were offered by teachers who saw her potential. She also solicited comfort and direction from the African American faculty members who gave her their support. "All my moms at school," she called them. These teachers "get on my case from time to time," she said—and she appreciated it.

But Alexis lamented the fact that there were not more African American teachers in the school. There were 6 out of a faculty of 114: two in PE (male), one in business (male), two in counseling (female), and only one in an academic subject (female). When the end-of-the-year staff cuts were announced, the African American history teacher was the first to go; she had been at the school for 2 years. Alexis was visibly upset when she found out that this teacher would be leaving:

> We need an African American teacher who knows something about our history. They [all students] need to know about our history so that in the end they would say, "I know why African Americans act the way they do." That would stop a lot of the racial slurs and tensions if we knew about each other's

history. We learn about Martin Luther King, but he was not the only one in the civil rights movement. What about Rosa Parks?

Alexis made a link between effective teaching of African American history and the presence of an African American faculty. The same link was made by an African American teacher:

> One of the reasons black students don't do well is that they have no black teachers. A lot of the black kids are not middle class; they are poor. Poor people often don't know how to help themselves, and so they need twice the reinforcement that white students do. When they do not receive that, the lag is great.

In the classes I attended with Alexis, I did not see very much constructive criticism of her work. In fact, she was always praised, and one teacher, when asked to comment on Alexis's abilities, said, "She is not a disruptive student!" Alexis's essays were often on black issues and contained unreferenced statements and generalized, repetitive rhetoric similar in style to political speeches. Her own speech-making style was the same. She said that she was never very good at English and confessed that she read very little. While allowing students the freedom to express themselves is important, the lack of direction and the lack of constructive comments on Alexis's work did leave one wondering why this was so when other students, like Jackie, received detailed critical analysis of their written work. In her final year at school, Alexis received a D in Literature; Jackie, an A. Was the unqualified acceptance of her writing and her rhetoric a racism of ommission?

For Alexis, success was in the recognition given her for making public the issues of the school's African American students. She wanted African Americans to have a greater say in the school and through her own reputation was able to give impetus to that cause. Alexis adopted the "speaking out" strategy identified by Cohen (1996) and discussed extensively by hooks (1989). She was noticed because of her public activities and used this credit to defend students when they were in trouble as well as to promote recognition of African American students and their needs. She advised other students to "get your homework done, and don't fight" as a recipe for success.

Alexis was the first to take a stand against perceived injustices, however, and, like her mother, was an activist. Unlike Fordham and Ogbu's (1986) students, who used a "raceless strategy" to become successful at school, Alexis used her very identification as an African American student leader to bring her success and recognition. She secured approval from teachers and counselors (Davies, 1983; Kerr, 1985; Weis, 1985), although not all of her teachers were convinced of her success.

Alexis had several of the key factors that Kerr (1985) found in the backgrounds of the successful women she studied: a mission in life, guidance and encouragement during adolescence, a refusal to accept the limitations of gender, and an ability to combine roles. The protective factors that enabled Alexis to become a successful student were found within the school. The teachers who gave her the greatest support were the African Americans. But they were few in number, and as Foster (1993) pointed out, "Rarely have African American teachers fared well in unitary school systems" (286).

Alexis sought opportunities to present herself in public, and she was given such opportunities by the school. She participated in speech competitions; she introduced public figures at school assemblies and she gained the attention of members of the administration and the teachers. They expected her to do well, even to the point of overlooking her performance in academics. Interestingly, Alexis was touted as an academically successful student, but the criteria for judging this were not so much her grades as her presence. She had developed a lot of idiosyncratic credit.

Sabrina: Life is an Endless Battle

Sabrina, a special education student since middle school, was a member of the National Honor Society and one of the first young women recommended to this study as a successful student. A special education teacher said, "Sabrina's deficit areas that make her eligible for learning disabilities services are written expression, applying phonics skills in reading, and difficulty with long- and short-term memory and auditory retrieval. She is in the average range intellectually (IQ of 96)."

Sabrina's definition of success was having a GPA of 4.6 achieved at the lowest academic level. In Sabrina's case, the school accepted this as one of the multiple pathways to success. For Sabrina, her teachers, and her family, success meant recognition of achievement, but for her, success also had other connotations: she did not want to be like her parents, her brother, or her sisters who, she said, did not value education. The school's acceptance of her definition of success aided her in gaining her prize. Sabrina achieved her educational goal the night she graduated; graduation was her success, the goal she had set herself. She did this by using the study hall, seeing her teachers as helpers (Davies, 1983; McCaslin & Good 1992; Weis, 1985), asking for help, organizing herself to get good grades (it didn't matter at what level), working hard, and applying determination. She made school her protection and her pathway to success.

Sabrina "did school" (Cohen, 1996). Her methods required her to be passive and not create trouble. This meant that she earned good grades and was described by both teachers and peers as successful. She followed carefully the teachers' prescription for success—"Ask if you need help"—and it worked. She received approval, recommendations, and rewards. Sabrina hated being labeled as a "special education student" and especially disliked its association with "being dumb." Paradoxically, even though the teachers tried to get her to take mainstream classes, she fought for the right to remain in the closely supervised study hall, where she received personalized attention. It was this individual attention that enabled her to learn how to do research and present quality assignments. It also enabled the teachers to take a close interest in her private life and monitor its effects on her schooling. By the time she reached her senior year, she was regarded as an independent learner and no longer required the services of the special education department. The ability to be independent of the support scaffold was the reason teachers recommended Sabrina as a successful student. She also was the teachers' success story.

Jasmine: My Two Personalities

There are close links between Jasmine's immigrant background and what she did to become successful. Her mother wanted her two girls to become successful through education and to make the most of the educational opportunities for women in the United States. Ogbu (1991) said this was typical of immigrants who come to the United States willingly. They wanted to utilize the new opportunities for success. So Jasmine studied long hours in her own room, which she set up as her place of study. She was a perfectionist, a great writer involved in many prominent extracurricular activities.

While Jasmine acknowledged that relationships were important, she didn't value interpersonal skills, such as working in groups, and she avoided relationships with those who were not interested in school. She had a strong need to be liked but was not sure what that meant in terms of reciprocity in relationships. Jasmine's volatile relationship with her mother encouraged her to succeed and, at the same time, prevented her from doing it the way she thought it should be done. She developed an elaborate network that supported the lies she told to her mother in order to do the things she wanted to do.

Jasmine primarily defined success in terms of getting good grades. She loved streaming (the ordering of students according to performance in a particular subject) and being compared with her peers. "That is what urges me to do better—if I can compare myself with others." But Jasmine's accomplishments seemed to exceed the usual explanations of success.

Some of Powell, Farrar, and Cohen's (1985) key experiences of advocacy, selective admissions procedures, restricted curriculum choices, and guidance in the choice of those subjects, together with high-caliber teachers, helped shape a successful school experience for Jasmine. The advocacy was limited to a few teachers and the social worker, even though she did not form warm relationships with them.

Wanting to take part in as many different school activities as possible brought her involvement in groups as diverse as the cheerleading squad and the National Honor Society. By securing leadership positions in clubs and classroom activities, she achieved her goal of becoming a successful student.

Jasmine said that she had no idols. She didn't watch TV or go to the movies very much, and so the people she admired were in books. She explained, "I like to read stories of people who are trying to overcome things in their lives. They make me realize that things in your life don't matter as much—I mean things in your life do influence you, but the one thing that can really let you succeed is yourself."

Jasmine was oblivious to structural constraints and blamed herself when she was not recognized or rewarded for her efforts (McCarthy, 1993). She was not a popular student with teachers because she did not seek the warm relationships that many other successful students fostered (Davies, 1983; Weis, 1985). She expected to be acknowledged and praised for her hard work and her contribution to the school. Jasmine couldn't understand why her hard work didn't stand on its own merits. She struggled to get teachers to cut the slack for her because she had not established idiosyncratic credit to the same degree as other students.

Xia: Brilliant but Erratic

Xia was recommended as successful by teachers and students. She had been one of the leading characters in the school drama and musical productions the previous year. At school, she was involved in numerous extracurricular activities: she was a peer counselor and a member of the Thespians, the school choir, the National Honor Society, the staff of the school literary magazine, and the staff of the yearbook. She was also a member of a youth advisory board at a local drug and alcohol center, and she worked two nights a week and one day on the weekend at a local restaurant. Xia had a GPA of 4.6, and she ranked in the 99th percentile in all areas on the national standardized tests, which she had taken each year that she was in high school. Her aptitude score was 141, with 100 being the mean.

Xia's notions of success were exemplified by her outstanding performances onstage, her ability to write and communicate effectively, and by the teachers and students who thought of her as a success. She often spoke of school as a means to an end. Xia sought and received counseling from the school social worker; she was a public figure, like Alexis, and was well-known around the school. She circumvented her problems with the school, for example, by auditioning for and being accepted by a community theater. She went elsewhere to get what she wanted, and that was to act. Xia bypassed obstacles preventing her from getting where she wanted to go—to a liberal arts college specializing in theater. She did not do her detentions after school, and she got away with it.

Contrary to Werner's (1989) finding that just being at school is a protective factor, Xia skipped a lot of school to do her work at home and to visit with her friends who were not in school. Xia was very much influenced by her close circle of friends, who were strong believers in the philosophy of "fulfillment of the whole person," and this included caring for other people, which she did as a peer counselor. Her extended family gave her support in the form of both financial aid and encouragement.

Xia tapped into the politics of the school very well. She established her credit with teachers by scoring well on standardized tests and performing brilliantly on stage. They were prepared to give her a lot of liberty because of her perceived successes. Xia was a calculating manipulator of the system, and this worked very well for her. There was a lot of tolerance of her behavior on the part of the school. But toward the end of the school year, this tolerance wore thin.

ESTABLISHING IDIOSYNCRATIC CREDIT

What each of these young women did at school was to build idiosyncratic credit from their freshman year on. By building idiosyncratic credit, I mean that they acted in ways that later allowed them to deviate from the norm and still be accepted by teachers and administrators. They showed, over a period of time, that they were capable of doing good work, thereby building up their teachers' high expectations of them. As they began to behave in ways that deviated from the norm, their behavior was accepted or ignored because of the credit they had acquired earlier. By the time they were seniors, they could afford to be a little different, even outrageously different, and get away with it.

Each of these young women had established enough idiosyncratic credit to last for some time. The fact that they could bend the rules by handing in assignments late or being absent and not get into trouble for it indicated that teachers and administrators perceived them as successful and therefore accepted their behavior. Acceptance of deviance was a system support for success.

One prominent example of idiosyncratic behavior is absence from school. Interestingly, most but not all of these students' absences were excused. That meant that a parent or a grandparent had called the school to say the young woman was ill or otherwise legitimately absent. A lot of this absence stemmed from involvement in extracurricular activities (for Xia, Jasmine, and Alexis), or counseling either for themselves or as part of the peer-counseling group (for Xia, Jasmine, and Alexis), and some of it stemmed from their own or their family members' illness (for Jackie, Sabrina, and Xia). Being absent from school or from class often created tensions between the young women and their teachers. Their poor attendance record and lack of responsibility in completing group work on time caused frustration for teachers and classmates, yet they still got good grades. The school's two attendance secretaries reviewed the five young women's records and made a comparison with the "average absences for most students." All the young women were categorized as being absent a lot more often than the average student, who stayed away approximately 4–5 full days and another 8–10 partial days per year. In contrast, the top five female graduates had very low absentee rates.

Table 8.1 shows the absences for the five young women and the average student. When the teachers were asked why these young women were allowed so many absences, their answers invariably referred to the fact that the absences were excused and so they couldn't do anything about it. The reasons the young women gave for their absences centered on their activities elsewhere: Jackie stayed home to look after her mother; Jasmine and Alexis attended other school-related functions, including counseling sessions; Xia was first involved in extracurricular programs, such as peer counseling, and second, making time for herself and her out-of-school friends.

Table 8.1. Days Absent from School

Student	Full Days	Partial Days	Total
Jackie	44	15	59/178
Alexis	12	25	37/178
Sabrina	8	15	23/89*
Jasmine	2	31	33/178
Xia	27	60	87/178
Average student	4–5	8–10	12–15/178

*First semester only.

None of the young women served a detention in the year of this study. All of this required the cooperation of the administration, and generally the young women were adept in gaining that. They were manipulators of the system. Many other students would not have been able to gain this cooperation. Manipulation of adults or the ability to find and gain adult supporters was a feature of these young women's lives.

One reason these young women received seemingly unqualified support from teachers was that they were considered to be mature. Each of them was mature beyond her years. All of them viewed themselves as more mature than their peers and were regarded by teachers and peers as being more mature. For teachers, maturity was the ability to relate to adults; it was being known as "sensible." Typical of comments by teachers is one made about Jackie. "Jackie is a very complex young lady....maturity-wise, she is beyond most of the students in [AP English]." A teacher said about Alexis, "The other girls in the cheerleading squad are not like her. They are high school girls, whereas Alexis is much more able to relate to those older than her. I think she is more mature and sensible."

These young women also liked the teachers and administrators to treat them as adults. They responded favorably when they received respect, which they interpreted as being treated as an adult. When they were treated as children at school, they actively tried to reframe the situation to their own liking, sat passively, or skipped class. Perceiving themselves to be adult, mature, and responsible for their own decisions enabled them to work the school system to their advantage.

For the young women, being adult and mature meant making decisions about which school regulations to follow without being unduly worried by what the school authorities thought of their behavior. Xia reacted to an administrator who called her out of class to discuss her absenteeism by commenting, "I could just shoot that administrator; he's always annoying me. He is irrational. Obstacles need to be taken care of if they are in the way of a goal, so nothing will stop me." Xia's attitude was to place herself outside the school rules, particularly with regard to attendance; she created the perception of herself as beyond school rules.

Of the five young women, Sabrina was the only one who openly admitted that she didn't want to cause trouble for the faculty. She wanted the teachers to maintain their positive attitude toward her, and she did this by being compliant. Sabrina accepted the teachers' perception of her as a successful student.

Although teachers agreed that these young women took advantage of opportunities, they did not always agree that the decisions they made were beneficial to their education, especially with regard to absenteeism. Nonetheless, having teachers whose attitude toward them was positive was one of their recipes for success.

In summary, it was responsiveness to opportunity that made these young women successful. They took control of their own learning situations, used opportunities for leadership as a means to being seen as successful, channeled their stress and anger into schooling, and focused on perfection while ignoring their limitations, thus pushing themselves on to success. They were supported by establishing idiosyncratic credit, which enabled them to deviate from expected norms without retribution.

CUTTING THE SLACK

There was an academic elitism in operation at school. From this academic environment come most of the prizes meted out at Awards Night, the possibility of attending a prestigious college, and leadership positions in the school. In tapping into the learning environment, the young women bought into the "special" side of the school (Powell, Farrar, & Cohen, 1985). They selected classes whose teachers they knew brought the curriculum alive, they made friends with teachers who "cut the slack" for them, they used the counseling services, and they seized opportunities for leadership in class and in extracurricular activities. They uncovered the caring side (Noddings, 1984, 1988) of the school, which was made up of people who understood and worked with the realities of these young women's lives. Some faculty members moved beyond what was required of them in order to support and help in any way they could. These caring people were very important to the success of the young women in this study. Two significant ways in which staff members manifested the caring side of the school were in cutting the slack for students and in providing counseling.

Cutting the slack occurs when a teacher bends the rules for a student whom the teacher knows is genuinely disadvantaged by school rules and regulations. This notion relates to and is an extension of idiosyncratic credit. There was a tacit belief among some staff members that "a little difference is delightful." Unspoken permissions, even if they went along with frustrations, were granted to students so they could control their lives, as long as these prerequisites did not disturb the general body of students.

What do teachers do when a student has to work until midnight and comes to school very tired with work unfinished? Jackie was the most obvious example of a student whose teacher cut the slack for her during the first period of each day when she was meant to be a teaching assistant. She was often absent and yet the teacher, knowing that she had worked until midnight the previous night, did not mark her absent. Other teachers also bent the rules in accepting late assignments from her. Although detentions were the usual punishment for those who broke the rules, in Jackie's case tardies and undone homework assignments were just not investigated.

When a student found a teacher who understood the stressors in her life and adapted the program accordingly, this made for success. Success for the young women in this study meant seeking out teachers who cut the slack for them. The teachers allowed these young women a lot of freedom to take control in these situations even if that meant the teachers risked being censured by the administration. Students who did not have the capacity to form trusting relationships that led to the slack being cut found it difficult to succeed at school.

For example, Cassie, a student who left the school because of pregnancy, found that the ability to establish good relationships with teachers who would cut the slack for her was missing. After having been away for 3 months for the birth of her baby, Cassie described her experience of returning to school as a "wall of silence." The teachers and administrators referred to her as having committed "academic suicide." It seemed that the teachers would cut the slack only for those they saw as deserving, those whose stress circumstances were "beyond their control." The five young women in this study fell conveniently into this category. It was obvious, however, that when Xia began taking too many days off of her own volition, the slack was not taken up as enthusiastically as it had been before. Teachers often said to me that they would be willing to make concessions for students who let them know their circumstances. But because they didn't know what Xia's problems were, they felt their "hands were tied."

Part of this "not knowing" was the result of an administrative procedure in that teachers would not automatically be told by the attendance office the reason for an absence; they had to find out themselves. If students were "excused," meaning they were listed as having a legitimate reason for their absence, the teacher was not required to take action. If the students were "unexcused," meaning their absence was not authorized, then the teachers had some power to intervene. For the young women in this study, tapping into the learning environment meant establishing relationships with teachers who would make allowances for deviance and with peers who didn't interfere with academic success.

IMPLICATIONS FOR TEACHERS AND STUDENTS

The politics of success was embodied in the teachers' and the administrators' values, which they expressed in what they did and did not do in areas that affected the students. Success was also affected by the students' responses to the school. If the students learned what the school valued and if they knew how to make that knowledge work for them, then they would be successful. If they did not learn the system, they failed or were ignored.

One way of gaining respect was by being seen as having ability, and having ability was demonstrated by joining clubs, taking AP classes, and doing high-quality work. Those who gained the respect of the teachers did not get many detentions or suspensions. The young women's idiosyncratic behavior was generously tolerated. Knowing what was acceptable, gaining the teachers' respect, and being viewed positively were part of being successful. Also part of being successful was performing in public, for example, by acting in a play or speaking before a group. The young women who used this method to achieve success were reinforced in their beliefs by the accolades they received. Again, teachers respected ability. By gaining a teacher's respect for her ability, a student could gain respectability. "Having the teachers positive toward you was a factor in success," said Jackie.

A further political act was the young women's relationships with their teachers and peers, which were protective of academic achievement. The young women associated with and learned from those teachers who related to them as "friends" (Jackie), as "moms" (Alexis), as "people I respect" (Xia), as "someone you can touch base with" (Jasmine), as "helpers" (Sabrina). All of the young women, except Jackie, indicated that their relationship with their teachers were different from those with their parents. The ones with their teachers were more adult. They were also more profitable in terms of academic success, although generally they were not deep attachments of the mentoring type. Alexis and Xia did form a trusting and close relationship with one of the counselors. Jasmine used the same counselor on many occasions but never referred to her as a friend.

It would seem that these young women cast their teachers in the role of provider. They wanted them to provide intellectual help, to pass on to them the skills they did not already have, to show them how to write and think. They saw this as the teachers' duty. These expectations were generally accompanied by appreciation when the expectations were met: the young women expressed gratitude toward and satisfaction with teachers who did their jobs effectively—but they were quick to criticize those who did not. They stayed away more often from classes they thought were not intellectually stimulating or beneficial. When a teacher showed a personal interest in them, they reciprocated by making an extra effort in class and voluntarily explaining their absences. There was no doubt that these young women sought out teachers with whom they could establish good working relationships, although there was variation in their approaches. That is, the young women approached the teachers variously as friends, helpers, persons to touch base with, mothers, or persons to respect.

Is it a surprise that these smart young women sound like any other smart young women? The differences between them and other smart young women lie not in their expectations but in how they went about becoming successful at school. It is evident from the many comments by their teachers that course requirements would be adjusted if the teachers knew the circumstances of their students' lives. There is a fine line, however, between adjusting course requirements and lowering standards. Most teachers would deny that they were lowering standards when they adjusted requirements, and these young women wanted to achieve just like the others; they did not want their teachers to lower their standards so that they could achieve.

The students in this study placed emphasis on grades, on having teachers who were positive toward them, on working hard themselves, on doing their best, and these qualities reflected what they thought success was. What differentiated them from the students in the comparison studies was not just how these students went about becoming successful, but the fact that certain factors in their lives necessitated them using a different route to achieve success. And what differentiated them from others who did not achieve success were having extra responsibilities at home, having focus, having the ability to build idiosyncratic credit, and having teachers who cut the slack. They were tough, resilient young women. Their resilience came from a combination of past and present strengths, protective factors, and their hopes for themselves in the future. What they aspired to differed little from what many other successful, smart students aspire to. What was different was that they went about becoming successful in ways that were different from the ways of those who did not have multiple stressors in their lives. The creation of different pathways to success is important to understand. The more that diversity is recognized, understood, and promoted, the more students will succeed.

What some teachers and administrators did for these young women was caringly "get in their faces" to show what was possible; critique their work (Goldenberg, 1992), except in Alexis's case; offer opportunities; and push for their continued application. Whereas some young people might reject this attention, these young women demanded it, sought it, and engaged their teachers in a way that made them respond to them. Why were they like that? Because of who they were: their biographies show significant events in their lives that made them strong, demanding people. They set their sights on the future and focused on getting there. The school reacted positively to that sort of focus.

ACKNOWLEDGMENT

I would like to thank Peter Lang Publishers who gave permission to use selected paragraphs from McGinty (1999).

REFERENCES

Benard, B. (1992). Fostering resiliency in kids: Protective factors in the family, school, and community. *Prevention Forum, 12*, 1–16.

Cohen, J. (1996). *Girls in the middle: Working to succeed in school.* Washington, DC: American Association of University Women Educational Foundation.

Connell, R. W., Ashenden, D. J., Kessler, S., & Dowsett, G. W. (1982). *Making the difference: Schools, families, and social division.* Sydney: Allen & Unwin.

Davies, L. (1983). Gender, resistence and power. In . S. Walker & L. Barton (Eds.), *Gender, class and education* (pp. 39–52). Barcombe, UK: Falmer.

Fordham, S., & Ogbu, J. (1986). Black students' school success: Coping with the burden of acting white. *Urban Review, 18,* 176–205.

Foster, M. (1993). Resisting racism: Personal testimonies of African American teachers. In L. Weis & M. Fine (Eds.), *Beyond silenced voices: Class, race, and gender in United States schools* (pp. 273–288). Buffalo: State University of New York Press.

Frame, J. (1982). *To the Is-land: An autobiography* (Vol. 1). Auckland: Random Century New Zealand.

Garmezy, N. (1991). Resiliency and vulnerability to adverse developmental outcomes associated with poverty. *American Behavioural Scientist, 34,* 416–430.

Garmezy, N., & Rutter, M. (1983, November). How, why do some kids flourish against all odds? *Behavior Today,* pp. 5–7.

Goldenberg, C. (1992). The limits of expectations: A case for case knowledge about teacher expectancy effects. *American Educational Research Journal, 29,* 517–544.

hooks, b. (1989). *Talking back: Thinking feminist, thinking black.* Boston: South End Press.

Howard, S., Dryden, J., & Johnson, B (1999). Childhood resilience: Review and critique of the literature. *Oxford Review of Education, 25,* 307–323.

Howard, S., & Johnson, B. (2000a). Resilient and non-resilient behaviour in adolescents. *Australian Institute of Criminology: Trends and issues in crime and criminal justice,* No. 183.

Howard, S., & Johnson, B. (2000b). What makes the difference? Children and teachers talk about resilient outcomes for students at risk. *Educational Studies, 26,* 321–327.

Kerr, B. A. (1985). *Smart girls, gifted women.* Columbus: OH: Psychology Publishing.

McCarthy, C. (1993). Beyond the poverty of theory in race relations: Nonsynchrony and social difference in education. In L. Weis & M. Fine (Eds.), *Beyond silenced voices: Class, race, and gender in United States schools* (pp. 325–346). Buffalo, NY: State University of New York Press.

McCaslin, M., & Good, T. L. (1992). Compliant cognition: The misalliance of management and instructional goals in current school reform. *Educational Research 21,* 4–17.

McGinty, S. (1999). *Resilience, gender and success at school.* New York: Peter Lang.

Noddings, N. (1984). *Caring: A feminine approach to ethics and moral education.* Berkley, CA: University of California Press.

Noddings, N. (1988, December 7). Schools face crisis in caring. *Education Week,* pp. 34–36.

Ogbu, J. (1991, April). *Cultural diversity and children's learning.* Paper presented at the annual meeting of the American Educational Research Association, Chicago.

Powell, A., Farrar, E, & Cohen, D. (1985). *The shopping mall high school: Winners and losers in the educational marketplace.* Boston: Houghton Mifflin.

Rutter, M., Maughan, B., Mortimore P., & Ouston, J., (1979). *Fifteen thousand hours: Secondary schools and their effects on children.* Cambridge, MA: Harvard University Press.

Weis, L. (1985). *Between two worlds.* Boston: Routledge & Kegan Paul.

Werner, E. (1989). High risk children in young adulthood: A longitudinal study from birth to 32 years. *American Journal of Orthopsychiatry 59,* 72–81.

CHAPTER 9

THE RELATIONS OF TEACHER EDUCATION STUDENTS' RESILIENCY, WORK MOTIVATION, AND SCHOOL-LEVEL RESILIENCE

Jon P. Gray
Lamar University

Schools today are faced with the difficult challenge of ensuring success for all students as well as fostering an environment in which teachers are committed to lifelong learning. University teacher education certification programs, therefore, are challenged with providing adequate preparation for preservice teachers who will take their places in meeting the challenges of the educational world.

Many university teacher education preservice programs are field based, with students spending many hours in school classrooms working with school faculty and students causing preservice teacher education students to be confronted earlier with the stresses associated with teaching. How to cope with stresses becomes an important task for the teacher education program. The psychological construct of resilience may provide a means for identifying why some preservice teachers not only survive but also succeed under stressful situations. A resilient person is one who has found a way to overcome or compensate for a problem that occurs; or a resilient person has the inner strength that will enable him/her to "bounce back" from the problems that would seem to doom the individual to certain failure (Brodkin & Coleman, 1996). Therefore, fostering educator resiliency should be a priority if educators want to have a positive influence on students and communities. Moreover, educators who are not resilient are most likely to be dissatisfied, frustrated, and poor role models for their students (Milstein & Henry, 2000). If an individual teacher's resiliency relates to other factors such as work motivation and school-level resilience, then valuable information may be provided for teacher educators and future teacher education programs.

Professors in teacher preparation programs struggle with balancing educational theory and the practical implications of teaching as a career. Veenman (1984) found that disciplining undesirable behaviors, motivating students, interacting with parents, getting along with colleagues, and meeting the needs of individual students are important concerns of prospective teachers. In helping new teachers cope with these problems, teacher preparation programs should prepare students with possible solutions. The teacher education students' resiliency level may be a positive characteristic that enhances their ability to deal with the difficulties of teaching and to reach constructive solutions for meeting student needs. Therefore, building individual resiliency in prospective teachers needs to be a central focal point of teacher preparation programs.

A better understanding of the contribution of resilience in schools may lead to the understanding of individual resiliency. Logically, teacher education students who possess high levels of work motivation and have positive perceptions of school resiliency will have an increased ability to deal with stress. Hence, the ability of teacher education students to meet the challenges of student teaching and become increasingly concerned with student needs rather than their own survival is important for teacher education programs as well as the schools they serve.

RESILIENCY

Resilience has been used to describe three major categories of phenomena in the psychological literature (Masten, Best, & Garmezy, 1990): (1) people from high-risk groups who have a better than expected outcome; (2) studies of individual differences in recovery from trauma; and (3) a positive adaptation despite stressful experiences. The latter resilience phenomenon may occur in student teaching when a student teacher encounters the stressful experiences associated with the transition from student to teacher. Synonymous terms have been used in describing resilient individuals.

"Hardy," "invulnerable," and "invincible" are terms that have been used to describe resilient characteristics (Wolin & Wolin, 1993). The common thread associated with the use of these terms is the focus on positive qualities or outcomes rather than on negative concerns. "Hardiness" has typically been the preferred term in the adult literature while "resilience" is the most accepted term associated with the literature that focuses on children, school-age youth, and adolescents; however, "resilience" is becoming the preferred term in the adult literature because resilience "best captures the active process of self-righting and growth" (Higgins, 1994, p. 1).

WORK MOTIVATION

The level of relative satisfaction that is obtained from an occupation may stimulate and motivate further work. Teachers come to teaching and stay in teaching because of different motives. The difference in individual motives to teach may be based on the needs of that particular person. Maslow's (1970) hierarchy of needs—physiological, safety, belongingness, self-esteem, and self-actualization—are based on human desires that are never-ceasing, and he contends that once the basic physiological needs are met, other psychological needs become important. Herzberg (1968) believed that satisfactory work motivation is closely tied to Maslow's fourth (ego) and fifth (self-actualization) levels of needs, where achievement, responsibility, recognition for achievement, work itself, and personal growth are all motivating factors comprising the concept of work motivation. Some researchers feel that these factors can contribute to an effective teacher in the workplace (Corothers, 1991; Parker, 1995; Russo, 1995). That is, when preservice teachers' basic needs are met, they may be motivated toward self-actualization, and ultimately may be more effective in the classroom. Wendt, Ward, and Jackson (1980) concurred that teachers who are more self-actualized are more concerned with students' needs. Saffici (1996) attempted to find connections between work motivation, hardiness, efficacy, and locus of control. Using 149 prospective teachers who were student teaching, Saffici found that work motivation, hardiness, and personal and teacher efficacy scores were positively ($p < .05$) related. He further explained that locus of control was positively linked to work motivation.

SCHOOL RESILIENCY

In the present study, school resiliency is defined simply as preservice teachers' perceptions of relationships associated with the work environment. In her review of school climate research, Anderson (1982) described school environment as a general "we-feeling" among staff members. Thus, preservice teachers who are a part of a field-based teacher education program become a part of the school staff and experience positive and/or negative feelings about the environment.

Although some protective factors are developed individually (such as personality), many can be learned (such as self-esteem). The aim of the resiliency-building literature is to build in enough factors that protect the individual and offset the impact of stressful life events. When the balance of protective factors is favorable over stressful life events, adaptation or resiliency is the outcome.

The organizational atmosphere or climate of the school, which is based on the overall school power structure and behavioral norms practiced by administrators and faculty, plays a major source of teacher alienation, burnout, and dissatisfaction. Ellis (1988) found that a good school climate is associated with teacher perceptions that teachers can trust their principal, get help when they need it, are respected professionals, and are involved in the decision-making process. Teachers must devote time to develop professional relationships with other staffs in order to build resilient schools (Krovetz, 1999). Milstein and Henry (2000) contend that the environments in which teachers' work can significantly affect resiliency and schools can change in ways that promote resiliency and meet the changing needs of students and faculty.

Individuals who express ego status and self-actualization needs have a greater potential for effective work than those who express basic and safety needs (Wendt et al., 1980). Teachers' work motivation may actually be a part of being resilient. Resiliency studies offer evidence of what practitioners have long suspected and hoped; more than any institution except the family, schools can provide the environment and conditions that foster resiliency in today's youth and tomorrow's adults (Henderson & Milstein, 1996). The purpose of this study is to determine if there is a relation between individual resiliency, work motivation, and school resiliency in teacher education students.

METHOD

Participants

Teacher education students ($N = 159$) from a large southwestern university were the participants in this study. Participants included those in elementary, secondary, and all-level programs from all major disciplines including those pursuing bachelor's degrees as well as those who have already attained degrees in other fields. The majority of the teacher education students were white and Hispanic, among which 87% were female and 13% were male. The majority of the participants were undergraduate preservice teachers seeking elementary certification and most of them were single and without children. In general, the participants ranged from 20 to 57 years of age ($M = 28.0$, $SD = 7.50$), had a favorable perception of the teacher education program (with about 80% describing their program as excellent or good), and responded that they were likely to become teachers.

Instruments

The Dispositional Resiliency Scale. The short form (30 items) of the Dispositional Resilience Scale (DRS), a 4-point Likert Scale, was selected as a measure for resiliency because it assesses the presence of control, commitment, and challenge tendencies. These resilient tendencies are described as a sense of personal *control* in handling life events, *commitment* to the people and activities in which one is involved, and perceiving change as a *challenge* (Bartone, Ursano, Wright, & Ingraham, 1989). For responses ranging from 1 (*not at all true*) to 4 (*completely true*), the sum of these items yields a composite resiliency score with a minimum possible score of 30 and a maximum possible score of 120. The internal consistency reliability coefficient of the DRS typically ranges from .78 to .94 (Bartone et al., 1989) for the total resiliency score.

The Work Motivation Inventory. Hall and Williams (1973) developed the Work Motivation Inventory (WMI) from Maslow's hierarchy of needs and Herzberg's theories of motivation. Herzberg's maintenance needs toward work are similar to Maslow's basic and safety needs. The motivator needs regarding work coincide with the ego and self-actualization needs of Maslow's hierarchy. There are 24 items in each need system of the instrument. In a test–retest with the original sample of business executives, the reliability was found to be .70 (Wendt, 1979). The validity coefficient with the California Psychological Inventory ($n = 61$) was found to be .70 ($p < .01$). A ratio score was created from the mean scores to reflect an individual's tendency toward motivator-seeking as opposed to one's tendency toward maintenance-seeking. The tendency was expressed as the following ratio:

$$WMR = \frac{Ego + Self\text{-}Actualization}{Basic + Safety} \text{ or } \frac{Motivator}{Maintenance}$$

The Social Support Scale. The Social Support Scale, adapted from the Work Relationship Index (Billings & Moos, 1982), is the best measure of school resilience because it represents the environmental relationships in which teachers function, and it has been found to be reliable with preservice teachers (Thomson, 1993). A 5-point Likert scale ranging from 1 (*strongly disagree*) to 5 (*strongly agree*) is comprised of three subscales originally developed for the larger Work Environment Scale (Insel & Moos, 1974). Each subscale contains nine items. These subscales measure *Involvement,* or the extent to which employees are concerned about and committed to their job; *Peer Cohesion,* or how friendly and supportive employees are to each other; and *Supervisor Support,* or the extent to which management is supportive of employees and encourages employees to be supportive of each other. Insel and Moos (1974) found the internal consistency reliabilities of the involvement, peer cohesion, and supervisor support subscales to be .84, .69, and .77, respectively. Pierce and Molloy (1990) found the total scale reliability to be .89. Higher scores on the Work Environment Scale are interpreted to indicate higher levels of social support (from peers and supervisors) that one perceives in the school environment.

Procedures

Approved by the Human Subjects Committee at a university in the southwestern region of the United States, this study included the Dispositional Resiliency Scale, the Work Motivation Inventory, and the Social Support Scale, which were administered during student teacher seminars and emergency certification class meetings conducted on and off campus. Data were collected at the completion of the preservice teaching semester when all participants had sufficient exposure to school conditions and interactions as a teacher.

RESULTS

Instrument Reliabilities

The overall reliability of the DRS was .73, which is consistent with Bartone and colleagues' (1989) earlier estimate. The subscale reliabilities for control, commitment, and challenge were less impressive at .52, .62, and .62, respectively. Items 5, 13, and 19 were not used in the analysis to improve the overall reliability of the DRS. The total resiliency score was used in the regression analyses to ensure that the findings were indeed reliable. Reliability for the Social Support Scale (school resilience) was .91, with subscale reliabilities of .84, .71, and .83 for involvement, peer cohesion, and administrator support, respectively. Items 13 and 18 were omitted from the analysis to improve the reliability for the peer cohesion subscale and the total school resilience construct. Reliabilities for the school resilience measure were slightly higher than that of Pierce and Molloy (1990). The test–retest revealed a reliability of .80 for WMI, which was higher than that of Wendt (1979). A convenience sample of 16 participants completed the WMI two weeks after the initial administration of the instrument. The convenience sample was randomly selected from a prestudent teaching methodology class as well as a student teaching seminar group.

Causal Comparative Data

Analysis of variance (ANOVA) was used to determine if significant differences of individual teacher resilience existed between ethnicity (white and nonwhite), grade level (elementary and secondary/all-level), and status (pre–student teaching, student teaching, and emergency certification) in the participant sample. Not all questions were answered because six participants chose not to complete the ethnicity portion of the demographic information.

An examination of the $2 \times 2 \times 3$ factorial ANOVA found no significant main effects for ethnicity (E), grade level (L), or status (S) on individual teacher resiliency. Furthermore, there were no other significant interactions found at any level. It should be noted that teacher education students' resiliency and the status of the teacher education student approached being significant ($p = .055$). Student teachers scored highest ($M = 92.3$) on resiliency, while emergency certification students had the lowest ($M = 89.5$) resiliency scores. Table 9.1 reports the results of the factorial ANOVA on the differences in individual teacher resiliency by ethnicity, grade level of certification, and status.

Table 9.1. Differences in Individual Teacher Resiliency by Ethnicity, Grade Level of Certification, and Teacher Education Student Status

Source of Variation	df	SS	MS	F	p
Ethnicity	1	58.98	59.98	1.05	.31
Grade level	1	135.55	135.55	2.41	.12
Status	2	332.60	166.30	2.96	.06
E × S	2	52.20	26.10	.46	.63
L × S	2	54.64	27.32	.49	.62
E × L × S	2	192.57	96.29	1.71	.18
Within	142	7982.13	56.21		

*$p < .05$

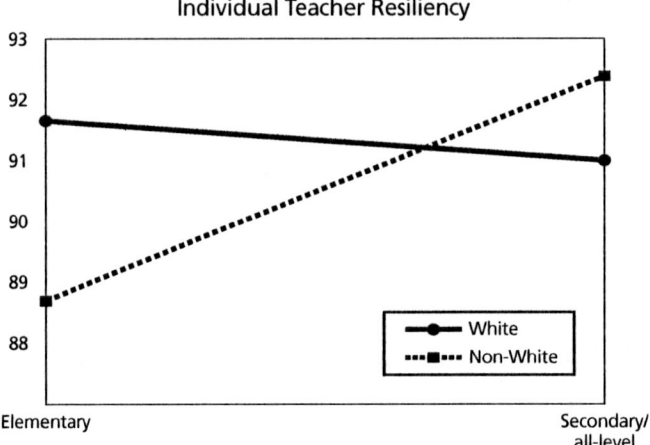

Figure 9.1. Interaction between ethnicity and grade level on individual teacher resiliency.

There was, however, a significant interaction between teacher education students' ethnicity and the grade level of certification on individual teacher resiliency ($p < .05$). White elementary teacher education students scored higher ($M = 91.8$) than white secondary/all-level teacher education students ($M = 91.0$) on resiliency, while nonwhite secondary/all-level teacher education students scored higher ($M = 92.3$) than nonwhite elementary teacher education students ($M = 88.6$) on resiliency. Figure 9.1 illustrates the interaction of ethnicity and grade level on individual teacher resiliency.

Descriptive Statistics

Table 9.2 reported that the descriptive statistics including minimum, maximum, mean, and standard deviations were calculated for total individual resiliency, work motivation, and total school resilience. The individual resiliency subscales of control, commitment, and challenge were also included as well as the school resilience subscales of involvement, peer cohesion, and administrator support. In the examination of descriptive statistics the participants scored higher on the commitment domain than on control, and challenge. The work motivation scores consisted of both maintenance and motivator seekers. The high work motivation ratio indicated a sample that leaned toward motivator seeking more than maintenance. Descriptive data also revealed that the participants scored highest on involvement on the school resilience measure. The total school resilience scores indicated participants that had both low and high perceptions of school resilience.

Table 9.2. Descriptive Statistics for Scales

Variable	M	SD	Min	Max
Resiliency	90.91	7.57	71.00	124.00
Control	31.17	3.03	23.00	39.00
Commitment	32.71	3.47	22.00	40.00
Challenge	26.94	3.94	19.00	54.00
Work Motivation	1.63	.80	.44	4.75
School Resilience	96.10	16.52	39.00	131.00
Involvement	33.43	6.37	12.00	45.00
Peer Cohesion	31.39	5.60	14.00	55.00
Admin. Support	31.33	6.40	9.00	45.00

Intercorrelation Analysis

In order to determine if the variables were measuring different constructs, intercorrelations among variables were examined. All total score and subscale score correlations of individual resiliency, work motivation, and school resilience were reported in Table 9.3.

Table 9.3. Intercorrelation Matrix

	CO	CM	CH	TR	WM	IN	PC	AS	SR
CO	1.000								
CM	.472**	1.000							
CH	.217**	.227**	1.000						
TR	.720**	.758**	.710**	1.000					
WM	.257**	.269**	.294**	.390**	1.000				
IN	−.044	.216**	.199*	.185*	.037	1.000			
PC	−.063	.192*	.204*	.178*	.042	.728**	1.000		
AS	−.051	.221**	.107*	.141*	−.039	.636**	.595**	1.000	
SR	−.055	.237**	.191*	.191*	.009	.901**	.876**	.854**	1.000

Note: CO, Control (subscale); CM, Commitment (subscale); CH, Challenge (subscale); TR, Resiliency (total score); WM, Work Motivation (work motivation ratio); In, Involvement (subscale); PC, Peer Cohesion (subscale); AS, Administrator Support (subscale); SR, School Resilience (total score).
*$p < .05$, **$p < .01$

In general, the individual resiliency subscales of commitment and challenge had a significantly low positive correlation with school resilience, and commitment, challenge, and control have a significantly low positive correlation with work motivation. The school resilience subscales of involvement and peer cohesion had a significantly low positive correlation with individual resiliency. Work motivation also had a significantly moderate correlation with individual resiliency. The school resilience subscales were more correlated with one another than the individual resiliency subscales. The school resilience subscales had moderate to high significant positive correlations while the individual resiliency subscales had low to moderate significant positive correlations with one another.

Multiple Regression Analysis

Multiple regression analysis was used to examine the total variance accounted for by work motivation and school resilience as a total construct on teacher education students' resiliency. Only the work motivation ratio and the total school resilience score were entered as independent variables in this regression analysis. The results are reported in Table 9.4.

Table 9.4. The Influence of Work Motivation and School Resilience on Individual Resilience

Variable	b-weight	Std.Err.	Beta	t	p	Tol.
Work Mot.	3.68	.72	.38	5.10	.00	1.00
School Res.	.09	.03	.19	2.56	.01	1.00

(R^2 =. 185; F = 16.39; p = .0001)

The results indicate that both work motivation and school resilience significantly influenced individual resiliency. Work motivation (β = .38, p < 0.01) and school resilience (β = .19, p < 0.05) accounted for 19% of the variance in teacher education students' resiliency. Work motivation influenced teacher education students' resiliency by accounting for 14% of the variance while teacher education students' perception of school resilience accounted for 5% of the variance in teacher education students' resiliency. Checks for multicollinearity revealed that assumptions were not violated. The high tolerance levels indicated constructs that are measuring different areas. It was hypothesized that there would be a positive relation between individual resiliency, work motivation, and school resilience. Therefore, I failed to reject the hypothesis.

DISCUSSION

The purpose of this study is to examine the contribution of work motivation and perceptions of school resilience in determining the level of resiliency in teacher education students. Work motivation was a positive influential determinant of the level of individual resiliency that the teacher education student displayed. With the combination of work motivation and individual resiliency, these individuals are the ones who accept change, feel personally involved, and are committed to their teaching. These students were motivator seekers, as found in other work (Wendt et al., 1980), indicating their tendencies toward emotional stability, sensitivity, thinking, and resourcefulness. Thus, a resilient teacher education student is able to overcome less than ideal situations and function positively for the students, certainly the kind needed in today's stressful school environment. Additionally, Thompson (1993) found that in less than desirable school environments, resilient student teachers still believe that they could help students, relate to other faculty, and function in their jobs despite the barriers they experienced.

What does this mean for schools and teacher education programs? There is no doubt that being resilient in this time of our history is a positive, critical characteristic to have. Having teachers who are committed to the education of their students, who can continue to work and cope despite the barriers with which they have to contend, and who can make meaningful contributions to school and society is certainly a goal for schools and teacher education programs. Milstein and Henry (2000) believe that schools should focus on creating resilient teachers, believing that a resilient teacher is a more effective teacher. In other words, resilient teachers promote resiliency in their students. All students deserve to have teachers who are resilient and who are concerned with meeting their needs.

REFERENCES

Anderson, C. (1982). The search for school climate: A review of research. *Review of Educational Research, 52,* 368–420.

Bartone, P. T., & Ursano, R. J., Wright, K. M., & Ingraham, L. H. (1989). The impact of a military air disaster on the health of assistance workers: A prospective study. *Journal of Nervous and Mental Disease, 177,* 317–328.

Billings, A. G., & Moos, R. H. (1982). Work stress and the stress buffering roles of work and family resources. *Journal of Occupational Behavior, 3,* 215–232.

Brodkin, A., & Coleman, M. (1996). What makes a child resilient? *Instructor, 1,* 28–29.

Corothers, C. L. (1991). *Principals' perceptions of their role in developing a motivated and committed staff.* Unpublished doctoral dissertation, University of Alberta.

Ellis, T. L. (1988). School climate. *Research Round-up of the National Association of Elementary School Principals, 4,* 3–6.

Hall, J., & Williams, M. (1973). *Interpreting your scores on the work motivation inventory.* Conroe, TX: Teleometrics.

Henderson, N., & Milstein, M. (1996). *Resiliency in schools.* Thousand Oaks, CA: Corwin.

Herzberg, F. (1968). One more time: How do you motivate employees? *Harvard Business Review, 46,* 53–62.

Higgins, G. O. (1994). *Resilient adults: Overcoming a cruel past.* San Francisco: Jossey-Bass.

Insel, P. M., & Moos, R. H. (1974). Work *environment scale.* Palo Alto, CA: Consulting Psychologists Press.

Krovetz, M. L. (1999). *Fostering resiliency: Expecting all students to use their minds and hearts well.* Thousand Oaks, CA: Corwin.

Maslow, A. H. (1970). *Motivation and personality.* New York: Harper & Row.

Masten, A. S., Best, K. M., & Garmezy, N. (1990). Resilience and development: Contributions from the study of children who overcome adversity. *Development and Psychopathology, 2,* 425–444.

Milstein, M. M., & Henry, D. A. (2000). *Spreading resiliency: Making it happen for schools and communities.* Thousand Oaks, CA. Corwin.

Parker, J. (1995). Secondary teachers' views of effective teaching in physical education. *Journal of Teaching in Physical Education, 14,* 127–139.

Pierce, M. B., & Molloy, G. N. (1990). Psychological and biographical differences between secondary school teachers experiencing high and low levels of burnout. *Educational Psychology, 60,* 37–51.

Russo, K. A. (1995). *A study of work motivation among intermediate elementary teachers.* Unpublished doctoral dissertation, State University of New York, Buffalo.

Saffici, C.L. (1996). *The relationship of hardiness, efficacy, and locus of control to the work motivation of student teachers.* Unpublished doctoral dissertation, University of Houston.

Thomson, W. C. (1993). *The contribution of school climate and hardiness to the level alienation experienced by student teachers.* Unpublished doctoral dissertation, University of Houston.

Veenman, S. (1984). Perceived problems of beginning teachers. *Review of Educational Research, 54,* 143–178.

Wendt, J. C. (1979). *Comparisons of prospective physical educators' work motivation, concerns and dogmatism during the professional preparation process.* Unpublished doctoral dissertation, University of Houston.

Wendt, J. C., Ward, W. R., & Jackson, A. S. (1980). Personality determinants of Herzberg's conceptualization of the maintenance-motivator. *Journal of Teaching and Learning, 5*(1), 34–43.

Wolin, S. J., & Wolin, S. (1993). *The resilient self: How survivors of troubled families rise above adversity.* New York: Villard.

part III

SCHOOLS, PROGRAMS, AND COMMUNITIES THAT ENHANCE RESILIENCY

CHAPTER 10

PRESENTING A RESILIENCE PARADIGM FOR TEACHERS

Sybil Wolin
Project Resilience, Washington, DC

A growing literature indicates that a positive school environment promotes resilience in children of hardship (Benard, 1991; Freiberg, 1994; Hawkins, Catalano, Kosterman, Abbott, & Hill, 1999; Hetherington, Cox, & Cox, 1979; Kelley & Wallerstein, 1977; Masten, 1994; Rutter, 1990). A related finding is that children who maintain developmental competence, despite severe challenges, have access to caring adults who give them practical help, serve as role models, offer affirmation and emotional support, and instill hope and courage (Garmezy, 1993; Masten, 1994; Werner & Smith, 1989). These adults may be, among others, family members, therapists, or figures in the child's neighborhood or religious community. Most often they are teachers. As Emmy Werner (1999), author of the most extensive long-term study of resilience in children, has noted, "One of the wonderful things we see now in adulthood is that these children really remember one or two teachers who made the difference. And they mourn these teachers when they die. They mourn some of those teachers more than they do their own family members because what went out of their life was a person who looked beyond outward experience, their behavior, their unkempt—oftentimes—appearance and saw the promise."

Based on the findings of Werner and other resiliency researchers; educators, preventionists, clinicians, and policymakers have been describing

Educational Resiliency: Student, Teacher, and School Perspectives, pages 189–204
Copyright © 2004 by Information Age Publishing
All rights of reproduction in any form reserved.

the drawbacks of a risk paradigm for understanding, programming, and serving youth who struggle with hardship (Bendtro, Brokenleg, & VanBockern, 1990; Burns, 1994; Henderson & Milstein, 1996; Rockwell, 1998; Saleebey, 2000). Their primary objections are to the emphasis the risk paradigm puts on the problems and deficits of children and youth, its use of diagnosis and negative labels, and its fix-it approach to intervention. As Benard (1991), an outspoken critic of the risk paradigm, has frequently noted, the term "at risk" is itself a risk factor.

What the critics of the risk paradigm advocate is a break with the long tradition of research and practice focused on the vulnerabilities of families, youth, and children of hardship. In its place they have advanced a "resiliency paradigm" that credits people with strength and the potential to repair from experiences of hardship. The resiliency paradigm vests power in them to help themselves and casts professionals as partners rather than as authorities, initiators, and directors of the change process.

I include myself in the contingent that is advocating for a new paradigm. At the same time, I have learned from my experience training hundreds of teachers, school and agency administrators, counselors, therapists, youth workers, and others that paradigm shifts are much more easily talked about than accomplished. Resistance is both natural and expected. It is especially pronounced in schools where teachers see children's difficulties as an impediment to their work not the object of their work, as beyond their domain, and as the responsibility of psychologists, counselors, and social workers. The contrast between their perception and the findings of resilience research regarding the positive influence teachers can play is an irony worth noting. Let's begin with the example of April, a 14-year-old student in an inner-city junior high school (Orenstein, 1994). Her story illustrates the difference between the risk and resiliency paradigms. It also provides some insight into the reasons for teachers' reluctance to shift away from the former and embrace the latter.

THE STORY OF APRIL

Upon entering junior high school, April was immediately identified as an at-risk student. The label paved the way to a convenient and familiar way of handling the difficulties she was having in her classes. Namely, she was brought to the attention of the guidance office and the special education screening team, who reviewed the "facts." April was disruptive in class, frequently calling out and making inappropriate remarks. All of her academic skills were 2–3 years below grade level. Her school record did not indicate a home address or the name of her father. Her mother, who was a teenager when April was born, was addicted to crack/cocaine. April was frequently absent or late to school. Notes sent home about her absences, her behavior, and her poor academic work were unanswered.

This recitation of "facts" is typical of the data cited by adherents of the risk paradigm to justify its grim conclusions. By documenting one problem after the next, the paradigm gives the impression of a teenager who is well on the way to repeating her mother's life. It predicts that because April is academically deficient and behaviorally and emotionally impaired, she is more likely than not to drop out of school. With few skills and little idea of a work ethic or the rules of the marketplace, she will be pushed to the margins of society. According to the risk paradigm, little in her past gives a reason to be hopeful about her future.

A resiliency paradigm comes to an opposing conclusion not by denying the "facts" cited by the risk paradigm but by looking at another part of the picture. For instance, resiliency thinkers would point out that at home April takes care of both her mother and her brother. Because her mother often skips appointments at the drug treatment center, April escorts her there, often waiting many hours until she is seen. April also goes along to the supermarket to be sure that her mother buys food rather than getting sidetracked and spending her money on drugs.

April cooks and prepares meals for her brother. When there is not enough food to go around, she cuts down on her own skimpy portion so that he will not go hungry. She insists that he attend school, even when she does not. April has also woven a safety net for herself by cultivating a relationship with her aunt, Edith. It is to Edith's house that she goes with her brother whenever her mother disappears or brings home a man.

By including these "facts" as well as April's school records and psychological and educational assessments, a resiliency paradigm holds out hope for her. It views her as someone with inherent strengths and the capacity to direct her future provided she is given the right support. It credits her maturity, morality, deep sense of obligation to her family, self-sufficiency, and common sense that exist paradoxically alongside all of her problems.

The issue for teachers is that in the arena of the classroom, the strengths that April and other students like her have seem not to apply. What stands out instead, to the point of obscuring her strengths, are her difficulties. Under these circumstances, teachers' skepticism about the relevance of the resilience paradigm to their work is understandable. The challenge for the resiliency field is to convince teachers otherwise. My own point of departure has been to analyze the obstacles that block teachers' acceptance of a resiliency paradigm and to design training that addresses those obstacles directly. In the following sections, I address four obstacles I have seen and propose ways of getting around them that are based on a training curriculum I have developed and my own experience implementing it both with teachers and other professionals (Wolin, 1995).

Obstacle #1: No one shifts paradigms easily, teachers included. Shifting one's paradigm requires personal change, and personal change requires hard work. How often do well-intentioned parents (you, perhaps) vow not to blow up at their teenage children only to find themselves in that very act the next day or the next hour? Or to begin a diet, or to start exercising, or to put your credit card away, or to stop procrastinating?

Compared to the difficulty of changing behaviors such as these, shifting one's paradigm is a different order of magnitude. Paradigms are not overt behaviors that people are aware of such as eating too much, exercising too little, or flying off the handle instead of being understanding and patient. Paradigms are deeply embedded in the self. As Steven Covey (1989) explains, a paradigm is a map inlaid in the mind that determines the way one sees the world. Paradigms are conditioned by one's inborn temperament, upbringing, family, friends, colleagues, schooling, and work environment. Deeply rooted as they are, paradigms are seldom scrutinized or questioned. Rather, they are accepted and drive the assumption that what one sees is a correct representation of reality. One's paradigm excludes other people's realities. When contradictions arise in an encounter with someone else's paradigm, they are dismissed as inaccuracies, misperceptions, or mistakes. The whole process repeats itself again and again without notice. It is not easily interrupted.

Solution: Being transparent about teacher's difficulty in embracing the resiliency paradigm and my wish for them to do so. I have found that in order to open the minds of teachers and other professionals to a resiliency paradigm, trainers need to be clear in their own minds about their agenda. In the training that I do, I rarely teach information about resiliency for its own sake. Rather, the information I present and the way I present it are chosen in order to influence how trainees think and act. I have two specific goals: encouraging trainees to (1) recognize and respect the strengths as well as the difficulties of students and clients and (2) see their role as building on their students' and clients' strengths rather than fixing their problems.

From the outset, I am transparent about my goals. I begin training by stating that my purpose is to persuade trainees who tend to think of students and clients more in terms of their weaknesses than their strengths to try a new approach. I add that for those who enter training with a strengths perspective, my purpose is to affirm and systematize what they are doing. I then universalize the difficulties I know trainees will have in considering a new paradigm and align myself with those difficulties by stating that no one (and I mean no one) changes his or her mind easily. To illustrate the point, I ask trainees to do a brief exercise that I do as well. It asks them to answer the series of questions below.

> Think of a time when someone told you that a deeply held opinion of yours was wrong. In trying to recall an incident, you may focus on one of the following issues or think of one of your own—gun control, abortion, legalization of guns, prayer in schools, how children should be raised, does God exist. Now recall the scene in detail.
> - Where did the incident take place?
> - What was your opinion?
> - Who tried to tell you that you were wrong?
> - What did he or she say?
> - What did you say?
> - How did the discussion end?
> - How did you feel during the discussion? Afterward? Now?
> - What did you learn about yourself from this exercise.
>
> (Wolin, 1995)

The purpose of debriefing, in addition to bringing the difficulty in changing one's mind to the surface, is to convey that I understand the problem, am sympathetic to it, and do not hold myself apart from it. Rarely has debriefing fallen short of my goal, especially if I offer my own experience first. Almost uniformly, it provokes laughter as trainees reveal their own foibles and other members of the group recognize the same ones in themselves. Typically people report that changing their mind about something important to them is a rare occurrence. Many say that discussions aimed at persuading them to do so usually end badly.

The exchange is disarming. By gently leading trainees to an awareness of their own closed-mindedness, it makes the challenge of training overt and, at least partially, shifts the responsibility for meeting that challenge from me as a trainer to them as learners. It establishes a culture for training that favors flexibility of thinking and diminishes the threat generally associated with considering a perspective other than one's own. Since I have been forthcoming about my own inflexibility of thought, trainees feel assured that their doubts, questions, and objections will not be regarded judgmentally.

Next, I lay out for trainees the principles of a resiliency paradigm that I would like them to consider. There are four. Children of hardship can:

- have strengths in addition to weaknesses
- learn, achieve, and build on their strengths
- break the cycle of poverty, violence, drug addiction, alcohol abuse, and other adversities
- become adults who contribute constructively to society (Wolin, 1995)

My purpose here is to maintain the transparency I established at the outset. To assure trainees that training will not run counter to their experience, I initiate a discussion of why accepting these principles may be hard. The inquiry gives trainees an opportunity to speak their minds openly. It also honors their experiences and it dismantles the usual hierarchical arrangement of trainer to trainee. The new arrangement not only contributes to the culture of change that I mentioned earlier, it also provides a model for interacting with students and clients.

My experience has been that given the combination of conditions I establish at the beginning of training, teachers and other professionals are receptive to accepting a new paradigm. This does not mean that 100% of the teachers I train shift paradigms and are transformed from deficit-based to strengths-based thinkers. It does mean that many are made aware of their basic assumptions about the children and youth they teach. More than a few begin to examine the accuracy and usefulness of those assumptions, and some consider the alternatives I offer.

Obstacle #2: The resiliency paradigm seems irrelevant to teachers who regard their role as providing instruction, not taking responsibility for the broad personal lives of their students. This obstacle requires very little explanation. Generally, teachers, especially those in secondary school, see teaching content and skills as their primary responsibilities. Their position is understandable. Little in their preparation or in the in-service supervision they receive prepares them to deal with the problems associated with poverty, racism, divorce, abuse, neglect and other social ills that children bring into the classroom with them each day. When these issues are addressed, it is usually from the perspective of the risk paradigm with more emphasis on describing early warning signs and the identifying characteristics of children of hardship than on ways to help them. It should come as no surprise, therefore, that teachers' most likely approach to problems in the classroom is to make a referral to other staff such as counselors and social workers who are trained to handle emotional and behavioral problems. When either the problem or the child does not go away, the suggestion that a new paradigm is in order has limited appeal.

Solution: Demonstrating to teachers how crucial their influence on children can be and how that influence can be exercised in the ordinary everyday interactions they have with children. Like the solution to the obstacle described above, an effective approach to speaking to teachers about resilience and their role in fostering children's strengths begins with the trainer's stance. A judgmental posture closes teachers' and everyone else's minds. So does dismissing teachers' points of view, preaching, and beseeching. By contrast, acknowledging and validating teachers' frustrations and bringing the question of their role and the extent and limit of their responsibilities into the open can set a tone that makes new ways of thinking possible. The approach also causes noticeable relief and solidifies a bond with me as a trainer. In the context of that bond, the findings of resilience research about the key role of teachers can seem relevant and helpful.

More often than not, the discussion uncovers many of the same points that research has made, allowing trainers to make their point by calling attention to what has been said, teasing out the implications, and relating them to the research. For instance, in one of my training sessions, a teacher was advocating loudly for the risk paradigm. He held the opinion that many children are irreparably damaged by their families and are beyond help. To bolster his point, he cited several examples of youth he had tried to help but then gave up on. "If they don't care and their families don't care, there is nothing I can do," he concluded.

As generally happens in groups, not everyone agreed. A third grade teacher who was present felt that it was never right to give up on a child or youth. She related the following experience: One of her most memorable students was a boy who entered her class with a reputation for being very difficult. Despite her best efforts, he managed to live up to his reputation. Nevertheless, she continued to believe in the value of her own influence and in his ability to repair. And she told him so every day. "I know that someday you are going to make something of yourself," she would say. At the end of the school year, the boy's behavior had not changed at all, nor was he different at the end of fourth, fifth, or sixth grade. When he left elementary school, she lost track of him. Many years later, at the time of the Gulf War, he showed up. She received a letter saying, among other things, "I am off to the war. I don't know whether or not I will come back alive. So before I go, I want you to know how much it meant that you didn't give up on me, and I want to apologize for the way that I treated you."

From a story like this (and there are many), the distance to resilience research and it's relevance for teachers is short. Building on the story, trainers can easily make the point that resilience research has a significant role that teachers can play in the lives of children. Having established the point, trainers can mobilize the group to explore why this is the case and how the teacher's influence is exerted. I have found that reliably, the group points to the restorative power of the personal support they can offer. They are also able to take the long view, accept that there is no quick fix, and see that they are not being asked to extend themselves unreasonably.

Based on my work interviewing youth about their resilience (Wolin, 1994) and analyzing narratives of resilience written by youth (Desetta & Wolin, 2000; Wolin & Desetta, 2000), I pull together the discussion by introducing the concept of "honoring the struggle." By "honoring the struggle," I mean acknowledging and affirming the efforts children and youth make to meet the challenges confronting them even when those efforts are small or not particularly successful. To demonstrate the power of "honoring the struggle," I ask trainees if they find it helpful when they are going through hard times to have the support of people who matter to them. I also provide anecdotal evidence directly from students' recollections, for instance, the case of Tanika.

An emancipated minor whose early years at home were difficult, Tanika recalled an elementary teacher who she felt helped her. The teacher noted that Tanika frequently came to school crying. The teacher called Tanika's mother, who was unresponsive. Tanika recalled that her mother didn't listen or do anything. Yet Tanika remembered the incident and felt helped by it (Wolin, 1994). I propose that Tanika did not expect the teacher to change her mother or the material circumstances of life at home. Nevertheless, she was touched and encouraged by the teacher's caring gesture and by the perception that her struggle at home was noted.

This incident, and others like it, demonstrate an important point for teachers. To encourage their students to persist in the face of difficult circumstances, they do not need to extend themselves unreasonably. Nor do they need to prepare resiliency lesson plans or get involved in areas of their students' lives that they are not equipped to handle (Bickart & Wolin, 1997). Rather, they can have an influence through small gestures that are easily made in their daily rounds.

If the observation presents any problem at all, generally it is not from the nay-sayers but from the teachers who are disappointed by the message and want something more. Seeing the severity of many of their problems displayed in their classrooms, these teachers believe that they need solutions that are equally big, complex, and dramatic as the situations their students face. The power of small gestures is hard for them to accept. The difficulty is increased by the element of time. Frequently the positive effects teachers have are not immediate but are seen only many years after children have left their class. Teachers have no way of knowing the good they have done. More likely, on a day-to-day basis they hear more about their failures than their successes. The situation casts the challenge of the trainer in a somewhat new form: from changing teachers' minds about the children they teach to helping them call on their own resilience in order to keep their own power in mind no matter how helpless they may feel in the moment.

Obstacle #3: Written materials about resiliency are either inaccessible to teachers or oversimplified to the point of losing credibility. Despite the key role teachers have been shown to play, little of substance about resilience has been written explicitly for them. Compared to articles and papers *about* the importance of teachers, material *for* teachers is scarce. For the most part, literature on resilience has been generated by research psychologists and is aimed at other research psychologists. This body of work includes reports of empirical studies, discussions of research methodologies, and historical overviews (Felsman & Vaillant, 1987; Higgins, 1994; Luther, Cicchetti, & Becker, 2000; Masten, 1994a, 1994b, 1999; Werner & Smith, 1989, 1992). Almost as plentiful are policy statements that describe how institutions, including schools, need to change in order to become a constructive force in the lives of children (Benard, 1993; Liddle, 1994; Reavis et al., 1999).

While many teachers search for answers to their questions about students in the resilience literature, they are as frequently frustrated by it as helped. Its format and technical language are inaccessible not only to them but also to others outside the research field. Policy papers generally focus on conditions beyond the individual teacher's control, and psychology and education papers—when they address teachers at all—usually provide an assortment of atheoretical tips that are context specific, on the one hand, or broad generalizations that leave much to the imagination on the other. The semi-professional literature does teachers an equal disservice. Typically, this writing depicts resilience as the story of exceptional superkids who transcend the most dismal of circumstances to achieve dazzling success (Blum, 1998; Shapiro, Friedman, Meyer, & Loftus, 1996).

Most teachers have not met these heroes, and know that they are not miracle workers who can transform the children they do see. The image of the superkid can demoralize them by setting impossible-to-reach standards and obscuring the small but more realistic victories that do occur in their classrooms. It also raises teachers' skepticism about resilience as a concept that could be useful to them.

Solution: Offering teachers a clear and convincing explanation of the field. A good point of departure for presenting the literature on resiliency to teachers is the work of Norman Garmezy (Garmezy, 1971, 1974, 1989, 1991, 1993; Garmezy, Masten, & Tellegen, 1984). A psychologist, Garmezy is the person credited with bringing the topic of resilience to the attention of scientists. Teachers can readily understand Garmezy's contribution and its relevance to them. Moreover, one need not avoid the statistics that are the heart of Garmezy's work in order to craft an explanation that teachers with no statistical background can grasp.

In the early 1970s, Garmezy objected to the singular focus on damage and vulnerability in children of hardship that was dominating research at the time. Concluding that this research was creating the mistaken impression that children of hardship are doomed, Garmezy reexamined a group of studies that looked at children who were at risk because they had been reared in poverty. While all the studies uniformly demonstrated that among children of poverty; behavioral, emotional, and learning problems occur at a higher rate than they do among children who grow up in more fortunate circumstances; Garmezy did not stop there. Instead, he asked an additional question that none of the researchers who had done these studies had posed; namely, did the findings justify the dire predictions about children at risk that they had produced? Garmezy correctly said no. He pointed out that in no study did more than 30% of the children included develop problems. In most studies, the percentage who succumbed was far lower.

Although Garmezy in no way intended to minimize the dangers of risk and the importance of helping children exposed to it, he did correct the misperception that being at risk is synonymous with doom. Garmezy's observations, which have come to be known as "flipping the coin of the risk statistics" (Garmezy, 1989), launched the first phase of resilience research that targeted children who do very well despite being at risk. This early phase was a backlash against the focus on problems that Garmezy questioned. Like most backlashes, it, too, became extreme and created a mistaken impression and distorted image of its own, namely, that some children are superkids who are invulnerable to hardship and who prevail no matter what. It is this image that gives teachers and other professionals pause.

Since Garmezy's initial breakthrough, many researchers have studied resilience, refining the concept and grappling with its application. The technicalities of this research, for instance its procedures and statistical analyses, are not particularly important for teachers unless they are specifically interested. The findings, however, hold considerable relevance. Current thinking is that resilience is not a miraculous comeback. Rather, it is "ordinary magic" (Masten, 1994a) based in the everyday normal processes occurring in children's minds, brains, and bodies, in their families and relationships, and in their communities. In other words, resilience develops in spheres of children's lives that are susceptible to the influence of teachers. The question is, how can teachers function in those spheres to make a difference?

While I do not mean to imply that this summary of resilience is the only way the field can be presented to teachers effectively, I have found that this narrative line is intelligible to teachers and, even more important, makes sense to them. I have observed that it speaks to teachers' skepticism about the field and can open their minds, just as Garmezy opened the minds of his colleagues, to a new perspective.

Obstacle #4: Compared to the risk paradigm, the resiliency paradigm carries considerable authority that is difficult to deny. Since the 1940s, when Rene Spitz first investigated hospitalism in institutionalized infants (Spitz, 1945), researchers have been studying the specific disorders of the mind associated with stress and hardship in early childhood. They have uncovered the myriad ways that children's psyches can be harmed by disruptions in their parent's, family's, and community's functioning. Their work has filled libraries with data on the maladies that beset children with schizophrenic mothers, divorcing parents, alcoholic fathers, handicapped siblings, abuse, and other similar traumas. This work with clinical observations is the foundation of the *Diagnostic and Statistical Manual,* or the *DSM-*

IV, which sets standards and provides the vocabulary for diagnosing mental illness (American Psychiatric Association 1994). It is hundreds of pages long and is replete with categories, subcategories, flow charts, and axes. Teachers may not know about the DSM specifically, but they are not strangers to its message about people's vulnerabilities.

Worthy as the investigation and identification of pathology have been, it is a one-sided endeavor, painting a distorted picture of human frailties and vulnerabilities and the insufficiencies of children to master their problems. In schools where the term "at risk" is freely used, teachers accept this picture and the associated idea that children who are hurt in early life suffer irreversible harm.

The resiliency model that fills in the picture is a relative newcomer in the service professions. Either teachers have not heard about it, or when they have, it is not nearly as convincing as the risk paradigm. Only a little more than three decades old, the resiliency paradigm lacks the aura of legitimacy that history, research, and a medical background bestow upon the risk paradigm. Next to the risk lexicon, a resiliency vocabulary is scant and pallid. The theory itself has only just begun to be applied clinically.

As a result, the resiliency paradigm is no match for the risk paradigm. Talking about inner strengths, protective factors, and the human capacity to repair from harm; professionals can feel that they are walking across unmapped territory. They grope for words and fear sounding unintelligent or naive when they replace pathology terminology with the more mundane vocabulary of courage, resourcefulness, hope, creativity, competence, and the like. Many prefer the familiarity and safety of the risk paradigm to the struggle of adopting a new framework.

Solution: Shortening the distance between the risk and resiliency paradigms. The distance between the resiliency and the at-risk paradigm, as each are typically described, is too great for people to cross comfortably. I have found that one way of reducing the advantages the risk paradigm has over the resiliency paradigm is to diminish the distance between the two. Specifically, the risk paradigm is often portrayed as the opposite of the resiliency paradigm. Therefore, for the resiliency paradigm to be accepted requires the unlikely event that people will stop believing that the children and youth they see in their classrooms and agencies each day have been severely damaged by the hardships they face. Instead, they will begin thinking that the damage in these children and youth is not as significant as the strengths and resources they have that had been previously ignored.

I believe that presenting the resiliency paradigm as the opposite of the risk paradigm is a misrepresentation and oversimplification that stirs up resistance rather than paving the way to change. A more accurate representation is that the risk paradigm, which I have called the Damage Model and the resiliency paradigm, which I have called the Challenge Model, complement rather than oppose one another (Wolin & Wolin, 1993).

The Damage Model (Figure 10.1) portrays the harm that troubles can inflict on children. It paints children as passive and without choices or the ability to help themselves. As a result, the best they can do is cope with hardship. However, coping takes its toll and gives way to pathology. As the process continues, pathologies are layered upon pathologies, and the child becomes an adult with serious and often irreversible problems.

The Challenge Model (Figure 10.2) starts with the same sequence. It does not require demoting or overlooking the deleterious effects of hardship. It does, however, add another dimension to the risk story. In the Challenge Model, hardship is not only destructive but also is an opportunity. Children are wounded in the Challenge Model, as they are in the Damage Model, and they are left with scars as adults. But they are also challenged by troubles to experiment and to respond actively and creatively. Their preemptive responses, repeated over time become incorporated into the self as lasting resiliencies, for example, April's maturity, self-sufficiency, and common sense.

Seen from the perspective of the Challenge Model, hardship has a paradoxical effect, causing strength and weakness simultaneously. In our work-

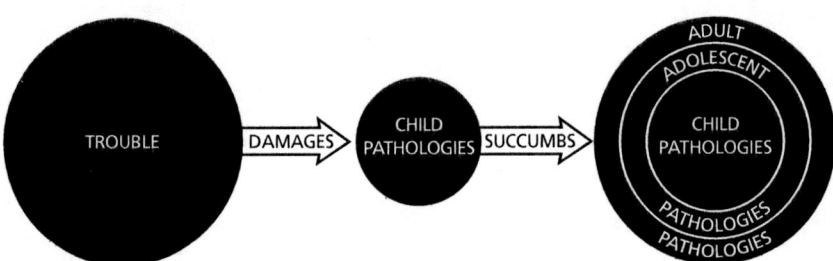

Figure 10.1. The Damage Model.

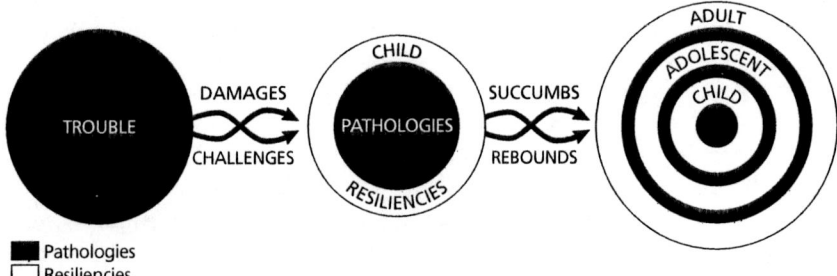

Figure 10.2. The Challenge Model.

shops, I have found that this notion of paradox is more easily accepted than the idea of dropping the risk paradigm completely and instead working with children who have been harmed from a strengths angle only. I also believe that a paradoxical formulation, in contrast to the either/or alternative of risk versus resiliency, is more clinically accurate and responsible.

Solution: Uncovering the subjective validity of the resilience paradigm. Although science and statistics carry considerable weight in our culture, people are just as prone to use their own personal experience to judge the efficacy of a claim. Thus, tapping the subjective experiences of trainees can provide support for a resiliency paradigm, especially when those experiences are credited with being a valid yardstick.

In training, I convey the value of subjective experience by explaining my own attraction and commitment to the resiliency paradigm. I note that for me, resilience is a very human and spiritual topic, by which I mean that resilience is a subject that concerns everyone who is alive. It is not a new subject, nor is it the exclusive domain of researchers, experts, and professionals. Everyone experiences hardship because in life, loss, rejection, failure, disappointment, and death are unavoidable. While most people are changed by the experience of hardship and many carry the hurt for their entire lives, resilience is more common than collapse. Likewise, information about resilience is not restricted to research journals and professional books. It can be found by turning inward.

The observation is an effective segue to turning teachers inward in order to reflect on how they have persisted in the face of hardship, what helped, and what they learned from the experience. Reliably the self-reflection yields the major points that I seek to make in resiliency training for teachers, namely that hardship does not necessarily spell doom, that it produces both strengths and weaknesses, that coming back is a struggle that may never be fully over, and that one powerful source of help is someone who cares and honors that struggle. When teachers and other professionals recognize the subjective validity of each of these points for themselves, the relevance for their students is hard to deny.

CONCLUSION

Teaching children of hardship can be a painfully uncertain enterprise. The education system provides few ways for teachers to know with any confidence whether a given activity, approach, or intervention is effective or not beyond the moment. What works with one student may backfire with another. Standardized test scores, which measure children's skills and knowledge, miss the intangible but equally important benefits of the personal relationships teachers have with their students. And sometimes the problems teachers see are so severe that they reach the mistaken but understandable conclusion that only monumental solutions can matter. Thinking this way, they devalue the accumulated power of the small everyday interactions they have with children. The risk paradigm, with its singular focus on the inevitable problems of these children, reinforces the misperception of their own influence.

Literature on resilience, which takes the long view of teachers' influence, gives them good reason to be optimistic both about the children they teach and their own role in those children's lives. Therefore, staff development should take teachers' skepticism about the concept of resilience into account. If it is designed and implemented in a way that makes sense to teachers, there is a reasonable chance that it could awaken their interest in a new paradigm.

REFERENCES

American Psychiatric Association. (1994). *Diagnostic and statistical manual of mental disorders* (4th ed.). Washington, DC:Author.

Benard, B. (1991). *Fostering resiliency in kids: Protective factors in the family, school, and community.* Oregon: Western Regional Center for Drug-free Schools and Communities Far West Laboratory.

Benard, B. (1993). *Turning the corner from risk to resiliency.* Oregon: Northwest Regional Educational Laboratory.

Bendtro, L., Brokenleg, M., & VanBockern, S. (1990). *Reclaiming youth at risk: Our hope for the future.* Indiana: National Education Services.

Bickart, T., & Wolin, S. (1997, November). Practicing resilience in the elementary classroom. *Principal, 77,* 21–24.

Blum, D. (1998, June). The art of overcoming: The new science of resilience. *Psychology Today, 31,* 32–38, 66–67, 69–70, 72–73.

Burns, T. (1994). *From risk to resilience.* Texas: The Marco Polo Group.

Covey, S. (1989). *The seven habits of highly effective people: Powerful lessons in personal change.* New York: Simon & Schuster.

Desetta, A., & Wolin, S. (Eds.). (2000). *The struggle to be strong: True stories by teens about overcoming tough times.* Minnesota: Free Spirit.

Felsman, J. K., & Vaillant, G. E. (1987). Resilient children as adults: A 40-year study. In E. J. Anthony & B. Cohler (Eds.), *The invulnerable child* (pp. 289–314). New York: Guilford Press.

Freiberg, H. J. (1994). Understanding resilience: Implications for inner-city schools and their near and far communities. In M. C. Wang & E. W. Gordon (Eds.), *Educational resilience in inner city America: Challenges and prospects* (pp. 151–165).Hillsdale, NJ: Erlbaum.

Garmezy, N. (1971). Vulnerability research and the issue of primary prevention, *American Journal of Orthopsychiatry, 41,* 101–116.

Garmezy, N. (1974). The study of competence in children at risk for severe psychopathology. In E. G. Anthony & C. Koupernik (Eds.), *The child in his family: Vol 3. Children at psychiatric risk* (pp. 77–97). New York: Wiley.

Garmezy, N. (1989), Foreword. In E. E. Werner & R. S. Smith, *Vulnerable but invincible: A longitudinal study of resilient children and youth* (pp. xiii–xxii). New York: Adams Bannister Cox.

Garmezy, N. (1991). Resilience in children's adaptation to negative life events and stressed environments. *Pediatrics, 20*, 459–466.

Garmezy, N. (1993). Children in poverty: Resilience despite risk. *Psychiatry, 56*, 127–136.

Garmezy, N., Masten, A.S., & Tellegen, A. (1984). The study of stress and competence in children: A building block for developmental pathology. *Child Development, 55*, 97–111.

Hawkins, J. D., Catalano, R. F., Kosterman, R., Abbott, R., & Hill. K.G. (1999). Preventing adolescent health-risk behavior by strengthening protection during childhood. *Archives of Pediatrics and Adolescent Medicine, 153*, 226–234.

Henderson, N., & Milstein, M. (1996). *Resiliency in schools: Making it happen for students and educators*. Thousand Oaks, CA: Corwin.

Hetherington, E. M., Cox, M., & Cox, R. (1979). Play and social interaction in children following divorce. *Journal of Social Issues, 35*, 26–49.

Higgins, G. O. (1994). *Resilient adults: Overcoming a cruel past.* San Francisco: Jossey-Bass.

Kelley, J. B., & Wallerstein, J. S. (1977). Brief intervention with children in divorcing families. *American Journal of Orthopsychiatry, 47*, 23–39.

Liddle, H.A. (1994). In M.C. Wang & E.W. Gordon (Eds.), *Educational resilience in inner city America: Challenges and prospects* (pp. 167–177). Hillsdale, NJ: Erlbaum.

Luthar, S. S., Cicchetti, D., & Becker, B. (2000). The construct of resilience: A critical evaluation and guidelines for future work. *Child Development, 71*, 543–562.

Masten, A. S. (1994a). Ordinary magic: Resilience processes in development. *American Psychologist, 71*, 227–238.

Masten, A. S. (1994b). Resilience in individual development: Successful adaptation despite risk and adversity. In M. C. Wang & E.W. Gordon (Eds.), *Educational resilience in inner city America: Challenges and prospects* (pp. 3–25). Hillsdale, NJ: Erlbaum.

Masten, A. S. (1999). Resilience comes of age: Reflections on the past and outlook for the next generation of research. In M. D. Glantz & J. L. Johnson (Eds.), *Resilience and development: Positive life adaptations* (pp. 281–296). New York: Kluwer/Plenum.

Orenstein, P. (1994). *School girls.* New York: Doubleday.

Reavis, K., Battalio, R., Osher, D., Rhode, G., Jenson, A., & Hofmeister, A. (1999, Summer). If you build it, they will come: A non-traditional approach for systems change. *Reaching Today's Youth, 3*, 15–17.

Rockwell, S. (1998, Spring). Overcoming four myths that prevent fostering resilience. *Reaching Today's Youth, 4*, 14–17.

Rutter, M. (1990). Psychosocial resilience and protective mechanisms. In J. Rolf, A. S. Masten, D. Cicchetti, K. H. Neuchterlein & S. Weintraub (Eds.), *Risk and pro-*

tective factors in the development of psychopathology (pp. 181–214). New York: Cambridge University Press.

Saleebey, D. (2002). *The strengths perspective in social work practice.* Boston: Beacon.

Shapiro, J., Friedman, D., Meyer M., & Loftus, M. (1996, November 11). Invincible kids. *Newsweek, 121,* 62–68.

Spitz, R. (1945). Hospitalism. An inquiry into the genesis of psychiatric conditions in early childhood. *Psychoanalytic Study of the Child, 1,* 53–74.

Werner, E. (1999). How children become resilient: Observations and cautions. In N. Henderson, B. Benard, & N. Sharp-Light (Eds.), *Resiliency in action* (pp. 11–20). Maine: Resiliency in Action.

Werner, E. E., & Smith, R. S. (1989). *Vulnerable but invincible: A longitudinal study of resilient children and youth.* New York: Adams Bannister Cox.

Werner, E. E., & Smith, R. S. (1992). *Overcoming the odds: High risk children from birth to adulthood.* Ithaca, NY: Cornell University Press.

Wolin, S. (1994). *The resiliency video series. Survivor's pride: Building resilience in youth at risk.* Wisconsin: Attainment Company.

Wolin, S. (1995). *Resilience in practice.* Unpublished training manual, Project Resilience, Washington, DC.

Wolin S., & Desetta, A. (2000) *A leader's guide to the struggle to be strong: How to foster resilience in teens.* Minnesota: Free Spirit.

Wolin, S. J., & Wolin, S. (1993). *The resilient self.* New York: Villard.

CHAPTER 11

DEVELOPING RESILIENT LEARNING COMMUNITIES TO CLOSE THE ACHIEVEMENT GAP

Robert Stephen Topf
Oak Grove School District

Virginia Frazier-Maiwald
Edenvale School

Martin L. Krovetz
San Jose State University

Excitement sparkles in the eyes of Juwan and Leticia. Like the other kindergartners in this inner-city San Jose, California, elementary school, they elatedly begin their formal schooling experience. Juwan is African American. Leticia is Mexican American. The majority of students at this school are, like themselves, students of color. Many are children of immigrants whose parents have had limited formal education. Most of the students are learning English as their second language.

If the trends hold true, Juwan and Leticia will probably not be as academically successful as their Asian or white classmates. As they proceed through the grades, they are apt to score lower on statewide tests, participate in fewer advanced placement courses, and be less likely to graduate high school directly into a 4-year university program.

There is an achievement gap in our nation's schools. As a whole, Latino and African American students are not achieving on par with their Asian and white classmates. Demographics indicate that students of color are now the majority population in California schools. Understanding the achievement patterns of these students and honestly tackling the real issues as to why the gap exists are essential to reversing the trends. "Their parents don't value education," "There are not enough books in the home," "They're poor." These comments are representative of many discussions that occur when educators come together to discuss the achievement gap.

However, conversations of this nature must not be used to excuse, justify, influence, or predict student performance. The whys beneath the disparities in achievement and notions about equality and equity must be honestly confronted. Research and experience show that what schools do matters tremendously. We feel passionately that there is both a moral and pragmatic imperative to close the achievement gap. By promoting equity and access to education, with particular attention to the needs of Latino and African American students, by meaningfully engaging families in the education process, by manifesting a spirit of critical inquiry, and as a concerned community, by maintaining a determined focus on developing a resilient learning community.

This chapter uses resiliency as a lens to describe how schools can assist students like Juwan and Leticia in reaching their academic potential. We look at the characteristics of resilient schools, as well as the attitudes, practices, and professional behaviors that help educators transform schools into resilient learning communities. We also provide vignettes that exemplify the kinds of schools and experiences that promote resiliency in Juwan and Leticia.

WHAT IS RESILIENCY?

Resiliency is the ability to overcome adversity. Based on longitudinal studies, researchers found that for every child who comes from an "at-risk" background who will need special intervention, there is a higher percentage of children coming from that same "at-risk" background who are able to become healthy, competent adults without intervention. The foundation for resiliency theory is based on the definitive research of Werner and Smith (1992). Their work focuses on identifying the protective factors within the family, school, and community that exist for the resilient student (Benard,

1991; Krovetz, 1999). Werner and Smith write that the resilient child is one "who loves well, works well, plays well, and expects well" (p. 192).

Resilient children usually have the following four common attributes (Benard, 1991):

- Social competence: the ability to elicit positive responses from others, thus establishing positive relationships with both adults and peers.
- Problem-solving skills: resourcefulness in problem resolution, seeking appropriate help from others.
- Autonomy: a sense of one's own identity and an ability to act independently and exert some control over one's environment.
- Sense of purpose and future: goals, educational aspirations, persistence, hopefulness, and a sense of a bright future.

Schools that recognize the critical importance of promoting resiliency in their students do everything possible to foster a feeling of social competence, the ability to effectively solve problems, the development of a sense of autonomy, and a perspective on what a bright future might look like. Students come to school possessing varying degrees of these four attributes. Whether or not these attributes are strong enough to help the student overcome adversity is largely dependent upon the existence of key protective factors in the student's daily environment.

WHAT DOES IT MEAN TO FOSTER RESILIENCY?

When these protective factors are in place: (1) caring, (2) high expectations and purposeful support, (3) ongoing opportunities for meaningful participation, and (4) effective instruction, a school community is fostering resiliency.

Take a moment to reflect upon your own experiences as a student. Who cared deeply about you? Who was it that held high expectations for you? Did you have qualified teachers that provided effective instruction? Where and when did you receive support to meet those expectations? In what ways did you participate in decisions about what you should learn and how to demonstrate your academic development? How did your family provide a voice in the decision-making process?

MOVING FROM RISK TO RESILIENCY

Practitioners in the social and behavioral sciences traditionally follow a problem-focused "medical model" when addressing the needs of people considered at risk. This involves identifying the risk factors—dysfunctional family, disease, illness, maladaptation, incompetence, deviance—and then seeking resources to develop programs to work with the "at-risk" population. This approach is reactive, in that programs are designed to help people who are already identified as being in trouble. In schools, many alternative programs are designed for these populations. Students who are behind academically may be placed in special education classes or receive remedial education services. Truant and behavior problem students are placed in in-house detention centers, in opportunity classes, on independent study, and into continuation schools.

The problem focus model offers little help to educational and community leaders who would prefer a more proactive position, who would prefer to build communities based primarily on protective factors that would reduce the need for special programs for at-risk students because fewer students would be at risk. A proactive position is based on building capacities, skills, and assets—building resiliency. It emphasizes strengthening the environment, not fixing kids.

The Problem

More than any other single factor, it is the lack of a deeply held belief in every child's ability to be academically successful that leads to students achieving at levels significantly below their potential. Most teachers enter the profession with the hope, dreams, and intention to help every student be successful. Unfortunately, the realities of being a teacher in the public school system diminish the strength of this belief system.

Current policies and practices often become obstacles in assisting all students to achieve their potential. Overcrowded schools with large class sizes, teachers feeling isolated, lack of instructional planning time, inadequate resources, poorly designed professional development, and an inability to stay focused on student learning all contribute to a tendency for teachers and educational leaders to lower their expectations for student achievement.

In most places, an elementary school teacher is responsible to teach reading, writing, math, social studies, science, physical education, and music to over 30 students. In the middle and high schools where teachers are responsible for 120–200 students, how can the teacher know each student and his/her work well? The task becomes increasingly more complex when teachers encounter multiple languages, poverty, drugs, student mobility, racism, the reality of serving students and families from different socioeconomic and cultural backgrounds than themselves, and families struggling to survive.

Where Do We Go From Here?

Any effort to improve the quality of life and learning for students must begin with an examination of our underlying beliefs. This requires a much deeper look than the usual efforts to write a school vision statement, by consensus, across various segments of the school community. Educators need to carefully examine why they come to work every day and what they believe about students as learners. Leaders must skillfully and courageously facilitate their colleagues to carefully analyze the data, especially student work, to determine if there is evidence that the students are indeed learning what is supposed to be taught.

Reflection

We invite you to think about an African American and Latino student that you know well. What is your school doing to foster resiliency for these students? Specifically, what do you see, hear, and feel on that campus that indicates that these students are cared for? How do you know that expectations are high and support is strong? What indications are there that students are being effectively taught and that the curriculum reflects who they are and their lifestyle? How do you know that their participation in the life of the classroom and school is valued? What do these students need in order to experience a more resilient learning community school? Use your two students as a lens as you continue reading. Our lens will be Juwan and Leticia.

The lack of daycare, medical care, and the impact of poverty on families create a tremendous burden for schools. More and more is expected of schools to meet the social and psychological needs of students. At the same time, schools are constantly criticized for not preparing graduates with the academic skills to be productive members of the American workforce.

Yet there are some districts and schools that address the tough issues of equity, race, resiliency, and the achievement gap. These places have high academic standards and serve as models for the attainable results when a community focuses on developing resilient learners. In these places, schools, teachers, principals, parents, administrators, and school boards are fighting for the hearts, minds, and futures of their students.

PROMOTING RESILIENCY: POWERFUL SOCIAL IMPLICATIONS

It is 4:52 PM. The late afternoon wind-down at school is interrupted with the dreaded missing child alert. Staff on campus appear injected with adrenaline. Announcements are made, the surrounding neighborhood is searched, and the school district office and police are contacted. Juwan's teacher reported seeing him walking across the school field with a group of students shortly after the last bell at approximately 2:40 PM.

This is not the first episode for Juwan. Staff suspect that he has found another student to go home with. The hope is that Juwan is in the neighborhood, sitting at a kitchen table sharing a snack with a friend's family.

Juwan's family became homeless less than 2 weeks ago. His father is in prison. The family has been evicted from the one room that they have shared during the past few months. Jude, Juwan's mother, is at the end of her financial resources. She is unable to stay at a job; even if she could find someone with the medical expertise to provide daycare for one of her other children, who has spina bifida, she is unable to pay for it.

Recently, the school helped Jude obtain catheters and diapers for her child. Jude waited for hours in the emergency room at the county hospital with the community liaison. She was then escorted to a room where she was questioned interminably. Jude struggles in dealing with the medical community, and is bothered by the endless personal questions. She has to endure the piercing stares of onlookers. Jude is poor. She has no home. She is a single mother, without a job, daycare, or medical insurance for her children. Jude does not know where to turn for help.

Finally, the crisis comes to a conclusion. Juwan reluctantly enters the principal's office that evening, where his anxious mother and siblings await. He is safe and physically okay. Juwan's disappearance, his continual tardies, daydreaming, and poor school performance must now be addressed in a positive way.

After conferencing with Jude and Juwan, the principal offers Jude a position as morning and noontime yard-duty supervisor. Her younger children can attend campus daycare. Jude will be close by if Johnathan, her special needs child, needs her. Jude and her children have become more meaningfully connected with the school. Jude feels a sense of pride in her newfound identity as she tells other parents about working at Edenvale School. Jude models social competence for her children. Juwan is proud of his mother as she roams the playground, maintaining safety and helping students. He sees his mother contributing, is reassured by her presence, and feels more motivated to perform better in class. Juwan is now on time each morning. He assists his mother in checking in students through the breakfast line.

OAK GROVE SCHOOL DISTRICT INITIATIVE TO CLOSE THE ACHIEVEMENT GAP

The Oak Grove School District, located in south San Jose, California, is a K–8 district, with 18 elementary and three intermediate schools, and a population of approximately 12,000 students. During the last 5 years, the district has had as a major focus an initiative to "close the achievement gap." Disaggregation of local student performance data informed district leaders that Latino and African American students were underachieving. A comprehensive document was developed outlining a vision of the attitudes, skills, and behaviors needed by students, parents, teachers, administrators, classified, and support staff to increase Latino and African American student performance.

The district has placed an emphasis on the instructional and interpersonal variables related to improving the achievement of these students. The superintendent, principals and instructional staff carefully analyze assessment data to determine which areas of the instructional program need greater emphasis, and which students require additional academic assistance. They monitor who is participating in the safety net programs offered in the district. This helps to ensure that Latino and African American students receive the assistance they need to be successful.

An essential tenet of the "Closing the Achievement Gap" plan is to provide Latino and African American parents increased access and a real voice in their children's education. Informal "Koffee Klatches" are held with African American parents. Latino parent meetings are conducted in Spanish. For many of the parents, this is the first time that schools have actively reached out to them. It is an opportunity for these parents to learn more about their child's academic performance, and also what they can do to work more closely with the schools.

At the same time, district employees are discovering how expectations about race, culture, and ethnicity affect the teaching–learning process. Instructional and administrative staff are increasing cross-cultural proficiency and developing new skills in working effectively with the district's diverse population. These are emotionally charged and challenging issues.

However, the district's courage in dealing with the complex issues associated with "closing the achievement gap" is beginning to show results. Upward trends are being seen in Latino and African American student performance. Academic Performance Index data show that African American and Latino students in Oak Grove School District are performing at a higher level on the Stanford Achievement Test 9 than their counterparts in other school districts in the state of California. Based on Spring 2000 data, there is still an achievement gap between Oak Grove's white, African American, and Latino students. The gap is narrower than what is seen in the rest of the state. In Oak Grove, white students scored 52 points higher than California's white students. African American students scored 151 points above the African American state average and Latino students 119 points higher than Latinos across the state. These results are encouraging and enhance the staff's motivation to close the achievement gap.

HOW ONE SCHOOL IS DEMONSTRATING THAT THE ACHIEVEMENT GAP CAN BE CLOSED

The school population at Edenvale consists of 92% students of color, 68% English language learners, 20% mobility rate, and 78% of students on free or reduced-price lunch. Teachers have adopted many powerful instructional practices, which help enhance student resiliency. At Edenvale, precious learning time is well protected. The first 2 hours of the day are considered "sacred time," and instruction is uninterrupted. Everyone provides literacy instruction at the beginning of the day. This allows students to be placed in reading and writing groups at their academic skill level. It allows teachers to focus more intensely on teaching a narrower range of skills. Flexible grouping of students, and departmentalization, based on the teacher's professional strengths and interests, helps to decrease the time pressures faced when attempting to organize powerful learning experiences in each curricular area for all students. Four grade-level team planning days are provided during the school year (substitutes provided) for collaboration and sharing of how to implement effective instructional practices.

The instructional staff is involved in mapping the curriculum. This helps ensure that classroom learning activities are aligned with state standards and assessments. Through the mapping process, teachers are able to see where the gaps exist in the school's instructional program, and also which academic concepts are being taught repeatedly. The staff makes special effort to design developmentally appropriate learning experiences for a multiplicity of learning styles. Curriculum materials that mirror the student population are utilized. The variety of cultures and life experiences of Edenvale students are also incorporated into the curriculum. Students in fifth and sixth grade complete projects on their family's cultural background. Parents are encouraged to participate in the classroom through the sharing of traditions, dress, food, and stories.

Edenvale teachers understand that hands-on learning experiences assist in the development of cognitive and academic abilities. Through cooperative learning, a variety of sheltered instructional strategies, and appropriate English language development support, instruction is comprehensible and meaningful. Edenvale has also successfully integrated technology into the curriculum. Students utilize the Internet for research, complete multimedia projects, and in the fifth and sixth grade, learn how to use PowerPoint in classroom presentations. All students participate in the Accelerated Reader Program. Every book in the school has been coded by level of difficulty, students are provided incentives for successful completion of comprehension tests, and the expectation is that when free time is available during the day, it should be spent productively on independent reading.

Edenvale has recently entered into a multi-year partnership with a school reform agency known as Partners in School Innovation. The goal of the partnership is to assist staff in identifying essential instructional areas that will improve the skills of teachers in order to facilitate improved student learning outcomes. Partners in School Innovation work in close collaboration with teachers to coach, expand, and strengthen best practices, evaluate its impact on student achievement, and develop systems that sustain these improvements. Partners support teachers in integrating these new practices in their classrooms, collecting and analyzing student data, and reflect upon the impact of these improvements.

The school's focused effort is helping to create a resilient student population. One indication of success is seen in Edenvale's statewide Stanford Achievement Test 9 results during the last 2 years. Their statewide Academic Performance Index increased 81 points. This demonstrates that high expectations and powerful instruction do produce positive student performance outcomes.

PROTECTIVE FACTORS THAT PROMOTE RESILIENCY IN SCHOOLS

Caring Environments

In a caring school culture, people are well known. Shared stories craft a culture and weave the tapestry of a school's identity. Trust is developed and lifelong bonds are forged.

Stories about the students and their success as well as the triumphs of staff members provide optimism and energy. Daily interactions, decisions, and problem solving are based on clearly articulated core values. When you walk into the school and through the classrooms you can sense that the staff feels a passion for teaching, students are well cared for, and that important learning is taking place. What a difference it makes when we acknowledge that every step we take along the way, every sentence we utter, and every reaction we have is an important part of the education of our students.

Through the Eyes of the Student

Leticia felt a wave of relief and great hope for success upon entering her third-grade classroom. Cruising the room, warmly greeting her students was Ms. Hernandez, a young Latina educator who actually grew up in a neighborhood close by. Leticia thought to herself that Ms. Hernandez was the most beautiful teacher she had ever seen, but she also knew that she was very strict. The students had heard that by the end of the first day of school they would have to recite the school's Behavioral Guidelines. While Ms. Hernandez is known in the community as being a no-nonsense "enforcer of the Edenvale way," her students are secure in her classroom as she consistently demonstrates a balance of warmth and affection with discipline.

Leticia remembered how difficult school was during second grade. In the middle of the year a new teacher appeared, and Leticia never saw Ms. Moore again. The substitute explained that due to complications in her pregnancy, Ms. Moore would not be able to return. She often walked home after school with tears streaming down her cheeks. Leticia spent most of the second-grade school year filling out worksheets that she did not understand and looking down at the floor when the teacher posed a question to the class. The classroom felt tense and chaotic. Leticia avoided being chosen to speak in class, as she recalled the look on the substitute's face, a signal of displeasure, which communicated to her that her English was not too good.

Through the Eyes of Teachers

Fortunately, Ms. Hernandez is cognizant of Leticia's strengths and weaknesses. Her academic program has been carefully designed to engage Leticia more fully with literacy development. Leticia will participate in small groups where she will hopefully feel more comfortable participating in class. Ms. Hernandez will work with Leticia twice a day and focus on her reading and writing skills. Transitional reading strategies and sheltered English instruction as well as the use of the primary language are some of the scaffolding strategies Ms. Hernandez will use to fortify Leticia's underdeveloped reading skills. Her teacher knows that Leticia has a beautiful voice, can sing in Spanish and English, and loves to perform with the school's Folkloric Dance Club. Ms. Hernandez too loves folkloric dance, having considerable performance experience herself. Leticia's talent will be recognized and incorporated into lessons by Ms. Hernandez. Ms. Hernandez begins the first math lesson of the year using a word problem involving the counting patterns in the "LingoLingo," Leticia's favorite dance, to reinforce multiplication. Leticia's face is illuminated. She gazes with affection at her teacher after realizing that Ms. Hernandez has chosen her especially for this first example. Leticia is already beginning to feel better about her mathematics ability.

Through the Eyes of the Family

Leticia races home from school this very first day with a special note from Ms. Hernandez. The note was discussed with Leticia so that she will be able to communicate about it with her grandmother. Leticia is to go to Homework Center daily after school for personal tutoring and homework support. Leticia is excited at the prospect of staying after school with Ms. Hernandez. Leticia will also be provided a special upper grade buddy.

Ms. Hernandez plays the same kind of music her grandmother listens to. This classroom is a sanctuary for Leticia. Ms. Hernandez is a role model for Leticia and links Leticia's interests to the school and formal curriculum in a meaningful way. A bridge has been erected. Leticia is no longer concerned that her family does not read or write English. Ms. Hernandez understands.

Leticia's grandmother is personally invited to attend English as a Second Language class at school. Though this is unfamiliar territory, Leticia's grandmother is comfortable talking with Ms. Hernandez and gives it a try. She finds her neighbors as well as dozens of other relatives of students at the school. The best part was meeting some people in the class who came to California from a neighboring village in Mexico. Leticia's grandmother attends classes three days a week now. She has become comfortable at the school and helps the teachers in other ways. Leticia feels a special bond with Ms. Hernandez. For the first time she is experiencing a feeling of status as a learner in this classroom.

High Expectations

At Edenvale Elementary School, academic, behavioral, and professional expectations are high. You feel this when you speak to the teachers and administration. For over 10 years, the school has provided the message that even if your parents have not gone to college, regardless of family background, you can graduate high school and attend college or a postsecondary vocational program.

Through the Eyes of the Student

Juwan races to school. He must get in the breakfast line early so that he is ready for the school year's first Adopt-A-College Program assembly. Juwan's mind is racing. He must remember his lines perfectly. This morning his class asks the principal's permission to participate in the Adopt-A-College Program. His class has written a rap about going to college. This is one of his favorite days of the school year. He will get to meet his college pen pal as well as important former Edenvale students. Juwan watches his teacher become emotional and tearful as the former Edenvale students greet their teachers, and pay tribute to this school and program that has provided the educational foundation for their current success. They are present to tell their college stories and the importance of working hard during the elementary school years.

The former students remind Juwan about the importance of doing his personal best, an important behavioral guideline at the school. Some of the former students have traveled far to join in this college day event. One former student, Christopher, is wearing his United States military uniform. Juwan sits in awe of the image that Chris' presence creates in the school cafeteria. His uniform is immaculate. As Chris passes by, Juwan notices his shoes. Chris has the shiniest shoes Juwan has ever seen. Juwan cannot pull his eyes from the image of Christopher saluting the American flag. Juwan wonders what it would feel like to wear such a uniform and walk in those shoes.

As the San Jose State football team strides past Juwan's class, an African American player stops and gives Juwan a high five. On this day, everyone at Edenvale wears a college shirt provided by donations from colleges across the country. Later, Juwan is selected to help lead the San Jose State cheer. This is the university Juwan's pen pal attends. Juwan has been to SJSU for a special tour. Juwan has also seen pictures of SJSU on TV, and his pen pal has written to answer all of his questions about the campus.

The assembly begins and his class takes the stage. The audience begins clapping along with the rap and begins to follow the words. The energy in the cafeteria grows and soon everyone is absorbed in the power of this day. Juwan stands at the front of the stage and delivers his lines. Everyone applauds. Next, Bobby Sanders, the state's 126-pound power weightlifting champion, takes the stage, performing to music and delivering his message about a healthy lifestyle and drug-free body. Like Juwan, Bobby is African American.

Through the Eyes of School Leadership

Former students have given speeches, and each class has performed. One class performed a rap, another, a PowerPoint presentation, and a third, a skit. Each class expressed their desire to participate in the Adopt-A-College Program. The former principal concludes the program with a heartfelt song performed on guitar and sung uniquely for the Edenvale students, staff, and parents.

Through the Eyes of the Family
Everyone joins in the song to the tune of "Johnny B Goode." It speaks of hard work and perseverance. Juwan replaces the word "Johnny" with his own name and hums the tune throughout the day and into the evening. The family's small apartment echoes with Juwan's version of the new Edenvale song. His little sister imitates his singing and Juwan speaks to her about going to college. Juwan has absorbed the message about college, and convinced his family about his plan. As Juwan reluctantly takes off his college t-shirt at the end of the day, he knows in his heart that he wants a college education to be a part of his future.

These elementary school students write to college buddies, participate in special assemblies, and visit college campuses. They are beginning to integrate a personal expectation that college is a part of their future. When this program began 12 years ago, 27% of the students from this school went on to college. This fall, 85% of Edenvale students were accepted to colleges and universities throughout the nation. This school culture emanates a heartfelt theme that our students will be successful learners.

Powerful Instruction

For schools to become resilient learning communities, students must be provided powerful instruction. Former president of the American Federation of Teachers, William Ayers, noted: " If you really care about the kids, give them the tools they need to succeed." To provide the right tools, we need to know which students are succeeding and which need additional instructional support. A systematic model of ongoing assessment informs teachers how students are progressing. This ongoing monitoring of student progress informs teachers which students need additional safety net support. This helps to increase the effectiveness of the instructional program.

Through the Eyes of School Leadership
How can instructional staff effectively monitor student progress? How do we know which students are successful, and which require additional support? Oak Grove School District adopted a practice developed in New Zealand known as the "Assessment Wall." During the 2000–2001 academic year, every elementary school within the Oak Grove School District committed to list by classroom teacher the reading and writing levels of all students. Each teacher prepared a record of student progress on large sheets of butcher paper. Statewide standardized test results, along with quarterly and monthly benchmarks (Gates MacGinitie, Running Records, and writing assessments), identify which students begin the year below grade-level standards and the degree of student progress during the year in reading

and writing skills. Race, ethnicity, gender, and language status are identified to provide disaggregated data.

Assessment Walls provide useful data for grade level and schoolwide meetings. Student performance is recorded and discussed by teachers. Strengths and weaknesses of the instructional program are analyzed, and instructional strategies are planned to more effectively meet the needs of all learners.

Through the Eyes of Teachers

At Edenvale School, teachers' voices and laughter fill each grade-level meeting room. As the instructional staff assembles, they organize themselves to create the Assessment Walls. The colorful scraps of paper that represent each child and his or her gender, ethnicity, special needs, and reading and writing levels are placed on the various Assessment Walls. Each child's journey through the school and his/her current level becomes vividly evident. The scraps of paper provide the reflection of the eyes, students' faces, hearts, voices, and minds. Teachers know their students well and recognize their talents, areas of weakness, and uniqueness of the students. They sense the essence of their students' learning, and what is required to help the kids become academically competent. Staff knows which children need support with vocabulary, which need help with fractions, and which need help with critical thinking skills.

Teachers begin to group students both homogeneously and heterogeneously depending upon their academic needs. The use of "sacred time" is at the core of the conversation. Sacred time is the first 2 hours of the school day. The goal is to engage every child in the most powerful literacy instruction possible. Some groupings are larger than others. Goals are set for each group. The journey for each student is now more clearly defined. The teaching team is clear on where to focus and how to more effectively collaborate in order to facilitate student success.

The grade level teams come together with the previous and subsequent grade levels to speak about their students. Each grade level's Assessment Walls are hung in the Professional Development Room. The sheets of butcher paper are then posted in chronological order from kindergarten through sixth grade around the room. A gallery walk of each grade level's students ensues.

The Professional Development Room is kept exclusively for teachers to analyze, reflect, and discuss a variety of data regarding student academic progress. The information in this room is confidential. Soon there is no discussion. The teachers are absorbed in writing their personal reflections in the journal each carries with him/her. Each teacher examines every grade level chart and looks for schoolwide achievement patterns.

Everyone is seated and privately reviews his/her reflections. Edenvale School's instructional gaps emerge from the work of the day. Clearly, the Hispanic population is low in reading, more specifically in the area of vocabulary and comprehension. A few specific schoolwide goals emerge. Each grade level agrees to focus on particular strategies to increase vocabulary and reading comprehension. The weaving of a school tapestry through the Assessment Wall process has sewn together purposeful and powerful instructional strategies at this school.

Through the Eyes of Families

The parent conference period becomes an opportunity for parents to become meaningful partners. The schoolwide collaborative effort of creating and analyzing Assessment Walls equips every teacher in the school with essential information to articulate to parents. Each teacher is able to discuss schoolwide and grade-level goals and individual student goals. Families receive specific data regarding their child and feel confident about the school focus and program. They are meaningfully drawn into conversation about their child's learning and gain a greater understanding about how the school works to promote their children's academic success.

Purposeful Support

How can a student who begins school with a more limited base of academically oriented stimulation, and a less developed vocabulary, eventually catch up and meet standards? Effective safety nets must be put in place. Oak Grove School District implemented pre-kindergarten and extended day programs, standards-based summer school, flexible grouping practices, Reading Recovery, and an effective Academic and Language Development Academy Model. Research-based small group instruction takes place before and after school, on weekends, and during the summer.

When necessary, students like Juwan and Leticia receive increased levels of prior knowledge instruction, after-school enrichment, and enhanced literacy and guided practice instruction. To further support academic development, the community liaison recruits parents to participate in culturally sensitive parent education. Two hundred parents a week are involved in parent programs on the Edenvale campus. Parent Institute for Quality Education classes as well as English as a Second Language classes take place in both the morning and evening. Parents report that these classes are helpful and continue to seek the information and skills required to help develop their children's academic abilities.

Through the Eyes of School Leadership

There is a melody of excitement in Leticia's classroom this morning. Students enter the room eagerly, absorbing the maps and new charts that adorn the classroom. The familiar roles and norms revisited at the beginning of each unit are clearly displayed. Ms. Jacobsen insists that every child is involved in decision making and sets clear expectations, goals, and learning outcomes. She helps students internalize social skills. They are developing the capacity to manage their own learning within the classroom. Through explicit instruction and practice of these social skills, students learn what can be accomplished through cooperation. This classroom is one of purposeful cooperation rather than competition.

Ms. Jacobsen, an exceptionally reflective practitioner, spent considerable time comparing her student work in social studies to articulated standards, knowing that standards are little more than theoretical ideals until they are purposefully taught utilizing a variety of instructional strategies to meet the needs of the diverse learners in her classroom.

The classroom becomes quiet as Ms. Jacobsen, like a symphony conductor, points to a chart displaying each student's assigned role. Each student responds with a characteristic nod and grin as her role is announced. Ms. Jacobsen has judiciously considered the many factors imaginable in formulating cooperative learning groups: race, gender, language ability, achievement and performance levels, social status, work style, motivation level, and personality. As she helps Leticia position her Facilitator Badge, she asks her about the questioning strategies that Leticia will use to help the group work (facilitating deeper levels of understanding below the surface). Ms. Jacobsen supports Leticia to grow into this challenging role. In turn, Leticia's status in the classroom is elevated. Her self-esteem as a learner will become a force of resiliency, enabling Leticia to narrow the academic achievement gap between her and students from the higher socioeconomic groups.

Orchestrating cooperative learning strategies within the classroom setting offers opportunities for students to experience purposeful support in a pivotal academic environment. Cooperative learning allows for interdisciplinary, thematic, and project-based work. Diversity of culture, experience, and opinion are explored. Classroom projects have relevance to students and they are able to have input and decision-making power around the questions they want to investigate. Cooperative learning structures individualize student roles, allowing for social development, which in turn enhances self-esteem and academic achievement.

Through the Eyes of Students

Leticia takes a deep breath and begins the class discussion with a thought-provoking question, "What are some reasons people leave their homes and migrate to new places?" The group's attention is focused on students who have lived as migrant farm workers or left their countries for important freedoms. The students listen attentively. A Caucasian boy kindly asks Leticia, "Why her family left Mexico?" In the midst of this group's work, cross-cultural understanding and emotional bonding are apparently taking place. Leticia has acknowledged the feelings, ideas, and contributions of others and the group members have developed an intrinsic commitment to purposefully care for and support one another. Leticia asks the group to compare and contrast their experiences with the pilgrims coming to America, the Recorder suggests that they make a Venn Diagram. The Harmonizer validates this suggestion. Leticia feels the warmth and satisfaction of having worked very effectively within this group of peers.

Through the Eyes of Families

"Tell me the story again, abuela (grandma). Why did you and abuelo (grandpa) come here?" "You know the story by heart, Leticia, I have told you many times. Why do you want to hear it again?" "It tells me who I am. It sounds so beautiful when you tell it. Please, abuela, tell me the story again." "Once we lived in a small, peaceful village. It had many things, handsome pottery, and an arroyo where we washed our clothes and a snow-capped mountain in the background. Everyone worked hard, in the fields, at the store, or in the kitchen. But the village had no school and we knew that this was important. We heard that California had lots of work, good schools, and the Brasero program. Your abuelo liked an adventure and was intrigued from the moment he heard about this. I was so very afraid of leaving the village and nervous about traveling and surviving in a new land," explained Leticia's grandmother. "Today, in school, abuela, I told this same story, just like you did. I felt strong and proud." "Your hard work in school is important, Leticia. I am so proud that I have a smart granddaughter."

Participation

For stakeholders to be collaborators, they must have a real voice. Inclusive practices, shared leadership, and effective communication maximize the talents of students, staff, parents, and community. To become a resilient learning community, leaders must recognize that schools exist within a neighborhood and a larger world. Schools must open their doors and become user friendly so that parents, businesses, and community agencies can provide and receive the vital resources that will enhance student resiliency.

Through the years, the Edenvale School campus has consistently been at the center of community life. The Edenvale Community Center was constructed through the visionary efforts of former principal Meril Smith, and community members who wanted to improve the quality of life in the neighborhood. In over 12 years of operation, it has functioned as a model of effective collaboration between the school, community, and the city of San Jose. The Center has hosted counseling programs, recreation and scouting programs, adult education, food and clothing banks, outreach medical services, and adult literacy projects.

The Edenvale Community Center concept was enhanced and enlarged in Fall 2000 with the official opening and dedication of the Edenvale Youth and Family Center. The Center, a triple-wide portable building, provides an attractive facility and recreational leaders who greatly benefit the community. After-school activities connected to school goals and objectives provide the community with a safe haven for children after school, during breaks, and throughout the summer. This project was made possible by a collaborative grant obtained by Edenvale School, Oak Grove School District, and the city of San Jose.

Through the Eyes of School Leadership

Each day at 3:00 PM, the school's campus transforms from the orientation of the rigorous work pace to the eclectic rhythm of children's spirits, talents, and playfulness. Manny Barbara, superintendent of the Oak Grove School District, enjoys his frequent visits to the Edenvale campus. Once an immigrant child at a similar Youth and Family Center in San Francisco, the nostalgia is evident in his eyes. He recalls a safe yet vibrant place where a plethora of languages were spoken and children from different backgrounds congregated daily.

With a large smile of recognition, Juwan hands Mr. Barbara a ping-pong paddle. The superintendent tosses his suit jacket onto a nearby chair and enthusiastically accepts the challenge. As Juwan sends his backhand spin over the net, Mr. Barbara asks Juwan what book he is reading. Juwan answers, "*Holes.* It's full of suspense and I'm at the part where the main character, Stanley, has just escaped from camp. It's desert all around the camp and Stanley could die from the heat or the lizards, but I don't think that is what is going to happen next." "I read that book a few months ago. I agree, it's an exciting book, I loved it. What do you think will happen next?" asks Mr. Barbara. "He finds his friend who has escaped and they somehow get the treasure. Is that really what happens, Mr. Barbara?" asks Juwan. As Mr. Barbara sends his best slam over the net, he assures Juwan it is a great ending and promises to talk to him again after he finishes the book. Juwan guarantees he will finish the book that very evening.

Through the Eyes of Students

"This school is cool, our homework's done, we read our book, and it's time for fun." Juakkila, Ardessia, Letisha, Shayenne, and other upper-grade girls are leading a younger group of girls in the latest cheers. Juwan's sister is part of the group. Juwan and his sister will be seeing their father for the first time next week. He has been in prison most of their lives. Both Juwan and his sister are happy to participate in this important after-school recreation program. As they bond with peers and caring adults, they are also developing into capable young people.

Through the Eyes of Families
Retrieving her grandchildren at the end of the day at the Youth and Family Center, Eloise takes a few moments outside the center to greet other families and show off her newest grandchild, a baby girl. Juwan now has a 5-month-old cousin living with him. Juwan is an avid participant in the school community, bubbling with motivation to excel. Juwan gleefully promenades up to his grandmother with an air of confidence and an ear-to-ear grin. "What in the world is up with you today, young man?" asks Juwan's grandmother. "You know grandma, I'm going to be the superintendent of this school district one day," responds Juwan. "Sounds mighty fine to me."

FOSTERING RESILIENCY IS WHERE WE MUST GO FROM HERE

Fostering resiliency in children is a long-term project, involving systemic change within the communities of children. It isn't something we do to students. It isn't a specific curriculum we teach to kids. It isn't something added to a school or community with short-term grant money. Supporting resiliency in children is based on deeply held beliefs that what we do every day in our schools makes a difference in their lives. It is about dedicating our hearts and minds to creating communities that are rich in caring, high expectations, and purposeful support, providing effective instruction and opportunities for meaningful participation. It is the understanding that the culture and daily practices of schools need to be redesigned in ways that help students achieve their academic potential.

If we care about every student, we will expect every student to become literate; we will offer extensive and appropriate support; we will know the students well and respond to the learning needs and lifestyles of our population. Curriculum, instruction, assessment, and professional development will be focused, research-based, and demonstrate measurable progress in student performance.

We feel passionately that if schools are committed to developing these protective factors, and purposefully fostering resiliency for students, then Juwan and Leticia will overcome their "at-risk" situations. The attainable goal for Juwan and Leticia is to achieve academically at a level that is commensurate with their Asian and white classmates.

What's in It for Me?

Whether you are a teacher, administrator, parent, student, grandparent, school board member, or community member, a resiliency focus is an opportunity to help build community, with and for my neighbors and myself, so that we all can have a more hopeful and productive future. Yes, we want to live in a place where people care about each other, where expectations and support are high, and where our participation is valued. We want this in our homes, our workplaces, and in the neighborhoods in which we live. Schools that have incorporated the protective factors of resiliency will be able to integrate the following positive aspects into the core of their culture:

- **Collegiality.** An important part of building a resilient school community is to create the time and expectation for teachers as professionals to know each other and their work well. True professionals share practices and generate much of their own knowledge base, just as engineers, doctors, and lawyers do. Bring a group of educators into a room for a professional development activity, and you cannot get them to stop talking. They do not want to listen to a presentation. They want to talk with one other! Why? Because educators have very little time to engage with their colleagues in meaningful professional conversation. There is so little time available to share ideas, concerns, and successes.
- **Intellectual stimulation.** In a school where these protective factors are flourishing, adults challenge one another to be reflective, share ideas, ask good questions, read widely, and be reflective practitioners. Adults want to know each student and their work well and, just as importantly, to know each adult and her/his work well.
- **Respect.** In a resilient learning community, the culture of the school is built on respect. If teachers, administrators, students, classified staff, parents, and community members know that they are valued as participants in the school, then effective collaboration toward closing the achievement gap can begin to take place.
- **Voice.** It is unlikely that any school will foster resiliency unless the members of that school community have significant voice in the workings of their own school. This is particularly true for teachers. Teachers currently have the traditional voice over their students that comes with the privacy of practice that results when a teacher shuts

her classroom door. Teachers are professionals, and professionals should have a say in their work lives. When teachers know that their voices are valued in the daily workings of the school, they are much more open to the voices of students, parents, classified staff, community members, and district leadership.
- **Increased job satisfaction.** When educators work to know students and student work well, when they commit to help every student learn to use both mind and heart well, the conversation changes. You no longer hear negative criticism of parents and students, peers and administrators. As the protective factors of resiliency become central to a school community, you can see, hear, and feel the difference in a school. You will see teachers and administrators engaging peers, students, parents, classified staff, and community in support of student learning. You will hear decisions being made based on what is best for students. You can sense the satisfaction that teachers feel when you hear them speak about the rewards of teaching.

JUWAN AND LETICIA IN THE FUTURE

It is the year 2015. Juwan and Leticia are high school seniors. They were fortunate to have attended schools that promoted student resiliency. Juwan and Leticia have become competent young people with the academic and social skills, confidence, and the belief that nothing can impede their success. Juwan and Leticia use their minds and hearts well. They communicate effectively, have strong problem-solving skills, and are motivated team players. They too want to make a difference and improve our world. Is this not our mission and purpose as educators? Can we develop resilient learning communities and close the achievement gap? As Asa Hilliard III (1991) writes: "We have the skill to do so. The remaining question is do we have the will?" (p. 14).

ACKNOWLEDGMENTS

This chapter is dedicated to Superintendent Manny Barbara, the Oak Grove School District Board of Trustees, the dedicated instructional staff, leadership team, students, and parents of the Oak Grove School District and the Edenvale School community. Without your leadership, professionalism, involvement, and desire to learn, the ideas that have come to life in this chapter may have never come to fruition.

REFERENCES

Benard, B. (1991). *Fostering resiliency in kids: Protective factors in the family, school, and community.* Portland, OR: Western Center for Drug-Free Schools and Communities.
Hilliard, A. G., III (1991). Why we must pluralize the curriculum. *Educational Leadership, 49*(4), 12–16.
Krovetz, M. (1999). *Fostering Resiliency: Expecting all students to use their minds and hearts well.* Thousand Oaks, CA: Corwin.
Werner, E., & R. S. Smith (1992). *Overcoming the odds: High risk children from birth to adulthood.* Ithaca, NY: Cornell University Press.

CHAPTER 12

RESILIENT COMMUNITIES

The Interplay between Community Development and Child Development Through Effective School Reform

Héctor H. Rivera
University of Houston

The resilience construct has been widely used in areas such as developmental psychology, general education, and learning environments (Garmezy, 1991; Matsen, 1994; Matsen, Best, & Garmezy, 1990; Rutter, 1987). In recent years its application to educational research has been emphasized. In the context of educational research, resilience can be defined as a heightened likelihood of success in a given context despite at-risk factors in the social environment. The environmental adversities brought about by early traits, conditions, and experiences have been discussed at the individual level of analysis. However, it is important to remember that the development of any individual also has a social component (Vygotsky, 1978).

This chapter examines the social component of resilient communities. Efforts to improve the educational development of Native American children through the process of school reform are examined. From a cultural-historical context, the characteristics of a resilient community represent an interplay between further developing the ecology of the community for its survival and success, as well as building students' capacities for their success in a dual world.

This chapter focuses on the collaborative work conducted at the Zuni Pueblo reservation in New Mexico. Over the past 20 years, this community has made an outstanding effort to improve the educational process for their children. The Zuni Pueblo community is one of the Native American communities about which much has been written by anthropologists and other researchers. However, most people are still unaware of the historical relationship between Europeans and Zunis, as well as the effect of the force colonization and political subjugation by Europeans on this community (Tharp et al., 2000). Fewer people still understand the central role played by schools in the process of colonization and socialization of Zuni children. The educational problems and conflicts now faced by Zunis and elsewhere in Native America are a condition of their history of relations and conflict with Europeans. This is still potent today in every aspect of the psychological experience and social process of the community. Historically, the primary intention of the schooling of Native children by European American institutions has been assimilation, achieved through the eradication of Native culture. Education has been the institutional mechanism used to systematically deny the Zuni community opportunities to practice their Native language, culture, and religion, thus aborting students' development as Native Americans (Tharp et al., 2000).

Previous research has seldom examined the interrelatedness of resilient communities to the development for successful educational programs. Resilient Native American communities assist in the development of effective programs, which in turn can bring about their children's development as Native Americans. What we now understand as sociolinguistic, contextual, and metacognitive strategies for teaching and learning are in fact elements emanating from everyday practices in a resilient community environment into the classroom setting (Wells & Chang-Wells, 1992). However, the historical context of intergroup relations continues to influence contemporary classrooms through institutionalized social relations, educational practices, and goals, all of which may be at odds with those of Native American communities and their perceived educational needs (Chavis & Newbrough, 1986; Darnell & Hoem, 1996; De Haan, 1999; McMillan & Chavis, 1986; O'Donnell & Tharp, 1990; Tharp et al., 2000; Tharp & Gallimore, 1988).

CHARACTERISTICS OF RESILIENT COMMUNITIES

Research in community psychology has identified three general characteristics among resilient communities involved in the process of school reform (O'Donnell & Tharp, 1990). These general characteristics of resilient communities include: (1) changing the landscape of the educational system, (2) empowering its members to action in school reform, and (3) seeking to model values and beliefs for the developmental growth of individual community members

Changing the Landscape of the Educational System

Resilient communities are focused on changing the ecology of the educational system through the rearrangement of school-related activities. The developmental continuum of any program must include an increase of community power to affect school systems. This is a process of acceptance of the detrimental nature of the educational conditions for the community and a desire to work toward changes that foster better community development (Darnell & Hoem, 1996). The literature suggests two important aspects of such community research. The first is that the current goals of education are embedded in the historical development of schooling. This realization has lead to the recognition of schooling as a socializing system. In return, this has prompted educators and communities to ask the question of whose values and beliefs are being taught in school and whose culture is being preserved through the schooling process. These questions have motivated the study of organizational structure of schooling in areas such as (a) locus of control; (b) the curriculum; (c) the language of instruction; (d) characteristics of teacher's professional development; and (e) the degree and type of parental involvement in schooling. Such research has focused on community activity practices, as a key for understanding individual development in the context of the sociohistorical experience of the community (Darnell & Hoem, 1996).

Empowering Community Members to Action in School Reform

Resilient communities recognize that their members need to have locus of control in educational policy and the direction of their children's development. The focus of community empowerment is on the development of community capacities in ways that foster their ability to achieve more satisfactory socialization of their children. Intervention is accomplished through a focus on community activities, intergroup relations, and on how those intergroup relations might change the activity settings, the ecological niche, and the dynamics under which intergroup participation dictates developmental goals for society through school developmental activity practices (O'Donnell & Tharp,1990). For example, a study by Saegert and Winkel (1996) indicates that personal participation in building activities also proved a good predictor of empowerment, indicating that empowerment operates at both the individual and group levels. Empowerment comes about through intertwined changes in behavior, self-concept, and actual improvement in the conditions of the individual, the group, and the community. Their study is consistent with the literature on community development. For example, a study conducted by Raeburn (1986) found that there needs to be community control and activities need to be of value to the cultural niche of the community in order for communities to be empowered (Moll, Amanti, Neff, & Gonzalez, 1992).

Seeking to Model Values and Beliefs for the Developmental Growth of Individual Community Members

This is based on the ideas that one does not practice what one has not learned. Therefore, resilient communities approach school reform as a process of modeling the conditions one wishes to achieve and perpetuate into future generations. Resilient communities provide their members with a map for their further developmental growth. This map is embedded in the cultural activities and practices enacted in the daily life of a community. According to Darnell and Hoem (1996), culture is the stored composite of knowledge that a nation or a people has at its disposal. It forms the basis for understanding and mastering for a single individual, a society, or a nation. It is the mechanism of group survival that is maintained through cultural activity practices.[1] Therefore, it follows that if diverse communities are to survive, and this is one of the basic dilemmas of indigenous peoples, their cultures must be transmitted from generation to generation through formal educational activities. The education system, regardless of form and locus of control, is inextricably a part of this process of community and child development (Darnell & Hoem, 1996). However, in order for the values and beliefs of a community to be shared across generations, the educational system needs to integrate the community's practices through connected and contextual activities in the classrooms. Also, its locus of control needs to include the community in the process of joint reform efforts.

Resilient communities seek to bring to their members a sense of community. This sense of community is guided by common symbols that are an integral part of the social world (Chavis & Newbrough,1986; McMillan & Chavis,1986). Raeburn (1986) found that comprehensive community projects and community houses were successfully developed by strategically making community members active participants and organizers of the project activities. Another aspect of importance was the need to implement programs and activities that are of value to the cultural niche of the community (Sasao & Sue, 1993).

THE IMPORTANCE OF RESILIENT COMMUNITIES (OUTCOMES)

It is the goal of resilient communities to see their children as functional members of their larger society as well as their future leaders adhering to the values, norms, and practices of their people. The development of each individual child is then interconnected to the continuous survival and development of the community and vice versa. However, schools have often assumed that there is a single trajectory for child development and social functioning. Therefore, the lessons and curriculum often represent Western European social values to be adopted and practiced in the classrooms. It is not always the case that the goals of formal schooling are opposite to the goals of a community. But it is often the case that for underrepresented groups, the school system often assumes to know what is best for their children. In some regards these educational assumptions are related to some of the existing forms of school reform efforts and they are related to the development of instructional programs that seldom provide lasting effects on students' academic achievement. Much of the research has placed a heavy emphasis on the study of the developing individual outside of his/her cultural context.

For Native American communities, one source of conflict has been the goals of the educational system versus their own goals as communities. Generally, education is defined as "the deliberate, systematic, and sustained effort to transmit, evoke, or acquire knowledge, attitudes, values, skills, or sensibilities" (Darnell & Hoem, 1996, pp. 10). However, a fundamental question is whose cultural values are being fostered in the classroom. Therefore, it is not only the issue of providing what we believe to be an optimal learning environment, but also of providing what students perceive to be a meaningful environment in which they can learn to be participants in a dual world.

FOSTERING RESILIENCY AT THE COMMUNITY LEVEL (INCORPORATION OF PEOPLE AND IDEAS)

A role of resilient communities is to develop their children's capacities in an interrelated process of community and child development. The work by Rogoff, Mistry, Göncü, and Mosier (1993) among communities in Salt Lake City and Guatemala suggests that the concept of development (e.g., skills and values) varies as a function of community goals, values, and beliefs. Analysis of observed interactions between toddler and parent, during activity, point to differences in the type of parental behavior and reinforcement as a way to elicit and foster specific social values to the child.

Socialization is also an adaptive response to ecological challenges that have shaped the family ecology of a community. Therefore, socialization also refers to the process by which individuals become distinctive and active functioning members of the society in which they live through community practices (Cole & Scribner,1975). Community values and beliefs guide the developmental activities of their children. For example, the work by Tharp and colleagues (1984) shows that the socialization system of Hawaiian children is not organized to train children for leaving the family, but to teach responsibility and competence within the family system. Hawaiian children are socialized to think of "success" in terms of contributions to the kin or peer group rather than as a matter of individual achievement. The training for specific acts of sharing and mutual assistance grow from basic social values for family life: interdependence, responsibility for others, sharing of work and resources, cooperation, and obedience and respect toward parents.

The profound effect of cultural context on the development of higher psychological functions is clearly stated in the work of Vygotsky (1978). His theoretical position asserts that interpsychological and social practices are internalized and become intramental. It is during the process of joint productive activity that higher psychological functions develop (Vygotsky, 1966; Wertsch, 1985). Therefore, teaching practices need to specifically address the concerns of students who come from different cultures and who often are trying to learn a new language. Teaching should involve the process of "assisting the performance of students through the Zone of Proximal Development (ZPD)" (Vygotsky, 1966, p. 31). The ZPD is the distance between the child's individual capacity and the capacity to perform with the assistance of others (Cole, 1985; Cole & Cole, 1997; Tharp & Gallimore, 1988). The relevance of the ZPD to teaching practices lies in the notion that learning and development occurs through assisted performance in the home/community environment as well as in the classroom. This neo-Vygotskian perspective finds much of its support in the educational literature on development of effective reform programs as well as in the developmental psychology literature on child development and socialization (Tharp & Gallimore, 1988). Therefore, development and social functioning are dependent on specific activities that in turn are dependent on the cultural-historical events that have led to the present conditions and activity practices (Bronfenbrenner,1986).

In summary, it seems that culturally based values, norms, and behaviors are transmitted from one generation to the next via overt and covert processes of socialization and they are functionally adaptive to the demands of the local environment (Seidman, Hughes, & Williams, 1993; Tharp et al., 1984). For example, studies in Aina Pumehana on rural Oahu suggest that a shared-function family system is the goal for development by the extended family during child rearing. This goal is accomplished through family behavior and the type of cognitive activities practiced and reinforced in the child by family members (Gallimore, Boggs, & Jordan, 1974).

BUILDING STUDENTS' CAPACITIES FOR ACADEMIC SUCCESS

An effective school environment that may lead to success for all students in the classroom requires community involvement. Effective instruction is notable for its family involvement, which allows for instruction to be meaningful and responsive to the local environment. Research also shows that there are important principles for achieving effective instruction in the classroom. These empirically derived principles form the basis for the success of all students (Tharp, Estrada, Dalton, & Yamauchi, 2000; Tharp & Gallimore, 1988).

The five standards for effective pedagogy are:

I. Joint Productive Activity: Teachers and students producing together.

II. Developing Language and Literacy across the Curriculum

III. Making Meaning: Connecting School to Students' Lives

IV. Teaching Complex Thinking: Cognitive Challenge

V. Teaching Through Instructional Conversation

These principles are interrelated factors for the achievement of academic success in the classroom. For example, research suggests that underrepresented students need opportunities to speak and write, to practice language use, and to receive the natural feedback of conversation from teachers and peers. This perspective implies that school success for children from culturally and linguistically diverse backgrounds should be viewed as a socially negotiated process involving interactions with persons, environment, resources, and goals. When they enter school, children have to adjust to the school-context behaviors and understandings that are unique to their culture. There are differences among cultures in the ways in which parents teach children at home, the ways in which parents expect children to behave, and the ways in which children and adults converse and interact. When teachers do not share their students' cultural background, the teaching and learning process may be impeded by misunderstanding and frustration. This makes community involvement more meaningful and necessary.

In summary, long before they enter the classroom, children attempt to make sense of the natural world (Bronfenbrenner, 1986). Many of the naive theories held by children arise from interaction with parents and family members. Efforts in the classroom should be focused on promoting communities of learners by taking advantage of children's innate curiosity and developed community orientation. The teacher's role is to facilitate the active learning of children by building on that curiosity and directing it into exploration. This approach to the social construction of knowledge is consistent with the underlying sociocultural approach to learning that is the basic framework for effective teaching and learning.

THE ZUNI COMMUNITY EFFORTS FOR SCHOOL REFORM

Historically, education for Native American communities has been an institutional mechanism used to systematically deny Native Americans opportunities to practice Native languages, cultures, and religions, thus aborting students' development as Native Americans. In a recent publication, Tharp and colleagues (1999) addressed the process for effective school reform in the context of the 500-year history of education as a battleground between European settlers and Native peoples. They review the history of the Zuni school reform movement, beginning with establishing the Zuni public school district. They also identified seven major obstacles to school reform as they have operated in Zuni and elsewhere among Native American communities. These obstacles are presented and elaborated in their article "Seven More Mountains and a Map: Overcoming Obstacles to Reform in Native American Education." Briefly, these obstacles include:

1. Disrespect of Native Americans by the school.
2. Student resistance—withdrawal and reduced achievement.
3. Lack of self-confidence in Native American leaders.
4. Passivity of Native communities in the face of school authority.
5. Teacher imperviousness to external influence.
6. Bureaucratic, legal, and policy constraints.
7. Vision conflicts between Native communities and the education power structure.

The obstacles to school reform at Zuni represent a microcosm of the experiences of many Native communities around the world. Many of these Native communities are struggling for the right to guide the development of their children so they may become the community leaders of the future, as well as in order to preserve the survival of their culture. In Native American communities, the goal of educational reform requires that schools educate their children within the context of the history, values, goals, and culture of the local tribal community. Through joint collaboration, the Center for Research on Education, Diversity, and Excellence (CREDE) and the Zuni community have been working in (1) the professional development of teachers; (2) the development of teacher portfolios and classroom assessment instruments; and (3) an increase in family/community involvement in school activities.

Through this joint effort and collaboration, a pedagogy that is effective for the academic success of Native American students has been developed (Dalton & Youpa, 1998; Tharp et al., 1994). An exhaustive analysis of the research on effective education for at-risk students resulted in the publication of "Five Standards for Effective Pedagogy" (Dalton, 1998; Dalton & Youpa, 1998; Tharp, 1989; Tharp et al., 2000). These standards are empirically derived from the existing knowledge in research across age and grade levels, cultural and linguistic groups, and subject matters. These standards are, therefore, consensual generic guidelines for effective pedagogy for all students. Not surprisingly, they are highly congruent with those standards independently developed by other organizations focused on the improvement of education for at-risk students, as well as with state-mandated standards for classroom practice (for details on the standards, see CREDE reports at www.crede.ucsc.edu).

A total of 200 people were randomly surveyed and 53 others volunteered to participate in the survey. Overall, the sample is also equally representative of men and women from 21 to 103 years of age. The data analysis involved descriptive statistics and multivariate analysis by *age, gender, socioeconomic status, schooling experience,* and *level of education* of participants. Overall, the findings show that there are no significant differences of opinions, values, and beliefs by *gender, age* or any of the other categories corresponding to the survey participants.

Principal component extraction is used as a means of identifying underlying processes among community members (Rummel, 1970; Tabachnick & Fidell, 1996). A principal component factor extraction with promax (orthogonal) rotation was performed using SPSS on the 57 items from the attitudinal survey. The presence of outliers, absence of multicollinearity, and factorability of the correlation matrices was assessed. No cases were deleted during the principal factor extraction.

A 14-factor solution was returned that explained 65.9% of the variance. Three factors were found to be not interpretable due to poorly written items. Upon conversations with Zuni community members, these factors were dropped from the solution. Variables are ordered and grouped by size of loading to facilitate interpretation. Overall, variables were well-defined by the factor solution. With a cut of .30 for inclusion of a variable in interpretation of a factor, 9 of 57 variables did not load on any factor. The loading across factors ranged from .42 to .84. Interpretive labels are suggested for each factor in the next section of the chapter.

KEY FINDINGS

Resilient community efforts are focused on the interplay between community development and child development through purposeful activities in order to build their children's capacities for success in a dual world. The main factors emerging from this study include:

1. Education should be contextualized.
2. Education should include the goals of the community.
3. Education should challenge students toward cognitive complexity.
4. Education should include language development in schools.
5. Education should include community involvement.

Education Should Be Contextualized

The Making Meaning Standard encourages teachers to use a variety of direct and indirect approaches to draw on students' familial and local contexts of experience. There is a wide range of social contexts and circumstances beyond the classroom and the school that influence academic accomplishment (August & Hakuta, 1997). The reality of students' lives is anchored in contexts outside school (August & Hakuta, 1997; Moll et al., 1992; Vogt, Jordan, & Tharp, 1992).

Research shows that resilient students who come from at-risk environments show characteristics such as high expectations, belief that life has meaning, goal direction, personal agency, interpersonal problem solving, social competence, responsiveness, autonomy, and a sense of purpose. According to the National Association for the Education of Young Children (1996), it is important to assess young children's progress and achievements during ongoing, strategic, and purposeful activities. The results can be used to benefit children—by adapting curriculum to developmentally appropriate tasks and by meeting the developmental and learning needs of children during and beyond the classroom activity (Dalton & Sison, 1994).

In the context of the classroom, these characteristics are promoted and fostered through an interactive synergy that occurs during meaningful, contextual joint activities that engaged the students by connecting school constructs and concepts to the students' everyday life. Good teaching uses meaningful content presented in life-like situations (Allington, 1990; Chalmot, 1992; Means & Knapp, 1991).

Education Should Include the Goals of the Community

Joint productive activity promotes resiliency by providing students with the opportunity to participate in meaningful learning classroom practices. This is an issue of concern that needs to be addressed when considering curriculum development, language programs, teacher professional development, and other aspects related to the teaching and learning of at-risk students. In the case of the Zuni community, formal education and the development of future community leaders are interconnected aspects. As pointed out by a survey participant:

> We need to keep up and make an effort to reach higher standards. We need to do something and find out what the community wants and how they want to address the problems of education. We need to get the schools involved in the community...this helps a lot. They [teachers and students] need to get involved in the community. For example, making and working on Shalako houses. This is where they are going to learn things about the community. It works both ways, it helps the community and it helps the schools. For our children, this is their culture anyway and they need to maintain it. It will be in their memories, they will never forget it. (Zuni, personal communication, March 1999)

Community members are of the opinion that if meaningful education is to be fostered in Zuni schools, it should create the conditions for their children to participate in community events. Joint activities teach students how to construct and incorporate new knowledge into their current repertoire and experiences, as well as it teaches them problem-solving skills in the context of social transactions and social discourse. When experts and novices work together for a common product or goal and they have opportunities to converse about the activity, learning is likely (Rogoff, 1993; Tharp & Gallimore, 1988; Wertsch, 1985). The use of joint productive activity increases exponentially the amount of communication and assisted performance available in the classroom. Therefore, joint productive activity does not only promote general resilience but it also fosters resiliency in domain-specific areas in which the child is considered to be resilient. The teacher becomes only one source among 30 or so peer resources. Research evidence also clearly supports the role of the constructive, productive activity; the critical feature is applying that knowledge in productive action with others (Boaler, 1999; Tharp & Gallimore, 1988; Vygotsky, 1978; Webb, Troper, & Fall, 1995).

Education Should Challenge Students Toward Cognitive Complexity

Standard IV reflects research evidence that the teaching of complex thinking by involving students in challenging tasks is a universal principle for effective instruction. Children learn what they are taught. If they are taught only facts and basic skills, they will learn only facts and basic skills. Cognitive complexity will be learned if it is taught. Of course, neither a challenge too low nor one too high will assist development. Through the activity-and-language-based interaction of the cultural-historical-activity-theory approach to pedagogy, "challenge" can be appropriately leveled. The appropriate level of cognitive challenge is to be found in the Zone of Proximal Development. For development to occur, challenge must constantly be set at the point where assistance is necessary (Au, 1980; Erickson & Mohatt, 1982; Rosebery, Warren, & Conant, 1992).

If school is a socializing institution, then we also need to be concerned with the means for teaching and learning. First of all, we need to teach students by using the most effective strategies for teaching and learning in the classroom. However, as pointed out by survey participants, currently Zuni children experience a different reality in the schools.

> My child was called "slow learner" but no one really told me what to do with my son at home as far as teaching him. All he got was labeled "slow learner." I don't know how to feel about a comment like this. (Survey participant, #532, 1998)

> The survey participant expressed that teachers should be more willing to challenge students. Her son at Zuni Middle School was labeled a "slacker" and he eventually only completed work that was expected of him and he didn't seek more. By the end of the year he had no motivation and complained about school being boring. (Surveyor notes, #1811, 1998)

As pointed out by a Zuni educator, "So far in our schools, a heavy emphasis and energy has been placed on the labeling of our students and on the assessment of their behaviors" (personal communication, 2001). However, for children with learning disabilities, as well as any other child, the focus in the classroom learning environment should be on the fact that they are growing, learning, and developing every day. In this way, the emphasis is placed on what they have accomplished and what they are capable of doing. Community members' comments on educational practices are consistent with educational research that defines teaching as " assisting the student's performance at the Zone of Proximal Development" (Tharp & Gallimore, 1988). This requires teaching strategies such as the ones Zunis have used throughout time in their teaching of complex religious ceremonies or arts and crafts to their children. Educational programs focused on promoting and fostering resilience among at-risk students require teaching to students' strengths, providing growth opportunities, and providing brainstorming activities. They also require the creation of an environment that allows for problem-solving activities, and the development of activities with clear goals that require critical thinking and reflection by students (Bernard, 1997; Bruce, 1995; Henderson & Milstein, 1996).

Education Should Include Language Development in Schools

One important aspect for promoting resiliency among at-risk students is providing growth opportunities for students. Oral and written language development can be fostered by restating, modeling, offering alternative phrasing, and questioning (Dalton & Youpa, 1998; Tharp & Gallimore,1988). Everyday language and academic language need continuous and integrated development. This is because academic language builds on and modifies everyday language and the thinking that it reflects. Academic discussion encourages students to move beyond everyday talk and use subject lexicons to express their understanding of concepts. The teacher's role is to involve students in activities that stimulate language use. In the case of the Zuni community, they are of the opinion that there cannot be Zuni cultural practices without the appropriate language due to the fact that many of their prayers and traditional activities are learned through oral teachings. The following quote from a survey participant points to the importance of the Zuni language.

> Learning and preserving the Zuni language is a "must" for the future survival of our traditions and heritage as A:shiwi[1] people. (Survey participant, # 196, 1999)

The teaching and learning of the Zuni language provide a medium for contextual and meaningful curriculum for classroom practices. This educational concern is also tied to other educational concerns expressed by the community. Proficiency in speaking, reading, and writing is key to academic achievement. Implementing the language development standard means that teachers seize informal opportunities to learn about students while encouraging student participation in the emerging academic community of their classroom. Language, thinking, values, and culture have deep interconnections; dialogue particularly during joint productive activity, supports students' academic achievement and affective development (Au, 1980; Cazden, 1986; Tharp, 1997; Vygotsky, 1978).

Education Should Include Community Involvement

A necessary condition for effective school reform includes the involvement of the community in the process of decision making, as well as in the everyday classroom activities. In the case of the Zuni community, it has been over 20 years since the community efforts for reform began. The resistance to change by the schools has been a prevalent issue in the process. However, the community understands that practices that have negated the importance of the community for the last 500 years cannot be changed in two decades. But they also understand that community involvement in decision making is vital in the process of changing the landscape of their educational system.

Community members also are of the opinion that community involvement is one way to begin the process of contextualizing and connecting education. In their view, Zuni parents/relatives and other community members also have knowledge and skills to contribute to the educational success of their children. They are also of the opinion that a successful education is one that allows for the integration (combining) of both school and community values in the schooling process of their children.

The following quote illustrates some of my experiences while conducting the survey interviews. The survey itself was an empowering process for the majority of the participants who wish to be involved in their children's education.

> I am glad that this survey is being conducted because as Zuni community people we don't get a chance to express our opinions. As a grandparent, I don't go to school meetings, but I am still interested in what my grandchildren are learning.
>
> Questions throughout the interview are all important, which also makes me feel important to be asked about my views. I have no negative feelings about the Zuni schools, only to let the teachers know that they are doing a good job. High school needs to improve more. More Zuni teachers at the high school level. (Survey participant, #485, 1998)

However, from the resilience literature on at-risk students we also find there are students that in spite of detrimental conditions are academically successful. Research suggests that these students benefit from a variety of protective factors such as family involvement in students' academic life and classroom practices pertaining to pedagogy that allows students' meaningful participation in classroom activities. Therefore, fostering and promoting such practices can be helpful to students who are at risk of academic failure.

Overall, research in community psychology suggests that resilience can be developed and fostered through these effective principles for teaching and learning. Educational research suggests that historically, school success has depended on the advantages that family and community institutions provide to children from birth. Many minority and low-income groups have had few language, literacy, and cultural resources in their families or communities that prepared them for success in schools in areas such as mathematics or science. However, when schools improve their teaching practices, students can improve their learning. The principles of teaching that are known to increase at-risk students' school success are equally effective for all students, but for at-risk students, they are a vital necessity (Dalton, 1998; Tharp & Gallimore, 1988).

CONCLUSION

Teaching and learning cannot be disassociated from developmental issues permeating the cultural environment. An effective classroom environment requires connectedness and contextualization of instruction in ways that are meaningful to the students. Effective school reform cannot be a one-dimensional approach that requires the involvement of some but not others. Meaningful instruction will require the involvement of parents and other community members not only for instruction to be meaningful in the classroom environment but also for instructional interventions to be lasting and sustainable.

The process of school reform is a process of changing the landscape of the educational system. There are sociohistorical implications on what education has meant to Native American people. At Zuni, this requires the rearrangement of school-related activities on issues of policy and decision making to include community opinions, values, and beliefs. Activities are goal-oriented practices that lead to the development and maintenance of any values system. However, the question is whose values and goals are being fostered in the classroom environment. The community survey has served as a tool for identifying the goals and values of the Zuni community. A refocus on what the community wants for their children may have some lasting effects on school reform. This effect is already apparent in the Zuni bilingual program, a program that has faced continuous resistance by some classroom teachers and administrators. However, the survey results have sparked new dialogue among bilingual educators by solidifying their belief on the importance of their efforts and program since survey results show an overwhelming endorsement by the community of their efforts on teaching and learning the Zuni language in schools.

Overall, efforts for educational reform to improve teaching and learning practices have moved classroom practices in directions that are generally considered to be an improvement in comparison to past history. However, this improvement has only occurred at the individual level for some teachers and administrators. But, in the last 5 years, evidence also shows the process of school reform has, in fact, left behind a legacy of new or improved curriculum frameworks, changes in a variety of educational policies, new institutions and partnering arrangements, and an increased number of competent local leaders of reform. The conditions are set for the development of educational programs that may aid in sustaining the community reform efforts. It is hoped the survey results will have a modest, positive impact on educational policy and on the trajectory and shape of school reform at Zuni. Identifying the educational goals of the community for their children is only the first step for effective school reform. These findings will be helpful in engaging the public in the discourse of educational reform. After all, these educational issues are not the concern of individuals alone but the concerns of a community in the context of their goals and objectives for the development and education of their future leaders.

IMPLICATIONS

Another important characteristic of resilient communities is to develop partnerships and ask for assistance when needed. This has led to joint efforts between researchers and community for the dissemination of the community survey findings. Since the completion of the survey, several activities have been carried out. A report was written and distributed among Zuni community leaders and other community members. A poster presentation was also done during the community's last educational summit. Some postinterviews with survey participants have been conducted in order to begin the process of identifying the type of programs that may aid the community in the process of their involvement in school reform. The findings were also presented during a recent "Teacher Summer Institute" at Zuni, a two-day teacher professional development workshop designed on applying the findings to classroom practices and providing teachers with community references and resources for the development of future integrated and connected classroom activities.

At the national level, the results have also been presented to Native organizations representing the interests of diverse Native groups. Future research is needed to organize an empirically derived set of community educational goals. The focus of the research is to identify shared goals among communities, as well as to identify the culturally specific need for different groups that may serve in the design of effective programs.

NOTES

1. "Since there are many definitions of culture, it is also important to state how I do not use it. In the literature, culture has also been used by others as a substitute for 'society.' Since I look upon culture as the stored knowledge of a society or subsociety that enables the society to survive as a group, it is an apparatus of, not a synonym for, society. From this perspective, people belong to, live in, or are members of social groups; they are not members of culture" (Darnell & Hoem, 1996, pp. 11).
2. A:shiwi is the name that Zunis give to themselves. It means "people of the middle place." It has a historical as well as a cultural reference to their current religious practices.

REFERENCES

Allington, R. (1990). Children who find learning to read difficult: School responses to diversity. In E. H. Hiebert (Ed.), *Literacy for a diverse society: perspectives, programs, and policies* (pp. 237–252). Bristol, PA: Falmer.

Au, K. (1980). Participation structures in a reading lesson with Hawaiian children: Analysis of a culturally appropriate instructional event. *Anthropology and Education Quarterly, 11*(2), 91–115.

August, D., & Hakuta, K. (1997). *Improving schooling for language-minority children: A research agenda.* Washington, DC: National Academy Press.

Bernard, B. (1997). *Turning it around for all youth: From risk to resilience* (ERIC/CUE Digest No. 126). New York: ERIC Clearinghouse on Urban Education.

Boaler, J. (1999). Participation, knowledge, and beliefs: A community perspective on mathematics learning, *Educational Studies in Math, 40,* 259–281.

Bronfenbrenner, U. (1986). Ecology of the family as a context for human development: Research perspectives. *Developmental Psychology, 22,* 723–742.

Bruce, M. A. (1995). Fostering resiliency in students: Positive action strategies for classroom teachers. *The Teacher Educator, 31*(2), 178–188.

Cazden, C. (1986). Classroom discourse. In M. S. Wittrock (Ed.), *Handbook of research on teaching* (3rd ed.). New York: Macmillan.

Chamot, A.U. (1992) Learning and problem solving strategies of ESL students. *Bilingual Research Journal, 16*(3&4), 3–27.

Chavis, D., & Newbrough, R. J. (1986). The meaning of "community" in community psychology. *Journal of Community Psychology, 14,* 335–340.

Cole, M. (1985). The zone of proximal development: Where culture and cognition create each other. In J. V. Wertsch, (Ed.), *Culture, communication, and cognition: Vygotskian perspectives.* Cambridge, UK: Cambridge University Press.

Cole, M., & Cole, S. (1997). *The development of children.* New York: W. H. Freeman.

Cole, M., & Scribner, S. (1975). Theorizing about socialization of cognition. *Ethos, 3*(2), 249–266.

Dalton, S. S. (1998). *Pedagogy matters: Standards for effective teaching practice.* Santa Cruz: Center for Research on Education, Diversity & Excellence, University of California.

Dalton, S. S., & Youpa, D. G. (1998). Standards-based teaching reform in Zuni Pueblo middle and high schools. *Equity and Excellence in Education, 31*(1), 55–68.

Darnell, F., & Hoem, A. (1996). *Taken to extremes: Education in the far north.* Oslo–Stockholm: Scandinavian University Press.

De Haan, M. (1999). *Learning as cultural practice: How children learn in a Mexican mazahua community. A study of culture and learning.* Netherlands: THELA THESIS.

Erickson, F., & Mohatt, G. (1982). The cultural organization of participation structure in two classrooms of Indian students. In G. Spindler (Ed.), *Doing the ethnography of schooling* (pp. 132–174). New York: Holt, Rinehart & Winston.

Garmezy, N. (1991). Resiliency and vulnerability to adverse developmental outcomes associated with poverty. *American Behavioral Scientist, 34,* 416–430.

Henderson, N., & Milstein, M. N. (1996). *Resiliency in schools: Making it happen for students and educators.* Thousand Oaks, CA: Corwin.

Masten, A. S. (1994). Resilience in individual development: Successful adaptation despite risk and adversity. In M. C. Wang & E. W. Gordon (Eds.), *Educational resilience in inner-city America: Challenges and prospects* (pp. 3–25). Hillsdale, NJ: Erlbaum.

Masten, A. S., Best, K. M., & Garmezy, N. (1990). Resilience and development: Contributions from the study of children who overcome adversity. *Development and Psychpathology, 2,* 425–444.

McMillan, D. W., & Chavis, D. M. (1986). Sense of community: A definition and theory. *Journal of Community Psychology, 14,* 6–23.

Means, B., & Knapp, M.S. (1991). *Models for teaching advanced skills to educationally disadvantaged children. Teaching advanced skills to educationally disadvantaged children.* Washington, DC: U.S. Department of Education, Office of Planning,

Moll, L., Amanti, C., Neff, D., & Gonzalez, N. (1992). Funds of knowledge for teaching: Using a qualitative approach to connect homes and classrooms. *Theory into Practice, 31,* 132–141.

National Association for the Education of Young Children. (2001). *NAEYC Guidelines Revision: NAEYC Standards for Early Childhood Professional Preparation* [Online]. Available: http:www.naeyc.org/

O'Donnell, C. R., & Tharp, R. G. (1990). Community intervention and the use of multi-disciplinary knowledge. In A. S. Bellack, M. Hersen, & A. E. Kazdin (Eds.), *International handbook of behavior modification and therapy.* New York: Plenum Press.

Raeburn, J. M. (1986). Towards a sense of community: Comprehensive community projects and community houses. *Journal of Community Psychology, 14,* 391–398.

Rogoff, B. (1981). Adults and peers agents of socialization: A highland Guatemalan profile. *Ethos, 9*(1), 18–36.

Rogoff, B. (1993). Observing sociocultural activity on three planes: Participatory appropriation, guided participation, apprenticeship. In A. Alvarez, P. del Rio, & J. V. Wertsch (Eds.), *Perspectives on sociocultural research.* Cambridge, MA: Cambridge University Press.

Rogoff, B., Mistry, J., Göncü, A., & Mosier, C. (1993). Guided participation in cultural activity by toddlers and caregivers. *Monographs of the Society for Research in Child Development, 58,* Serial No. 236.

Rosebery, A. S., Warren, B. W., & Conant, F. R. (1992). Appropriating scientific discourse: Findings from language minority classrooms. *The Journal of the Learning Sciences, 2*(1), 61–94.

Rummel, R. (1970) *Applied factor analysis.* Evanston, IL: Northwestern University Press.

Rutter, M. (1987). Psychosocial resilience and protective mechanisms. *American Journal of Orthopsychiatry, 37,* 317–331.

Saegert, S., & Winkel, G. (1996). Path to community empowerment: Organizing at home. *American Journal of Community Psychology, 24,* 517–550.

Sasao, T., & Sue, S. (1993). Toward a culturally anchored ecological framework of research in ethnic-cultural communities. *American Journal of Community Psychology, 21,* 705–727.

Seidman, E., Hughes, D., & Williams, N. (1993). Cultural phenomena and the research enterprise: Toward a culturally anchored methodology. *American Journal of Community Psychology, Special Issue, 21*(6), 687–703.

Tabachnick, B., & Fidell, L. (1996*). Using multivariate statistics.* New York: Harper-Collins.

Tharp, R. G. (1989). Psychocultural variables and constants: Effects on teaching and learning in schools. *American Psychologist, 44,* 349–359.

Tharp, R. G. (1997). *From at-risk to excellence: Research, theory and principles for practice.* (Research Report No. 1). Washington, DC: Center for Applied Linguistics and Center for Research on Education, Diversity, and Excellence.

Tharp, R. G., Dalton, S. S., & Yamauchi, L. (1994). Principles for culturally compatible Native American Education. *Journal of Navajo Education, 11*(3), 33–39.

Tharp, R. G. Estrada, P., Dalton, S. S., & Yamauchi, L. (2000). *Teaching transformed: Achieving excellence, fairness, inclusion.* Denver, CO: Harmony Westview.

Tharp, R. G., & Gallimore, R. (1988*). Rousing minds to life: Teaching, learning, and schooling in social context.* Cambridge, MA: Harvard University Press.

Tharp, R. G., Jordan, C., Speidel, E. G., Au, K. H., Klein, W. T., Calkins, P. R., Sloat, M. C., & Gallimore, R. (1984). Product and process in applied developmental research: Education and the children of a minority. In M. E. Lamb, A. L. Brown, & B. Rogoff (Eds.), *Advances in developmental psychology* (Vol. 3). London: Erlbaum.

Tharp, R. G., Lewis, H., Hilberg, R., Bird, C., Epaloose, G., Dalton, S., Youpa, D., Rivera, H., Riding In-Feathers, M., & Eriacho, W. (1999). Seven more mountains and a map: Overcoming obstacles to reform in Native American schools. *Journal of Education for Students Placed at Risk, 4*(1), 5–25.

Vogt, L. A., Jordan, C., & Tharp, R. G. (1992). Explaining school failure, producing school success: Two cases. In E. Jacob & C. Jordan (Eds.), *Minority education: Anthropological perspectives* (pp. 53–66). Norwood, NJ: Ablex.

Vygotsky, L. S. (1978). *Mind in society: The development of higher psychological processes.* (M. Cole, V. John-Steiner, S. Scribner, & E. Souberman, Eds.). Cambridge, MA: Harvard University Press.

Webb, N. M., Troper, J. D., & Fall, R. (1995). Constructive activity and learning in collaborative small groups. *Journal of Educational Psychology, 87*(3), 406–423.

Wertsch, J. (1985). *Vygotsky and the social formation of mind.* Cambridge, MA: Harvard University Press.

Wells, G., & Chang-Wells, L. (1992). *Constructing knowledge together: Classrooms as centers of inquiry and literacy.* Portsmouth, NH: Heinemann.

CHAPTER 13

PROMOTING RESILIENCY IN YOUTH, EDUCATORS, AND COMMUNITIES

Doris "Annie" Henry
New Mexico Highlands University

Mike M. Milstein
University of New Mexico

Resiliency is an approach that expands our thinking about students, schools, and communities beyond problem identification and resolution to strengths identification and actualization. Problem solving draws one's attention directly to deficits and how to repair them, whether we are talking about students, educators, schools, or communities. Problem solvers have a mind map that focuses on shortcomings and difficulties, which ultimately leads to a fixation on why things don't, can't, and won't work.

In contrast, resiliency thinking concentrates on why things do work, can work, and will work. We need to encourage educators and communities to shift their mind maps away from problem solving and toward resiliency as a frame of reference. A problem-solving mentality can, at best, lead to reduction or elimination of a problem, but a resiliency mentality can expand abilities beyond mere problem resolution and toward creativity, growth, and realization of potential.

This chapter focuses on resiliency as a powerful path to school and community improvement. It includes perspectives on resiliency, major shifts in our own thinking about resiliency, and an update of our resiliency model for youth, adults, organizations, and communities. Finally, we provide some case examples of our applications of the resiliency model and explore the role of educators as leaders in building resiliency.

RESILIENCY AS A POWERFUL PATH TO SCHOOL IMPROVEMENT

Resiliency can be a powerful path to school and community improvement for the following reasons:

1. **It is a positive approach that focuses on strengths and potentials.** So much of the work to change schools has been grounded in negative frames of reference. Those who have been participants in these efforts have grown weary of being consistently criticized.

2. **It is an easily understood language that can be communicated and shared by everyone—students, teachers, administrators, staff, parents, and other community members.** Many times when we bring these role players together, we use professional educator language that is not easily comprehended by others. Learning and practicing commonly shared resiliency language and concepts together can help to bridge the language barrier that too often exists among participants.

3. **Resiliency is a holistic framework.** It encourages participants to focus on all of the elements that promote resiliency. Too often, simple, "magical" solutions or quick fixes are sought for comprehensive and complex dilemmas. Resiliency thinking causes people to look across the landscape, to inventory current practices and identify gaps that need to be addressed in order to promote resiliency for all participants.

4. **Resiliency promotes widespread involvement.** Resiliency research findings (Werner & Smith, 1992) support the contention that people need to participate in meaningful activities to enhance their resiliency. It would be contradictory to the ends being sought if resiliency initiatives did not include appropriate and meaningful involvement for all participants.

5. **Resiliency energizes and motivates participants.** The more that participants are actively involved, challenged to achieve, experience caring, and are taught life skills in an environment that uses boundaries

to promote safety and security, the more likely that there will be an expansion of positive energy directed toward agreed-upon ends.

6. **Resiliency does not require schools and communities to discard strongly held beliefs about specific educational philosophies and programs.** Rather, it is about attitudes, how we communicate, and how we decide upon things. The shift is in the thinking toward a resiliency mentality instead of a "fix-it" mentality.

PERSPECTIVES ON RESILIENCY

Is the glass half full or half empty? This well-known phrase is a good starting placing to understand resiliency. In working with schools and their communities, we ask participants how they see their world. Is life full of challenges to be met or problems to be solved? If we interpret our situation as replete with positive challenges, we will likely be enthusiastic and feel empowered to embrace them as they arise. Perceptions shape our beliefs about our reality. People who think and behave resiliently think and behave differently from problem-focused people.

Resilient people may have had as many hardships in their lives as those who do not exhibit resiliency, but they cope with them differently. Resilient people bounce back from adversities stronger and quicker, learn from experiences, develop new skills, and gain more self-confidence in the process. They are aware of what they need to do to get through difficult situations and bring internal and environmental resiliency building blocks into their lives.

Internal and Environmental Resiliency Building Blocks

All of us, whether young, middle-age, or older, have the potential to respond to life's dynamics with resilience, but there is great variation in how people do actually react to challenges. Some collapse, others survive, while those who exhibit resiliency become stronger.

How do we build strength and become stronger? A part of this is rooted in what we, as individuals, bring and what our environments contribute to the situation. A review of the literature developed by Henderson and Milstein (1996) and adapted by Milstein and Henry (2000) has resulted in a summary of the key individual and environmental protective factors that serve as building blocks to resiliency. First, let us look at the factors that are characteristic of resilient individuals (see Table 13.1).

Table 13.1. Internal Protective Factors: Characteristics of Resilient Individuals

1. Gives of self in service to others or a cause or both.
2. Uses life skills, including good decision making, assertiveness, impulse control, and problem solving.
3. Is sociable and has ability to be a friend and form positive relationships.
4. Has a sense of humor.
5. Exhibits internal locus of control, i.e., belief in ability to influence one's environment.
6. Is autonomous, independent.
7. Has positive view of personal future.
8. Is flexible.
9. Has spirituality, i.e., belief in a greater power.
10. Has capacity for connection to learning.
11. Is self-motivated.
12. Is "good at something," has personal competence.
13. Has feelings of self-worth and self-confidence.

Each of us has some, if not all, of these characteristics. They are based on genetics, personality, and how we respond to life experiences. The extent to which we possess them is affected by avoiding or eliminating dysfunctional habits and learning new and more effective ways of coping.

The environments that surround us—for example, our families, organizations, and communities—also significantly affect our ability to cope and bounce back. If our environments are depleting, it may be necessary to consider changing, leaving, or avoiding them, if possible, in favor of environments that are more supportive of our growth and development needs. What does a supportive environment look like? (See Table 13.2.)

Table 13.2. Environmental Protective Factors: Characteristics of Families, Communities, and Organizations That Promote Resiliency

1. Promotes close bonds.
2. Values and encourages education.
3. Uses high warmth, low criticism style of interaction.
4. Sets and enforces clear boundaries (rules, norms, and laws).
5. Encourages supportive relationships with many caring others.
6. Promotes sharing of responsibilities, service to others, "required helpfulness."
7. Provides access to resources for meeting basic needs of housing, employment, health care, and recreation.
8. Expresses high and realistic expectations for success.

Table 13.2. Environmental Protective Factors: Characteristics of Families, Communities, and Organizations That Promote Resiliency

9. Encourages goal setting and mastery.
10. Nourishes development of positive connections (such as altruism) and life skills (such as cooperation).
11. Provides leadership, decision making, and other opportunities for meaningful participation.
12. Appreciates the unique talents of each individual.

Most of us live in multiple environments, including families, neighborhoods, communities, friendship groups, and the organizations in which we participate. These environments can negatively affect our ability to behave resiliently if they do not provide the enrichment factors identified in Table 13.2. It is difficult to remain optimistic and motivated if we live in depleting environments. But if our environments are responsive to our developmental needs and our attitudes, beliefs, and skills are supported, we are likely to become more resilient. What may be required is to work to change our environments in ways that more closely reflect the factors noted in Table 13.2. However, at times what may be required is to leave negative environments or, at least, minimize exposure to them as much as possible and to seek out substitutes that support our ability to live resiliently.

Our lives will play out differently based upon our internal resources and the extent to which our environments are supportive of our ability to bounce back from adversity. No doubt we will face challenges throughout our lives. How we respond to them will vary from loss and submission to growth and success, depending on whether we have honed our resiliency capabilities and the extent to which our environments are fertile soil for rebounding, adapting, and growing. Figure 13.1, which was adopted and modified from Richardson, Neiger, Jensen, and Krumpfer (1990), visualizes these dynamics.

CHALLENGES AND RESPONSES

As noted in Figure 13.1, there are multiple ways that we might respond to stress and adversity.

If we do not have the skills or the environmental support required, we probably will end up feeling overwhelmed and seek to withdraw from the situation (*dysfunctional response*). If we learn how to scrape by, to survive and respond in ways that are at least minimally successful, we will continue to struggle (*survival*). If we persist and learn more adequate responses, we will return to where we were at before the challenges came our way (*comfort*

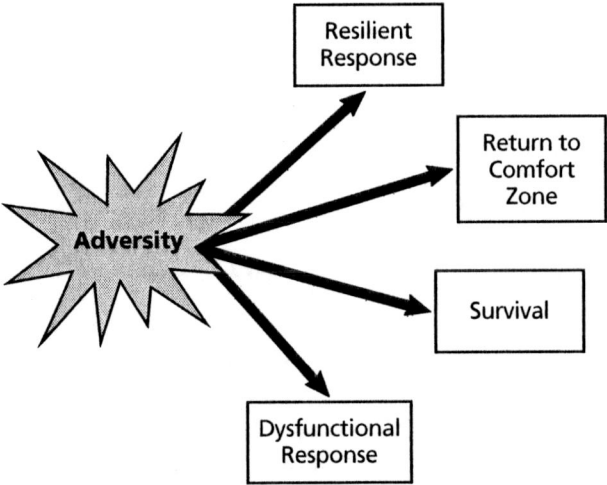

Figure 13.1. Multiple ways to respond to stress and adversity.

zone). Lastly, if the disruptions we are dealing with result in new insights, new skills, increased self-confidence, and better support from our environment, we may become more resilient than we were at the outset (*resilience response*).

The ability to confront life's challenges in ways that lead to improved capabilities and a better sense of self is what resiliency is all about. How well we do at this is dependent upon our capacity to respond effectively to these challenges. To respond effectively we need to: (1) have a clear understanding of what the underlying elements are that promote resiliency; (2) be honest as we assess our current state of development regarding these resiliency elements; and (3) seek ways of closing the gap between our current realities and what we need to be able to do to respond to life's challenges more effectively.

SHIFTS IN OUR THINKING ABOUT THE RESILIENCY ELEMENTS

Our own work has been built around the Resiliency Wheel that was initially developed by Henderson and Milstein (1996). It has proven to be durable; useful to individuals, schools, and communities that we have worked with that are seeking ways of promoting resiliency and bringing people together to work cooperatively and with purpose. However, the language of the six factors in the Resiliency Wheel has been difficult for some participants to assimilate, so we have developed language that seems to resonate with peo-

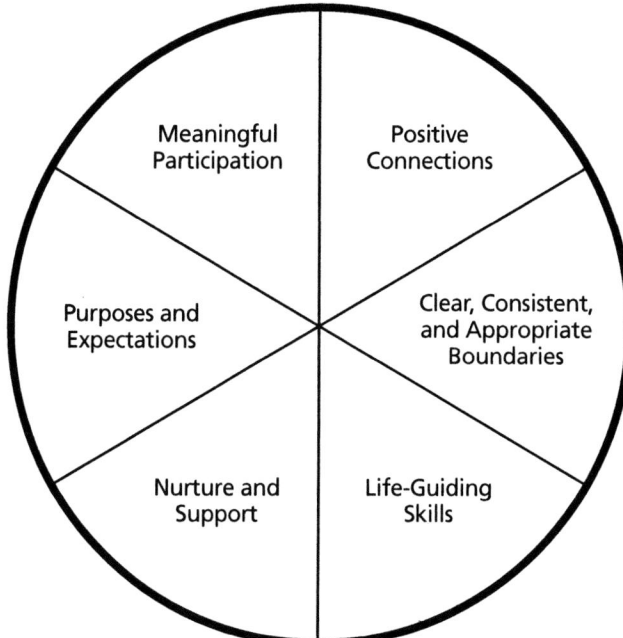

Figure 13.2. The Resiliency Model.

ple better. We have simplified the terms used to depict the elements and we have tightened and clarified the definitions for these six elements. (See Figure 13.2.)

THE RESILIENCY MODEL

The six elements depicted in the updated Resiliency Model summarize the key findings of the resiliency and at-risk literature. While resiliency researchers have mainly focused on youth, their findings are equally applicable to all of us: students, educators, parents, and community members. The more we possess these elements as individuals and the more we are supported by our environments, the more likely it is that we will live positive, healthy, and meaningful lives.

Positive connections. People, activities, programs, institutions, communities, and society, as well as the core values that underlie them, are related in profound ways. These connections help us know who we are and how we fit in with those around us.

Most of us need positive connections that are healthy and supportive so our lives can have meaning and value. We need to maintain and nurture positive connections and seek out new ones that support our sense of belonging and meaning.

Clear, consistent, and appropriate boundaries. These include expectations that are communicated in writing, such as laws, policies, and procedures, as well as expectations that are informal but powerful, such as norms and cultural preferences.

Our behaviors are greatly affected by the expectations of others. If they are clearly and consistently enforced, and appropriate to the needs and abilities of those who are expected to abide by them, they can serve as a safety net, providing guidance for appropriate behaviors. Creating boundaries is also important for growth and development, which are more feasible if one feels safe and secure.

Life-guiding skills. Competencies that are needed to navigate life's twists and turns include goal setting, planning, problem solving, decision making, communications, conflict resolution and management, and the ability to be reflective.

It takes more than good intentions to navigate life's twists and turns. Life skills need to be developed, honed through experiences, and applied flexibly as conditions change and life progresses.

Nurture and support. We thrive when nurtured and supported by those around us, whether they are relatives, friends, or others. Life is more worth living when we matter to others.

We are most fully alive when we experience unconditional regard from others. Everyone from newborns to centenarians need to be loved and cared for, to be touched and held. Learning how to ask for and receive such attention is important. Being able and willing to give others nurturance and support is also important for our sense of well-being.

Purposes and expectations. When we have clear goals and priorities and the motivation to achieve them, we are more likely to engage with life's challenges. With purposes and expectations, we are motivated to grow and develop.

Meaning is the driving energy in life. Clarity of purposes and expectations and the motivation to achieve them provide the impetus to engage with life's challenges. Without purposes and expectations we are likely to become alienated, which leaves us adrift and with little drive beyond mere survival. Our purposes and expectations are suggested by teachers, parents, and others, but we must ultimately choose and prioritize our own expectations—for example, to become independent, to become financially secure, find a mate, raise a family, and do well in our chosen lines of work.

Meaningful participation. As social beings we need to be engaged with our families and friends, as well as with volunteer efforts and the communities we live in. Meaningful participation confirms that we are not alone, that we have something to offer; and that we have the responsibility to give back to the environments that have nurtured us.

People may have the time, the life experiences, and the knowledge to participate meaningfully, but they need to be invited to participate appropriately.

APPLICATIONS OF RESILIENCY

There are many examples of individuals and groups who have made a commitment to help their schools and communities become healthier and stronger. Often times these efforts begin with just one person who takes the lead to coalesce people who see the potential of working together for healthier schools and communities. Communities that have conducted resiliency initiatives with our help vary in size, types of challenges, readiness, resources (time, people, finances, and space), location (rural, suburban, small town, or urban), and protective factors available at the outset. What these communities do have in common is a willingness to face their challenges, the belief that all community members are important and should be invited to participate, a willingness to develop necessary infrastructures that can support well-being, and the desire to promote shared values and beliefs.

When people are motivated, they can be mobilized to conduct resiliency improvement efforts. Some of the places that we have worked include Ashland, Oregon (schools and community), Memphis, Tennessee City Schools (mental health providers), Kalamazoo, Michigan (educators), Tennessee superintendents (Leader Roles), Shelby County Schools, Tennessee (school teams), and Robertson High School in Las Vegas, New Mexico (site faculty). The Ashland story is one of total community involvement. The others are within educational systems, but vary from system level to cross-site and to school site levels. Each of these settings recognized the need to grow stronger and healthier.

COMMUNITY-WIDE INTERVENTIONS

When all the forces within a community join together to enhance resiliency of its members, the outcome can be powerful. Problems educators face in schools are also problems in the community.

Our belief is that you can't have resilient youth if you don't have resilient educators. You can't have resilient educators without a resilient school. The school cannot maintain their resiliency unless the community is also resilient. The goal, then, is to build resiliency at the community level.

Ashland, Oregon

Ashland is a community of approximately 20,000 residents with a diverse population. The superintendent at that time, Dr. John Daggett, believed that the schools could only be resilient if the community was resilient. From an initial conversation we had with him, a process of involving the entire community—including students, teachers, administrators, businesspeople, city officials, and the university community, was developed, in addition to an assessment and a plan to promote resiliency. Efforts to build resiliency have grown over the years and are now widespread throughout the community. Resiliency has become a lens that is being used to guide the schools' and the community's well-being.

SYSTEM-WIDE INTERVENTIONS

Sometimes communities are not ready to commit to something that may seem to be as overwhelming as bringing the entire community together. Infrastructures may not be in place. Readiness may be lacking in the schools. We know that change can only happen if there is readiness, so starting resiliency initiatives should be aimed at points of contact that exhibit sufficient readiness.

Memphis City Schools Mental Health Providers

The resiliency concept is derived from the mental health field, so working with this group became a logical way to bridge into the system. Over 200 mental health providers in the Memphis City Schools, which has over 115,000 students, worked for two days learning about resiliency and developing resiliency-promoting strategies to incorporate in their work with youth and adults. Cross-job teams were created so there would be support at various levels. Divisions worked together and gained mutual support during the process. The support of the superintendent was also critical in bringing these professionals together.

Kalamazoo, Michigan Educators

Another system-wide approach is to have all of a school district's educators learn about resiliency at the same time. A two-day workshop was provided that focused on basic resiliency concepts. A support team within the district became the infrastructure that worked with teachers and administrators to continue to build resiliency.

Tennessee Superintendents

This was a strategy to build understanding and readiness across school systems in the state. Superintendents throughout Tennessee came together for several professional development days to learn about resiliency. Following these initial meetings, districts could request additional funding to support implementation of resiliency plans within their districts. Having the leaders of the districts become involved gave credence, as well as understanding, to the shift in thinking from deficit to wellness.

CROSS-SITE LEVEL

Shelby County Schools, Tennessee

The suburban district of Shelby County Schools brought together eight Title I school teams comprised of teachers, the principal, and other staff members for two weeks to write school improvement plans, using resiliency as their model. Each school individualized its plans to fit its needs. They also developed a strong connection with the other schools as they worked together during the training.

SITE LEVEL

Robertson High School in Las Vegas, New Mexico

Robertson High School staff devoted five professional development days spread throughout one school year to improving the school. The school had experienced a tumultuous past with a new principal nearly every year, students who were not achieving expected academic success, low teacher morale, and a fragmented staff. The first day was dedicated to assessing where the school was and where staff wanted it to be. Two months later, the entire staff spent three days learning about resiliency and developing plans for implementation of resiliency initiatives for both students and teachers. A steering committee met every other week and four working committees met during alternate weeks. By the final professional development meeting at the end of the year all four committees had accomplished at least part of their plans and concluded that it was important to continue their efforts.

The focus on resiliency remains central to the school's decision making about resource allocation.

Each of the noted situations is different, but there are some significant similarities in the outcomes. Resiliency concepts were learned and applications to fit the individual school, school district, or community needs were initiated. Resiliency initiatives can build enthusiasm, create energy, and synergize people because the focus is on positiveness, possibilities, and being proactive.

EDUCATORS AS LEADERS IN BUILDING RESILIENCY

The glue required to hold resiliency initiatives together is the group in the middle—educators. Without their active and positive involvement it is unlikely that students and parents and other community members will engage in resiliency development over the long haul. Teachers, administrators, counselors, and other specialists are in the best position to initiate and sustain efforts aimed at promoting resiliency. They interact with students and parents on a daily basis. They monitor the system and the impact it is having on students regularly. They can communicate needs and hopes of youth to parents and the community in general.

To be able to play these important roles, educators must understand the importance of promoting resiliency for students and communities. They must also exhibit resiliency in their own professional and personal lives. If they don't, they will not be in a position to influence others to develop and exhibit resiliency behaviors. In fact, they may even become a major impediment in the resiliency promoting process.

We should not take it for granted that educators fully understand resiliency concepts, let alone live resilient lives. The significant challenges that confront educators daily, such as extremely diverse and sometimes uninterested students, intensive and growing pressure to "produce" better test results, insufficient resources to do the job, and lack of community appreciation for their efforts, frequently combine to wear down their enthusiasm and motivation.

Educators with many years of service who have made repeated efforts for improvements that fall short of the mark are particularly susceptible to becoming cynical and exhausted. Having fought the good fight but coming up short quite frequently, they are likely to withdraw or at least minimize their participation in school improvement efforts.

As educators progress through their professional life cycles, they tend to shake out into three groups:

1. **Educators Who Remain Resilient Throughout Their Careers.** These educators somehow find ways of remaining enthusiastic day-by-day and year-by-year. They figure out strategies to stay engaged and enthused. They do so in various ways. They might change their work. For example, some teachers change grade levels or simply change the content they teach; some teachers become counselors, diagnosticians, or administrators; and some specialists and administrators take on central office leadership roles. Or they might seek professional development opportunities or volunteer for school- or system-wide initiatives. Whatever activity is chosen, the common denominator is recognition of the importance of growing and developing as educators and as human beings.

2. **Educators Who Exhibit Low Resiliency at Some Point in Time but Bounce Back.** These educators tend to have ebbs and flows as they move through their careers, but somehow find their way back over time. The slippage may be due to any number of factors, including stressful situations at home, being shifted from school to school, the frustration of seeing key leaders leave, or just simply not continuing to make the efforts required to grow as educators. Through reflection and decision making these educators find ways to make the commitment to reestablish their sense of professionalism and modify their on-the-job behaviors in ways that they are proud of and enhance their self-esteem. Sometimes finding their way back may require support from others in the environment—colleagues, leaders, parents, or others. The trigger mechanism might be embedded in individual awareness or it might be environmentally stimulated, but the effort is ultimately based on the clear recognition that they became educators because they believed that this is a special calling; one that is critically important to the improvement of the lives of their students and their communities.

3. **Educators Who Do Not Exhibit Resiliency.** These educators feel stuck and miserable and make those around them unhappy and frustrated. They avoid anything that looks like it might require risk taking. They take a lot of sick days and they count the days until the end of the week, the semester, the year, and ultimately until the time that they can retire. Unfortunately, we can all tell too many stories about educators who comprise this group. Their dissatisfactions quickly spill over into the school environment. They are poor role models for students as well as for their colleagues. They are the roadblocks that stand in the way of efforts to promote resiliency.

Building Resiliency in Educators

Those in the first group somehow manage to persist as resilient individuals regardless of their school situations. But if they can find themselves in more supportive situations, they might do even better. Those in the second group need supportive school environments to help them bounce back and regain their enthusiasm. Those in the third group require focused attention to help them either overcome their negativity or leave education. In short, we need to make every effort to develop and maintain a resilient educator workforce. We need to do so for them and for the well-being of those they impact—students, colleagues, parents, and the community.

STRATEGIES THAT PROMOTE EDUCATOR RESILIENCY

Using the Updated Resiliency Model (Figure 13.2) as a way of thinking is a useful beginning point in the development of strategies that can be employed to promote educator resiliency.

1. **Positive connections.** Educators typically play out their roles in splendid isolation from each other. However, there are ways of mitigating this situation and promoting positive connections. For example, team teaching and curriculum development groups can be encouraged. Similarly, site-based shared decision-making teams, study groups, visitations to other schools, and participation in state, regional, and national professional conferences can be supported. In addition, opportunities for school staffs to develop visions, goals, purposes, and programs, if facilitated effectively, can do much to enhance motivation, involvement, and ownership. Promoting norms of cooperation and support can do much to break down the isolation many educators experience.

2. **Clear, consistent, and appropriate boundaries.** Boundaries are necessary for all of us to grow, be creative, and achieve. They also provide a modicum of security. Strategies that focus on involving educators in establishing, interpreting, and implementing rules and policies contribute to deepening their understanding, acceptance, and support of these boundaries. Communicating policies in writing clearly and frequently and checking for clarity can avoid misinterpretations. This is also true for setting and following norms. If the norms are clear, understood, and shared, they can diminish conflict and help new staff members become acquainted with them without undue stress.

3. **Life-guiding skills.** With the different challenges that educators face, both those who are relative novices and those who are more experienced, it becomes imperative that their skills be upgraded and new ones learned so they can be engaged in the growth of a school. Seeing educators as whole people who have different facets changes the way we think and plan professional development. We need to survey educators to determine what *they think they need* from professional development initiatives and activities. We also need to practice adult learning principles. Learning should be relevant to these adult learners. They should participate in the definition of what is to be learned. We need to provide resources and support to continue the learning. Attending a conference or workshop is a great start, but follow-through is what strengthens the implementation. Schedule times for educators to meet and collaborate. Recognize the talents that educators at the school have and encourage them to share their expertise with colleagues, present at conferences, and publish in practitioner journals.

4. **Nurture and support.** Let educators know that they are valued and supported by providing purposeful and regular feedback, identifying the positive contributions they make as well as behaviors that need to be strengthened. Too often educators lack feedback on their teaching and the contributions they make as staff members. Create events that recognize and celebrate their efforts. These symbolic events send the message of what is valued. Likewise, a "Sunshine" committee can be an effective means of recognizing life events. Discourage negative criticism and encourage positive attention and support of educators on the part of the community, and vice versa. The local newspaper and TV stations are excellent avenues to pursue in this effort. Establishing a community–school appreciation day can connect people in positive ways.

5. **Purposes and expectations.** Educators can send messages of appreciation for efforts made and recognition for achievements accomplished. Our expectations are shaped by the feedback messages we receive. If the messages sent are negative or critical we will likely play it safe and not risk taking on challenges that are outside our comfort zone. Involving others in the development and clarification of the school's mission, vision, and goals also promotes a sense of purpose and expectations for achievement. We are likely to be more enthusiastic about missions and goals when we have participated in their development. Creating ongoing planning and action teams that bring diverse groups together can also do much to maintain and expand commitments to purposes and expectations. Finally, commu-

nicating progress, as well as problems, regarding goal attainment promotes engagement and commitment to purposes.
6. **Meaningful participation.** Educators are discovering the value of having more people participate in meaningful discussions and decisions. School Councils and site-based improvement teams encourage educators to work together as well as with the community. The essential ingredient to make this work is to have administrators who have the skills and motivation to facilitate the process. Having the skills to convene, intervene, and bringing consensus gives a clear message that everyone's voice is important and heard. Leaders who lead effective meetings ensure that agendas are delivered ahead of time so that everyone can be prepared at the meeting to discuss the issue, time for discussion is scheduled into the meeting, and that discussions can lead to actions. With experience, cooperative efforts can become a part of the fabric of the school.

IN CLOSING

In brief, resiliency is about encountering disruptive and stressful challenges, learning coping skills, and becoming more effective in dealing with life events in ways that promote healthy well-being for everyone. Resilient individuals, organizations, and communities emphasize potentials and possibilities rather than shortcomings and limitations. Resiliency focuses on adaptability, strengths, development of solutions to problems, and a "can-do" attitude.

REFERENCES

Henderson, N., & Milstein, M. (1996). *Resiliency in schools: Making it happen for students and educators.* Thousand Oaks, CA: Corwin.
Milstein, M., & Henry, D. A. (2000). *Spreading resiliency: Making it happen for schools and communities.* Thousand Oaks, CA: Corwin.
Richardson, G. E., Neiger, B. L., Jensen, S., & Krumpfer, K. L. (1990). The resiliency model. *Health Education, 21*(6), 33–39.
Werner, E. E., & Smith, R. S. (1992). *Overcoming the odds: High risk children from birth to adulthood.* Ithaca, NY: Cornell University Press.

CHAPTER 14

FUTURE DIRECTIONS FOR EDUCATIONAL RESILIENCY RESEARCH

Hersh C. Waxman
Ann Brown
Hui-Li Chang
University of Houston

Our nation faces very serious challenges in serving students at risk of academic failure. Progress has been made in isolated areas, but to sustain this progress and to extend it to much larger numbers of schools, a more solid research base must be provided for the many suspected connections between instructional processes and student outcomes, and for the level of effectiveness of various promising programs in diverse contexts (Rossi & Stringfield, 1995). More studies are needed to examine how some students overcome adversity and become successful in our schools. These students, often called resilient learners, often face enormous hardships in their lives but nevertheless succeed. Although threatened by a variety of risks, they overcome apparently insurmountable odds to build promising futures (Masten, 1994). Through the study of resilience, educators can identify factors that have been found to be effective in providing support for students at risk of failure and then apply them to similar students from disadvantaged backgrounds who have not done well in school (Padrón, Waxman, & Huang, 1999; Waxman, Huang, & Padrón, 1997).

Many of the educational interventions in the past few decades have had little long-term effect on students at risk of failure because researchers have failed to consider the multitude of intervening home, family, and community factors that prevent schools and teachers from succeeding with their students. As many of the chapters in this book have indicated, we need to address the crucial factors of health and social welfare of children. We also need school-linked comprehensive services to address the problems of poor housing, inadequate food, poor health, and chronic unemployment.

Furthermore, to confront the achievement gap between white and minority students, it is essential that educators understand the achievement patterns as well as attitudes, practices, and professional behaviors of educators. Promoting protective factors (equity and access to education, caring, high expectations, purposeful support, ongoing opportunities for meaningful participation, and effective instruction) may help us transform schools into resilient learning communities where *all* students can attain their academic potentials.

CAUTIONS RELATED TO PROMOTING RESILIENCY

While the chapters in this book provide many excellent examples of educators successfully promoting resiliency in teachers and students, it should be pointed out that this is not necessarily easy to accomplish. Cappella and Weinstein (2001), for example, found that 15% of the at-risk group significantly improved their reading proficiency from the lowest level in eighth grade to the intermediate or advanced levels in 12th grade whereas 85% either dropped out of school or remained in the lowest or basic proficiency levels. These disturbing, but insightful results based on a national, longitudinal database (NELS:88) mean that students facing low reading proficiency upon entry into high school are susceptible to continued low achievement or failure by the end of high school. These findings also suggest that there is a need to study and understand those students who improved in order to design interventions that prevent students' continued low achievement or dropping out of school.

Another cautionary aspect related to resiliency is that in today's accountability-driven educational climate, educators may perceive that it is very difficult to implement resiliency programs. Teachers throughout the United States, for example, are being held accountable to improve students' test scores. Many teachers we've talked to over the past few years frequently told us that they were aware that the various components of resiliency are important, but the teachers also stated that they only were going to be held accountable for increased test scores on the state-wide assessment tests. As

Merrow (2001) puts it, "this constant focus on high-stakes tests creates intense pressures on teachers and administrators and unfortunate decisions are being made as pressure for 'accountability' overwhelms common sense" (p. 655). While many schools try to foster a collaborative learning culture for teachers, it often is still not enough to help them overcome some of the federal, state, district, and school policies that they perceive limit their capacity for helping students in their classroom.

The high-stakes testing context contributes to teachers' feelings of powerlessness and alienation, which results in a weak sense of teacher self-efficacy and self-belief (Padrón, Waxman, Powers, & Brown, 2002). When teachers have a strong sense of their own efficacy, they can make a real difference in the lives of their students (Ashton & Webb, 1986). On the other hand, when teachers lack hope, optimism, and self-belief, schools and classrooms will "become barren wastelands of boredom and routine" (Hargreaves & Fullan, 1998, p. 1).

Schools need to provide continuous, quality professional learning experiences for all teachers. These learning experiences need to help teachers become optimistic, hopeful, and empowered so that they believe they can help improve the education of all children. The chapters in this book describe several meaningful, school-based projects that focused on reculturing or changing the entire school climate so that teachers and administrators create more collaborative, supportive work cultures that enable them to be "out there" in ways that make a difference for all students (Hargreaves & Fullan, 1998). As many of the authors in this book have indicated, in order for resiliency to be promoted, the school needs to be a learning community for students, teachers, and administrators.

A final noteworthy concern related to promoting resliency in schools is that teachers sometimes have difficulty discussing issues related to fostering students' resiliency because they do not know their students well. As Darling-Hammond (1997) puts it, the teacher's job is to get into the hearts and minds of their students. Many teachers know some basic demographic or background information about their students (e.g., number of siblings, employment status of parents), but how many teachers know about the goals and aspirations of their students? During the past decade, we have conducted hundreds of classroom observations across the United States. Unfortunately, we seldom observed teachers discussing social or personal issues with students (Waxman & Huang, 1998; Waxman, Huang, & Padrón, 1995). Schools today are often very depersonalized and teachers appear to spend very little time learning about their students. This has to dramatically change in order to promote students' resiliency.

FUTURE DIRECTIONS IN THE STUDY OF EDUCATIONAL RESILIENCY

This section highlights six areas of resiliency studies that hold promise for improving education: (1) school-based programs, (2) survey feedback professional development projects, (3) research design and methods, (4) programmatic research, (5) contextual research, and (6) neuroscience research.

School-Based Programs

In recent years, many school districts across the United States have adopted and implemented comprehensive reform models for their schools. These models are designed to help alleviate teachers' decision making in the classroom by explicitly telling them "what" to teach and "how" to teach it. While there is some evidence to support some of these models, there is also quite a bit of controversy involving their use. Some educators argue that adopting such models represents an "act of desperation on the part of educators because they do not believe that the school can reform and succeed on its own" (Becker, 2000). Others are critical of school reform models because these generic models assume that students, teachers, and schools throughout the United States are similar. As Jackson and Davis (2000) put it, "ultimately, no one size educational program can possibly fully capitalize on the diversity of student and faculty interests and talents, and community resources, that define each and every...school" (p. 225). We also agree with Jackson and Davis that teachers need to adapt and tailor effective teaching practices that build on students' and educators' diversity and strengths.

Despite these cautions about programs and reforms, Wang, Haertel, and Walberg (1998), for example, examined 12 educational programs and comprehensive school reforms that include resilience-promoting attributes. Although they found that there was a great deal of variability among these programs and reforms in terms of promoting resiliency, it is apparent that many do incorporate resiliency-promoting aspects. Thus, continued research on the effects of these comprehensive school reform models and school-based programs on students' resiliency are important, especially since we still need to have more empirical evidence on how these programs promote resiliency and improve the education of students.

Survey Feedback

Another aspect that is especially promising is the "survey feedback" approach to professional development. In survey feedback professional development projects, researchers provide teachers with systematic feedback or classroom profiles from their own class(es) related to their classroom behaviors. These approaches may be especially important in the field of educational resilience because teachers need to initally examine their own beliefs and practices before they will make major changes in their own teaching.

Padrón, Waxman, Brown, and Powers (2002), for example, found that one of the most effective components in the Pedagogy to Improve Resiliency Program (PIRP) was the specific feedback from the classroom observation and learning environment measures that were provided to the teachers in the program. This approach has been found to be very effective in helping teachers understand their current instructional strengths and weaknesses (Fraser, 1991; Fraser & Fisher, 1986; Stallings & Mohlman, 1988; Waxman & Padrón, 1995; Waxman et al., 1995). The feedback profiles provided to the PIRP teachers contained the teachers' individual data and a summary of the aggregated data across the elementary school. The class means for each of the indicators on both of the classroom observation and learning environment surveys were presented along with the overall school mean value. This allowed each teacher to compare their class means to the school's average. Furthermore, differences between resilient and non-resilient student behaviors were also included in the profiles. Feedback from these profiles was used to stimulate dialogue and discussion about instructional strengths and weaknesses in the school. The profiles also helped initiate discussion about specific instructional areas that needed to be improved in the school and how resilient and non-resilient students behaved differently in the classroom.

The feedback profiles provided some guidelines for practice; they were not attempts to tell teachers what to do. These profiles provided teachers with concepts and criteria that they could use to reflect about their own teaching (Nuthall & Alton-Lee, 1990). The researchers did not view the feedback session as one where they would apply their research findings into specific rules or guidelines for teachers to follow. Rather, the observational and survey feedback was intended to be used as guides for teachers where they and their colleagues could reflect about their practices on their own and decide what action to take. Quality staff development is one of the keys to successful school reform, and feedback from classroom observation and survey data can be the catalyst for this process.

Research Design and Methods

Another area that may change research in the field and improve education is the use of newer and better research designs and methods. Experimental research, for example, should be placed at the forefront of educational resiliency studies. It is incumbent for the resiliency research community to design, administer, document, and publish the findings from experimental resiliency studies. There are many books and articles on how to "foster" resiliency or how to have resilient children, resilient schools, or resilient communities or be resilient as an adult, but what is needed is empirical evidence that these prescriptions/guidelines/programs work. There also is a need for longitudinal studies on educational resiliency, including data on students (academic and personal) and on implemented programs and/or interventions. Critical qualitative data from students to include their interaction with their families, their interaction in their classroom, their interaction outside of the classroom with their peers, their involvement in their community, and in-depth interviews may advance our understanding of the field.

Future research also can include conducting long-term impact studies to see if providing recommended protective factors leads to enhanced student achievement, though academic outcomes are only one measure of the results of education. More longitudinal studies, recording the development of a group of students over a long time span (e.g., from elementary to middle school to high school and to college) after exposing them to a rich protective environment (i.e., teachers provide a less stressful, risk-free learning environment, expect all students to master their tasks that are tailored to their learning styles and pace, encourage the students to try their best and reach their potential with the constructive method of teaching to facilitate students to construct their own understanding and learning) are needed. The results of such longitudinal studies may add a dimension of understanding of how resilient attributes, fostered by the teachers, impact the students' mathematics understanding, appreciation, confidence, and communication in the long term.

Programmatic Research

There have been several exemplary programs of research in the field of resiliency, but more programmatic research is needed. Although there have been several federally funded national research centers that have had specific research programs focusing on educational resilience (e.g., Center for Research on Students Placed at Risk (CRESPAR), Center for Education in the Inner Cities (CEIC), and Center for Research on Education, Diversity, and Excellence (CREDE), most of these centers have not been reauthorized for continuation. This lack of federal funding may seriously curtail resiliency research and hinder the progress made in the area. Professional organizations such as the National Youth At-Risk Conference and the American Education Research Association's Special Interest Groups on Education Development in Urban Cities and Talent Development for Students At Risk of Failure, however, may facilitate some programmatic research through its conferences and by encouraging concerted research efforts. The efforts of some of the organizations described in this book also are critical to continued emphasis on programmatic research on resiliency.

Contextual Differences

One of the persistent problems in education is that we often talk about best practices in education without consideration of context or possible interaction effects (Eisner, 2001). In the past two decades, there has been a proliferation of summaries of research and collections of "best practices" in education. Furthermore, there has been a number of school-based research projects. The new federal agenda of "Leaving No Child Behind" insists that we include scientifically based research on what works in education. More specifically, there is a real interest on developing a research base that can explicitly indicate (a) what works in education, (b) for what type of student, and (c) under what conditions. The last two directives constitute the "contextual perspective on best practice in education."

Unfortunately, much of the research in resiliency as well as in other substantive areas do not address important contextual differences. For example, in the area of English language learners (ELLs), many studies and reviews of research have merely prescribed generalized best practices for ELLs without taking into account the important individual and contextual variables that represent the great diversity of conditions or risk factors that students encounter. There is much variability, however, within the population of ELLs. García (2001), for example, points out that 45% of the current ELL school-age student population are foreign-born immigrants, while the remaining 55% are U.S.-born. Foreign- and native-born students as well as other subgroups of students have different dialects, levels of schooling, and degrees of access to preschool experiences, all of which differentially impact their achievement in school. This heterogeneity makes it highly problematic to describe a "typical" ELL and, therefore, appropriate interventions. This example is quite relevant to all facets of resiliency research. Many conceptual articles and studies generalize to a larger population without taking into account the great diversity among types of resilient and nonresilient students. Consequently, recommendations from research should take into account this diversity.

Neuroscience

A final area that holds promise for the resiliency field is recent research on neurodevelopment. Physicians, psychologists, and other researchers have begun to focus on neurodevelopmental dysfunctions that hinder the academic success of children (Levine, 2003). Weaknesses in neurodevelopmental areas such as motor function, memory, language, and organization have been found to impact the academic success of many children. From the neuroscience perspective, the pertinent research question is, "How do some children overcome serious dysfunctions, while others don't?" It appears that getting help makes a difference as does believing in yourself and preserving a sense of optimism (Levine, 2003; Seligman, 2002). Although an emphasis in this area may appear to be a "deficit-based" approach, the advances uncovered in neuroscience indicate important learning differences among students that include both strengths and weaknesses in learning. Fostering childrens' learning strengths may be the key to their academic as well as social success.

SUMMARY

While the term *research* often has a negative connotation for educational practitioners and policymakers, it is the best criterion we have for determining effective practices in education. The conceptual work and research presented in this book have suggested several consistent relations among resiliency and teacher and student outcomes. Further descriptive, correlational, longitudinal, and especially experimental research is needed to verify these results. In addition, studies should attempt to replicate some of the previous studies and projects in other settings, especially in urban school settings where many more students are at risk of dropping out and not furthering their education. These and other issues previously discussed still need to be examined so that we can continue to understand how resiliency influences teacher and student outcomes.

Today's world is a mix of good news and bad news. The good news is that an emphasis on promoting resiliency may likely improve teaching and student learning more than many other educational interventions. Promoting resiliency might provide opportunities to radically improve schools and classrooms that would not be available under the current educational fiscal crisis. The bad news is that schools and students are changing so rapidly that once we think we understand important relationships that promote resiliency and the quality of teachers and student learning, the school context will have changed dramatically. We'll be back in the position of needing to do additional research to understand new relationships. Research takes time to plan, conduct, and evaluate. But the context of schools and students that is the focus of that research will continue to change, and the relationships we establish for one type of student, classroom, and school may not transfer to other settings.

One possible response to this state of affairs is to become overwhelmed at the prospect of never reaching the end of the quest. However, the energy and enthusiasm of the people who have contributed to this book are certain to act as an antidote to the lethargy that tends to result from feelings of being overwhelmed. Understanding the role of resiliency in education is an enormous challenge. We believe, however, that our colleagues are not only qualified to meet that challenge but also dedicated to fostering resiliency to serve the purpose of improving the education of *all* students.

ACKNOWLEDGMENT

This research was supported in part by a U. S. Department of Education, Office of Educational Research and Improvement grant from the National Center for Research on Education, Diversity, and Excellence. The opinions expressed in this chapter do not necessarily reflect the position, policy, or endorsement of the granting agency.

REFERENCES

Ashton, P., & Webb, R. (1986). *Making a difference: Teacher's sense of efficacy.* New York: Longman.

Becker, A. (2000, June). *International perspectives in language diversity and teacher training.* Paper presented at the Teaching English Language Learners: Effective Programs and Practices Conference, Storrs, CT.

Cappella, E., & Weinstein, R. S. (2001). Turning around reading achievement: Predictors of high school students' academic resilience. *Journal of Educational Psychology, 93,* 758–771.

Darling-Hammond, L. (1997). *The right to learn: A blueprint for creating schools that work.* San Francisco: Jossey-Bass.

Eisner, E. W. (1998). *The kinds of schools we need: Personal essays.* Portsmouth, NH: Heineman.

Fraser, B. J. (1991). Two decades of classroom environment research. In B. J. Fraser & H. J. Walberg (Eds.), *Educational environments: Evaluation, antecedents and consequences* (pp. 3–27). Oxford: Pergamon.

Fraser, B. J., & Fisher, D. L. (1986). Using short forms of classroom climate instruments to assess and improve classroom psychosocial environment. *Journal of Research in Science Teaching, 5,* 387–413.

García, G. N. (2001). The factors that place Latino children and youth at risk of educational failure. In R. E. Slavin & M. Calderón (Eds.), *Effective programs for Latino students* (pp. 307–329). Mahwah, NJ: Erlbaum.

Hargreaves, A., & Fullan, M. (1998). *What's worth fighting for out there.* New York: Teachers College.

Jackson, A. W., & Davis, G. A. (2000). *Turning points 2000: Educating adolescents in the 21st century.* New York: Teachers College.

Levine, M. (2003). *The myth of laziness.* New York: Simon & Schuster.

Masten, A. S. (1994). Resilience in individual development: Successful adaptation despite risk and adversity. In M. C. Wang & E. W. Gordon (Eds.), *Educational resilience in inner-city America: Challenges and prospects* (pp. 3–25). Hillsdale, NJ: Erlbaum.

Merrow, J. (2001). Undermining standards. *Phi Delta Kappan, 82,* 653–659.

Nuthall, G., & Alton-Lee, A. (1990). Research on teaching and learning: Thirty years of change. *Elementary School Journal, 90,* 546–570.

Padrón, Y. N., Waxman, H. C., & Huang, S. L. (1999). Classroom behavior and learning environment differences between resilient and nonresilient elementary school students. *Journal of Education for Students Placed At Risk, 4,* 63–81.

Padrón, Y. N., Waxman, H. C., Powers, R. A., & Brown, A. (2002). Evaluating the effects of the Pedagogy to Improve Resiliency Program on English Language Learners. In L. Minaya-Rowe (Ed.), *Teacher training and effective pedagogy in the context of student diversity* (pp. 211–238). Greenwich, CT: Information Age.

Rossi, R. J., & Stringfield, S. C. (1995). What must we do for students placed at risk. *Phi Delta Kappan, 77,* 73–76.

Seligman, M. E. P. (2002). *Authentic happiness: Using the new positive psychology to realize your potential for lasting fulfillment.* New York: Free Press.

Stallings, J. A., & Mohlman, G. G. (1988). Classroom observation techniques. In J. P. Keeves (Ed.), *Educational research, methodology, and measurement: An International handbook* (pp. 469–474). Oxford: Pergamon.

Wang, M. C., Haertel, G. D., & Wulberg, H. J. (1998). *Building educational resilience.* Bloomington, IN: Phi Delta Kappa.

Waxman, H. C., & Huang, S. L. (1998). Classroom learning environments in urban elementary, middle, and high schools. *Learning Environments Research: An International Journal, 1,* 95–113.

Waxman, H. C., Huang, S. L., & Padrón, Y. N. (1995). Investigating the pedagogy of poverty in inner-city middle level schools. *Research in Middle Level Education, 18*(2), 1–22.

Waxman, H. C., Huang, S. L., & Padrón, Y. N. (1997). Motivation and learning environment differences between resilient and non-resilient Latino middle school students. *Hispanic Journal of Behavioral Sciences, 19,* 137–155.

Waxman, H. C., Huang, S. L., & Wang, M. C. (1997). Investigating the classroom learning environment of resilient and non-resilient students from inner-city elementary schools. *International Journal of Educational Research, 27,* 343–353.

Waxman, H. C., & Padrón, Y. P. (1995). Improving the quality of classroom instruction for students at risk of failure in urban schools. *Peabody Journal of Education, 70*(2), 44–65.

Waxman, H. C., Padrón, Y. N., & Arnold, K. A. (2001). Effective instructional practices for students placed at risk of failure. In G. D. Borman, S. C. Stringfield, & R. E. Slavin (Eds.), *Title I: Compensatory education at the crossroads* (pp. 137–170). Mahwah, NJ: Erlbaum.

CONTRIBUTING AUTHORS

Diane Barone is a Professor of Literacy Studies in the College of Education at the University of Nevada, Reno. She teaches courses in early literacy, literacy and diversity, and qualitative research. Her research explores the literacy development of children who are deemed to be at risk in school settings. She has completed a longitudinal study of the literacy learning and instruction of children prenatally exposed to crack/cocaine. She is currently involved in a seven-year study of children attending a school labeled at risk to learn more about their literacy development and instruction. Her research has been published in journals such as the *Journal of Literacy Research, Urban Education, Research in the Teaching of English,* and the *Elementary School Journal.* She is also the outgoing editor of *Reading Research Quarterly.*

Joel H. Brown is an educational researcher with rare experience in blending resilience-oriented educational research with program development, training, and competency-based evaluation research methods. Currently, he is an Associate Professor of Educational Leadership and Policy Studies at the University of Oklahoma. Dr. Brown is also Executive Director of the Center for Educational Research and Development (CERD) (www.cerd.org), a Berkeley-based nonprofit program and research organization committed to the development of resilience-based policies and programs. Among numerous nationally noted and resilience-based educational evaluations and publications, he was the director of the nationally noted research project titled "In Their Own Voices: Students and Educators Evaluate California School-Based Drug Alcohol and Tobacco Education (DATE) Programs." Dr. Brown is lead author of *Resilience Education*. His commentary has been solicited in myriad media outlets, including CNN, NPR, and the *New York Times*.

Ann Brown is a research assistant for the Texas Institute for Measurement, Evaluation, and Statistics (TIMES) at the University of Houston. Her research focuses on educational resiliency, multicultural education, and second language learning.

Hui-Li Chang is a Postdoctoral fellow in the Center for Research on Education, Diversity, and Excellence (CREDE) at the University of Houston. Her research focuses on mathematics education and educational resiliency.

Virginia Frazier-Maiwald is currently Principal of Bernal Intermediate School, formerly serving as Principal of Edenvale Elementary School. She is also an adjunct faculty m ember in teacher education at San Jose State University, specializing in bilingual and multicultural education, second language acquisition, emergent literacy, and special education. She is also the author of *Keys to Raising a Deaf Child* (1999).

Jon P. Gray is an Assistant Professor of Health and Kinesiology in the College of Education and Human Development at Lamar University and the Teacher Education Coordinator for the Health and Kinesiology Department. His research interests and efforts have focused on educational resiliency, teaching effectiveness, and teacher certification and supervision. Dr. Gray has also taught grades Pre-K–8 and served as Athletic Director and Mid-Management Administrator in a number of school districts in Texas.

Doris "Annie" Henry is Professor and Coordinator of Educational Leadership at New Mexico Highlands University and a partner in the Resiliency Group, Limited. Her teaching, research, and writing interests focus on resiliency, restructuring, change, organization development, and school improvement. Dr. Henry has facilitated resiliency at the classroom, schoolwide, and community–school partnership levels. She was formerly Professor of Educational Leadership at the University of Memphis and at the University of Nebraska at Omaha, an elementary school principal for nearly a decade in Arizona and Oklahoma, and a classroom teacher. She has published widely in her areas of interest, most notably as coauthor of *Spreading Resiliency: Making It Happen for Schools and Communities* (2000) and of the national study *Becoming a Superintendent: Challenges of School District Leadership* (1997).

Martin Krovetz is Professor of Educational Administration at San Jose State University. He is Codirector of the LEAD Center, a regional center of the

Coalition of Essential Schools. He is also the author of *Fostering Resiliency: Expecting All Students to Use Their Minds and Hearts Well* (1999). From 1977–1991, Dr. Krovetz served as a high school principal in Santa Cruz, California.

Kathy Marshall is Executive Director of the National Resilience Resource Center at the University of Minnesota. For more than 25 years, she directed systems changing prevention and education programs in school, community, and public policy arenas. She was Assistant to the Director for the University of Minnesota Center for Applied Research and Educational Improvement, and directed U.S. Department of Education Drug Free Schools programs for both the Midwest Regional Center of the North Central Regional Educational Laboratory and the Educational Cooperative Service of Southwest Minnesota. Marshall administered a philanthropic nonprofit organization, headed a state Department of Social Services public information office, lobbied for women and children's issues, and was on the faculty of California State University. She earned a master's degree in Speech Communication and completed doctoral courses at the University of Southern California as a National Defense Education Act fellow. Marshall has consulted with the U.S. Center for Substance Abuse Prevention and a variety of local, state, and federal education and health and human services agencies, and has presented and written *Reculturing Systems with Resilience/Health Realization* for The Carter Center in Atlanta. Most recently, she wrote *Bringing Out the Best in Our Kids: A Parent's Guide to Resilience/Health Realization*.

Sue McGinty is Director of Research in the School of Indigenous Australian Studies at James Cook University, Townsville, Australia. Her research centers on school–community relations and community capacity building in that context. Her most recent projects have been an investigation into retention to year 12 or equivalent for indigenous students, and teacher education preparation and professional development for teaching indigenous students. McGinty has recently published *The Politics and Machinations of Education Research: International Case Studies* and *Karrayili: Adult Education in a Remote Australian Community*.

Mike M. Milstein is Professor Emeritus at the University of New Mexico and a partner in the Resiliency Group, Limited. His teaching, research, and writing interests are in the areas of resiliency and organization development. He has been actively engaged in school and community resiliency development efforts. The resiliency initiatives Dr. Milstein has facilitated include classroom instruction and curriculum improvement efforts, schoolwide activities that enhance the resiliency of educators, and school–community partnerships that support resiliency development for both children and adults. He has written 12 books, including coauthoring *Resiliency in Schools* (2002) and *Spreading Resiliency: Making It Happen for Schools and Communities* (2000).

Yolanda N. Padrón is Professor at the University of Houston and Chair of the Curriculum and Instruction Department where she also teaches courses in the areas of bilingual and second language education. In addition, she is currently serving as Codirector and Principal Researcher at the National Center for Research on Education, Diversity, and Excellence (CREDE). The predominant area upon which Dr. Padrón's research has focused is on improving classroom instruction and reading instruction for English Language learners. Specifically, she has concentrated on bilingual students' cognitive strategies in reading and resiliency.

Judy Radigan is a Lecturer in Cultural Studies in the College of Education at the University of Houston and at the Center of Education at Rice University. She is the Research Coordinator for a 5-year longitudinal study at Child Advocates in Houston. Radigan has recently published articles in *Ethnography and Schools: Qualitative Approaches to the Study of Education* and *Critical Ethnography and Education, Studies in Educational Ethnography*.

Héctor H. Rivera is an Assistant Professor (Research Track) in the Psychology Department, as well as a Scientific Advisor for the Texas Institute for Measurement, Evaluation, and Statistics (TIMES) at the University of Houston. His research focuses on child and community development, classroom learning environments, school program development, and teacher professional development in urban and rural settings. Dr. Rivera has recently published on those topics in *Information Technology in Childhood Education; Journal of Education for Students Placed at Risk; Center for Applied Linguistics (practice report);* and *National Society for the Study of Education.*

Ruth Silva is currently an Assistant Professor in Teacher Education at North Texas University. She previously was a Visiting Assistant Professor at the University of Houston in the Center for Research on Education, Diversity, and Excellence and a Principal Researcher for the Annenberg Challenge Evaluation at Rice University. Prior to coming to the United States, she was a teacher, principal, and administrator at the high school level in Sydney, Australia. Dr. Silva's research interests include critical research methodology, post-structuralist theories in teacher roles in the classroom and instructional supervision. She has recently published on these topics in *Critical Ethnography and Education* and *Debates and Developments in Ethnographic Methodology*.

Robert Stephen Topf is currently Principal at Parkview Elementary School, in the Oak Grove School District, in San Jose, California. He obtained is BA at the University of Colorado in Psychology and his master's degree in School Psychology at San Jose State University. He also holds a license as a marriage and family therapist. Topf is well grounded in systems theory, and has had a long-term professional interest in assisting students and families in being academically successful and meaningfully engaged in the education process.

Hersh Waxman is a Professor of Educational Leadership and Cultural Studies in the College of Education at the University of Houston, a Principal Researcher in the National Center for Research on Education, Diversity, and Excellence, and a Principal Investigator in the Mid-Atlantic Regional Educational Laboratory for Student Success. His research focuses on classroom learning environments, school and teacher effectiveness, urban education, and students at risk of failure. Dr. Waxman has recently published articles on those topics in journals such as *Journal of Educational Research, Learning Environments Research: An International Journal, Journal of Education for Students Placed At Risk,* and *Urban Education.*

Sybil Wolin, a developmental psychologist, is co-director of Project Resilience—a private organization in Washington, DC that provides training, resources, and educational material to schools, clinics, and prevention agencies. She is co-author of *The Struggle to Be Strong* (Free Spirit, 2000), a curriculum to foster resilience in youth, and *The Resilient Self: How Survivors of Troubled Families Rise Above Adversity* (Villard, 1993). She is featured in "Survivor's Pride: Building Resilience in Youth at Risk" (Attainment Co., 1994), and eight-part educational video series. She is widely published in magazines and journals and has lectured and consulted to numerous agencies seeking to implement a strength-based approach to working with children and youth. In October 2001, she was the recipient of Strength Based Services International "My Brother's Keeper" award for her contribution to the field of youth development.